Diary of a Musician

by

Paul Griggs

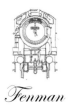

Fenman

Diary of a Musician

Introduction

I was given a diary as a present every Christmas and always had good intentions of writing down my daily events. This usually lasted until around February when I would miss a few days and then give up. In 1960 I managed to keep it going and kept a small pocket diary up to date until the late eighties.

I was fifteen years of age when I started the diaries and they cover my time as a budding musician who was inspired to take up the guitar by discovering Lonnie Donegan. The trials and tribulations of starting my own band, the Cortinas, and eventually bringing in my brother Nigel on bass guitar. There are the amazing times I had in the sixties both as a musician and as a fan. Seeing the Beatles live on stage ten times and playing with my band at London's Speakeasy Club in front of Jimi Hendrix.

When groups named after cars became unfashionable the Cortinas became Octopus and almost immediately signed to Larry Page's fledgling label Penny Farthing Records. We moved away from being a pop group, becoming more progressive and playing regularly at London's famous Marquee Club. After making one album, Octopus disbanded in 1971.

In 1974, at thirty years of age I completely changed my musical direction and my life. Lying about my age, I joined the newly formed Guys n' Dolls (I'm still not sure why). The group was signed to Magnet Records owned by the infamous Michael (now Lord) Levy. We achieved instant success reaching number two in the charts with "There's a Whole Lot of Loving" a record that was made before the group was formed. This meant that none of us sang on it, which caused problems and press controversy. In 1977 there was an acrimonious split in the group when David Van Day and Thereze Bazar were unceremoniously sacked and we continued as a four piece. David and Thereze would achieve success as Dollar. A year later Guys n' Dolls appeared with Frank Sinatra for a week of concerts at the Royal Festival Hall which was one of the major highlights of my career.

Guys n' Dolls would have two separate careers, although our success was subsiding in the United Kingdom it was on the rise in Holland where we relocated in 1981, virtually becoming a Dutch group. We had a string of hits there and never performed in the UK again. Guys n' Dolls finally disbanded in 1985.

I soon went back to performing as a solo artist which I still do to this day. As I was completing this book, almost out of the blue and against all odds, the original six members of Guys n' Dolls put aside any past differences and reformed for a major Dutch television show in March 2008 with the possibility of concerts later in the year.

Lonnie, you sure started something.

My musical career began, I suppose, around the time Hatfield music teacher Mrs. Johnson tried to teach me to play pieces like "The Blue Danube" and "The Emperors Waltz" on the piano. It was 1951 and at seven years of age my mother would send me to piano lessons once a week at a cost of two shillings and sixpence (12.5p to you). I would be made to practice for thirty minutes every day, ten minutes on each of the two pieces I was given by Mrs. Johnson, and ten minutes of scales which I found so boring. That was usually the longest half hour of the day playing music I didn't really like and when Mum wasn't looking I would push the hands of the clock forward a few minutes to lessen my ordeal. I realized that I could work out tunes by myself, and spent hours busking away, until I finally persuaded Mum that piano lessons were a waste of time. At one point I almost took up the piano accordion before discovering the man who would change my life.

In 1956 the only record player in our house was an old wind up model with a sound box directly above the needle which had to be changed every time you had played about five records. The record collection consisted of a few old 78s like, "The Sabre Dance" and "Buttons and Bows". One day my father came home with the latest "hi tech" arm for our record player which meant you could plug it into a radio. We had to update our record collection so with my hard earned pocket money I bought my favourite record of the day "The Dam Busters March", while Mum bought the latest record by a certain Lonnie Donegan called "Don't You Rock Me Daddy-O". Soon I was playing "Don't You Rock Me Daddy-O" most of the time, and when Lonnie's next record "Cumberland Gap" was released, and reached number one in the charts, I was hooked and began buying everything he had ever recorded.

When I bought Lonnie's first album "Showcase" I found a track that has always been one of my all time favourites, "Frankie and Johnny". It's such a heavy track, and I've always likened it to Ravels "Bolero", fourteen verses that build to a frantic crescendo at the end, and Nick Nicholls opening drum pattern is heavy enough to grace any modern day Rock track. It was the first track recorded along with most of the "Showcase" album on 22nd August 1956 and in those days there were no overdubs, you went in recorded the performance and that was it. The performance on Frankie and Johnny is amazing except that at one point Lonnie forgets who is doing what to whom, because he says that Nellie shot Johnny when in fact it was Frankie.

In 1957 around the time of Lonnie's next release, the double sided number one hit "Putting on the Style" / "Gamblin Man", I was in hospital with a serious kidney complaint. When I got out of hospital I had several months off school and by now all I wanted to do was play the guitar and sing like Lonnie. I pestered my father for a guitar and he, being a woodworker by trade, decided to make me one. A few months later the guitar was finished and I started to learn how to play. At first I would tune the top two strings until I thought they sounded OK and bash out Lonnie's songs before buying a book (not Bert Weedon's) which taught me how to play the chords properly. I would practise every spare moment I had playing and singing along to Lonnie's records. Sometimes I would be Lonnie singing and playing rhythm guitar and other times I would be Denny Wright or Jimmy Currie. (Lonnie's lead guitarists) and concentrate on playing the lead guitar parts.

The Satellites. The Griggs Brothers first public performance 4th January 1958 4.16pm. (left to right) Nigel Griggs, Paul Griggs, and Colin Hurst.

Lonnie Donegan was at the height of his popularity and I decided that I wanted a Skiffle Group, so I recruited my brother Nigel, who was only eight at the time, to play washboard and Colin Hurst, a school friend on tea chest bass. We called ourselves the Satellites which was a pretty cool name at the time as Russia had recently launched the first ever space satellite called "Sputnik 1. My father worked at De Havillands aircraft factory in Hatfield, and secured our first booking playing for the children's Christmas parties in the works canteen. We did three consecutive Saturdays playing the same three Lonnie Donegan songs, "My Dixie Darling" "Gamblin' Man" and "Jack O' Diamonds". We were paid three pounds for these shows and I was well impressed thinking that at the age of 13, I was already a professional musician.

Poster for the first concert I attended. Lonnie Donegan at The Finsbury Park Empire 14th February 1958

On Friday February 14th 1958 I saw Lonnie on Stage for the first time at the Finsbury Park Empire in North London. In those days there were no Pop Concerts, just variety shows which featured various variety acts and a top of the bill. I still have the programme for this show and among the acts with Lonnie were, Freddie Harrison (The Tricky Pianist), The Three Brittons (Juggling Cyclists), Jimmy Webster and Jill (Thrills on Wheels), and a certain Mr. Des O'Connor (Comedy in the Modern Manner). Finally after what seemed like an eternity of nine acts and an interval Des O'Connor announced "Ladies and Gentlemen Lonnie Donegan and his Skiffle Group". The curtains opened and there was the man himself singing "Wabash Cannonball" a track from his first LP. This may sound a bit daft in this day and age, but my first reaction was, "it's in colour". In the days before colour television and magazines I had only seen Lonnie and his group, and their instruments in black and white, now here before me was the real thing and in colour. Lonnie's guitarist Jimmy Currie was playing a beautiful sunburst Gibson L175 guitar. I was transfixed and wanted one immediately. The show was over far too quickly but the night was complete when Lonnie came out to the stage door to sign autographs and I was one of the lucky ones. I understand that when Lonnie played The Liverpool Empire around this time a certain George Harrison was getting his own autograph book signed.

I only had to wait four weeks to see Lonnie live again, as he performed a Sunday Concert at St. Albans Odeon on March 9th 1958 , five miles from my home in Hatfield. I saw him again in St. Albans on Sunday 12th October 1958 with his new guitarist Les Bennetts.

In 1959 I bought a second hand Rosetti Cello Electric guitar that was really more of a Jazz guitar. It had a flat finger board which was a bit of a pig to play but was a step up from the guitar that Dad had made for me, (which I still own). I began playing at school with a guy called Mick Searl who played double bass, and we used to bash out Lonnie Donegan songs in the lunch hour, and even performed a few local gigs.

**With my Dad.
The Guitar that he
built for me in 1957
is bottom right.**

I needed an amplifier for my electric guitar and Dad decided to build me one from scratch. My earliest memory of Dad was that he was always making things, mostly furniture which was in short supply after the war. I can remember him making Nigel and I our first proper single beds. He did this completely from scratch (no flat packs in those days) even managing to upholster it himself. Dad came from a generation that was very practical through necessity.

To me, Dad's finest achievement came in the early fifties when we wanted a television. They were very expensive to buy and there were only two or three in our street. Dad went out and bought a book "How to Build a Television" and set to work. There were no kits in those days, he would go to a shop which sold war surplus electrical parts, buy a mass of bits and pieces and then spend hours soldering them together on the kitchen table. After about a year this mass of valves and wires was ready to be switched on and I can remember that there was a cowboy film on at the time and the picture was upside down, but it worked. Dad made a beautiful polished cabinet and that was it. Just one BBC channel but we thought it was marvellous and in June 1953 sat in front of it to see the Coronation of Queen Elizabeth II.

I went to Welwyn Garden City High School and one of my GCE (no "S" in those days) subjects was music, under the very tolerant Miss Britten. One of the conditions of studying music for GCE was that you had to be in the school choir and the school orchestra. For someone who lived and breathed Lonnie Donegan this was a little hard to take. At first Miss Britten persuaded me to have double bass lessons along side Mick Searl but I soon tired of that and ended up playing Timpani drums in the orchestra. One of the GCE papers was called "Set Works" where we were given pieces of music to listen to, dissect and analyse. One of these pieces was Handel's Messiah, which we were forced to listen to incessantly and if it was being performed anywhere locally the GCE music group was forced to go and see it. This led to me hating Handel's Messiah with a vengeance and even today should I hear the Hallelujah Chorus I get a feeling of doom in the pit of my stomach.

1960

Friday 1st January 1960

The sixties have always been known as a great period in Pop Music, but musically the sixties didn't really start until 1963 when the Beatles became the biggest pop act in history. In the first week of the sixties the number one record was "What Do You Want to Make Those Eyes at Me" by Emile Ford and the Checkmates. Also in the Top Ten this week were Tommy Steele who had forsaken his Rock n' Roll roots and was at number six with "Little White Bull", at number nine was Cliff Richard who was also starting to leave Rock n' Roll behind singing the country tinged "Travellin' Light", and at number four, the rather silly "Seven Little Girls Sitting In The Back Seat" by "The Avons". All I did on the first day of the sixties was to go to my local record shop and try and get the number three record "Oh Carol" by Neil Sedaka, but they had sold out.

Today Bill Shankly officially took over as manager of Liverpool Football Club, which would become my team.

Sunday 3rd January 1960

One of the most popular programmes of the time was Val Parnell's "Sunday Night at the London Palladium", which was a one hour variety show hosted by, among others, Bruce Forsyth who became a big favourite in our household. He was in his early years as a top name, in a career that has spanned six decades. Little did I know that in 15 years time I would be working with his daughter Julie when we both joined "Guys n' Dolls".

"Sunday Night at the London Palladium" was a must see show in the days of only two television channels, and on this first show of 1960, Anthony Newley topped the bill along with Musical and Comedy actor Stanley Holloway. The show also featured "Beat the Clock" which was an audience participation game, and a forerunner to Bruce's "Generation Game".

Friday 22nd January 1960

My Lonnie Donegan Club Card, and Badge. (Member No. 2198)

I couldn't concentrate at school too much today because in the evening I was going to see Lonnie Donegan on stage once again. I caught the train from Hatfield to Finsbury Park and walked the few hundred yards to the Empire Theatre where I had first seen Lonnie back in 1958. He was appearing in the pantomime Robinson Crusoe playing Robinson's brother Billy Crusoe. (What do you mean he didn't have a brother?) I was by now a fully fledged member, number 2198, of the Lonnie Donegan Fan Club, and had written to Sylvie Symonds who ran the club asking if I could get to meet Lonnie as I had found a song that might suit him. Sylvie wrote back saying that if I asked for Peter Huggett, his bass player, in the interval it might be possible.

The interval came and I nervously asked one of the attendants if I could see Peter Huggett and he took me back stage. I had to walk past Nick Nicholls drums that were on a small platform ready for the end of the show when Lonnie would perform with his group, and was introduced to Peter Huggett. Peter took me to Lonnie's dressing room, knocked on the door and we went in and there he was, my hero. I can't deny it I was awestruck, but I managed to explain that I had this record by a guy called Vernon Dalhart called "Get Away Old Man Get Away" that might be the sort of song he could sing. Behind Lonnie I could see his Martin guitar and his banjo lying on a table ready to go. I had wanted a Martin like Lonnie's from the time I first saw him so I was even in awe of the guitar. We had a short chat, I thanked him for seeing me and I went back to my seat in a bit of a daze and watched the second half of the show which was great. Robinson Crusoe and his girlfriend (what do you mean he didn't have a girlfriend) lived happily ever after, and Lonnie finished the show with a magnificent set. I went home with a smile on my face. Lonnie never recorded that song but would make up for it 36 years later and record a song that I had written specially for him.

Sunday 21st February 1960

Today I went to the Empire Pool Wembley for the annual New Musical Express Poll Winners Concert. Every year the New Musical Express had a poll to decide best male and female singers best groups etc. culminating with a concert featuring the winners. This year Lonnie was on and I managed to get a ticket. Also on the bill were Gene Vincent and Eddie Cochran and it was always a bit special to see top acts from the states and they were both great.

Friday 26th February 1960

My school were putting on a performance of Shakespeare's "Twelfth Night" and as I was the only pupil who could "allegedly" play guitar, I was cast as the musician. I had complete Shakespearian costume including some rather fetching yellow tights, and the idea was that at the beginning of the play I would walk down the aisle playing medieval music, then onto the stage drawing the audience into Ilyria. I didn't know any medieval music only Lonnie Donegan, but there was a song that Lonnie had recorded call "My Lagan Love" which sounded a little "Celtic". This was the closest I was going to get to anything Shakespearian, so I learned the instrumental section which seemed to work. I had never been so nervous in my life walking what seemed like a mile from the back of the hall, and I felt rather exposed in my yellow tights. I heard someone mutter "here comes Elvis" as I climbed onto the stage, sat down, stopped playing, and heard the immortal words, "If music be the food of love play on"-----

Saturday 9th April 1960

Nigel had been following Liverpool FC for a while and today Dad took Nigel and I to see Liverpool play Leyton Orient. I must admit my love for Liverpool FC was not fully realised and I spent the first half down the road at Stratford, train spotting. Yes I admit it, but most boys went train spotting in those days. Liverpool were in Division Two at the time and Nigel informs me that the team for this match was: Slater, Molyneux , Byrne, Wheeler, White, Moran, Liddell, Hunt, Hickson, Melia, A'Court. There were no substitutes in 1960.

This was the start of my love of Liverpool FC.

Sunday 17th April 1960

American singer Eddie Cochran was killed in a car crash in Chippenham Wiltshire today, less than two months after I had seen him sing live at Wembley. He was on his way back to London to fly to America, after finishing his British tour at the Bristol Hippodrome.

Saturday 13th August - Saturday 20th August 1960

"She Came
Down From
Birmingham ---"
Butlins Clacton
18th August
1960

It was Holiday time and the whole family set off for Butlins Holiday Camp in Clacton. Today these types of holidays are rather ridiculed and have been sent up in the comedy series "Hi De Hi", but for a fifteen year old in 1960 they were brilliant. Once you were in the camp all of the entertainment from the fairground to the shows was free, and there was some excellent entertainment. The main theatre at Butlins was called "The Gaiety Theatre" and every night there were top class shows. The second night we were there we saw comedian Roy Castle topping the bill. There was also the Rock Ballroom where every night a group called the Dominoes were playing and I thought they were great.

I had taken my guitar with me as heats of the "The People's National Talent Contest" were held every week. Unfortunately I discovered that you had to be sixteen to enter, so naturally I lied about my age. I got through the heats and the semi final and took part in the final in the Gaiety Theatre singing, what else, a Lonnie Donegan song, "Wabash Cannonball." I didn't win.

Thursday 8th December - Saturday 10th December 1960

It was back into tights (red this time) for another school Shakespearean production, this time it was "The Merchant of Venice" and once again I was a victim of type casting, playing the musician. I had to provide the backing for a girl called Ilona Lloyd to sing a short song and to provide a piece of appropriate music to cover a costume change. Once again Lonnie's "My Lagan Love" came to the rescue and I even got a short burst of applause, although I'm not sure that's strictly allowed during Shakespeare plays, but it did help to massage my ego.

1961

Saturdays 7th, 14th, 21st, January 1961

With Mick Searl trying to entertain the kids at De Havillands Childrens Christmas Party January 1961. 4.52pm

Dad had secured me another booking playing to the kids at the De Havilland's children's Christmas party and this time I played with Mick Searl on Double Bass. We performed two shows in the works canteen each week, (upstairs and downstairs) and were each paid £5.00.

Friday 13th January 1961

Today the world famous percussionist Jimmy Blades visited my school to give a lecture, and demonstrate percussion instruments. When it was over I grabbed my guitar and Mick Searl collected his double bass and we asked Jimmy if he would play a couple of numbers with us. He said yes and we played two of Lonnie's songs "Wabash Cannonball" and "The Wreck of The Old 97" and with Jimmy Blades playing drums it was fantastic, the first time I had ever played with a real drummer.

Jimmy Blades was most famous for providing the sound of the gong that preceded films produced by the Rank Organisation and worked extensively on film soundtracks having a long association with the composer Benjamin Britten. He died in 1999.

Sunday 5th March 1961

My Photos of
Adam Faith and
Hank B. Marvin.
Empire Pool
Wembley
5th March 1961

Today I set off with a school friend, to the Empire Pool Wembley for the 1961 "New musical Express Poll Winners Concert". We arrived early as we wanted to see the acts arriving. I had with me my Brownie 127, a real bottom of the range camera, which was able to take only eight photographs on each roll of film so you had to be very selective. Lonnie Donegan was on the show, but in the last year the Shadows had come on to the scene and I was looking forward to seeing them as well. Before we went in we saw Adam Faith and Hank B. Marvin (he has now dropped the B) of the Shadows arriving and I managed to get a couple of photos.

The full line up of the show was, Jerry Lordan, The Mudlarks, Bert Weedon, Billy Fury, Alma Cogan, Lonnie Donegan, The John Barry Seven, Adam Faith, Mark Wynter, Russ Conway, The King Brothers, Connie Francis, The Shadows, Cliff Richard, Ted Heath (the band leader not the ex. Prime Minister), Emile Ford and the Checkmates. With the exception of American singer Connie Francis this was the cream of British Pop but apart from Cliff, Adam, Billy, Lonnie and The Shadows the rest, in my mind, was just padding, and even Lonnie's career had peaked as he was only a year away from his last ever top ten hit. John Barry went on to fame and fortune as a film composer and co-wrote The James Bond Theme.

Saying that, I did enjoy the show, Lonnie was great and so were the Shadows, who looked so cool with Hank Marvin and Bruce Welch playing identical red Fender Stratocasters and Jet Harris a red Precision Bass, all through matching Vox amplifiers. They only performed one number their latest hit FBI before Cliff Richard joined them to a chorus of boos from a mainly male section of the audience who felt that the Shadows should have performed for longer, and so did I.

After the show we were invited to stay in our seats as all the acts returned to perform a couple of numbers each, which was recorded by ABC television and broadcast on Saturday 25th March. Lonnie sang "Miss Otis Regrets" and "Gamblin' Man" which sounded a bit untogether from where I was sitting.

Lonnie Donegan would sometimes change the way he would perform a song live. He would occasionally move verses or lines around, (I never knew if it was intentional or a bad memory) and the guitar solos were usually different. This could be interesting if the changes worked but could be frustrating to hard core fans like myself who would prefer him to stick more to the recorded version.

Wednesday 8th March 1961

George Formby and conductor Sir Thomas Beecham died today.

Sunday 9th April 1961

Lonnie Donegan appeared on TV, in an advert for "Chivers Jelly".

Thursday 13th July 1961

I was in the middle of taking my GCE exams and today I had a meeting with the headmaster, Mr. Gilbey, about what I was going to do next, i.e. stay on in the sixth form or go out into the big wide world and get a job. I was quite an average pupil when it came to exams and the minimum target was five GCE O levels where the only career choice in those days seemed to be the bank or the Civil Service. I mentioned to Cyril (all the pupils called the headmaster by his first name behind his back) that I quite fancied a career in music, but the only sort of music he really understood was classical, and he said that there were no guitar players in orchestras. This was 1961 and Rock n' Roll was in it's infancy, so the teachers of the day were of an age that did not understand what the pop music world was about, and it was inconceivable to them that you could make a career from it, but forty seven years on and I'm still getting away with it.

Wednesday 9th August 1961

Today I bought my first brand new guitar, a Futurama 3, probably the first Fender Stratocaster copy ever. These guitars were really good for the price (£45) they were of Czechoslovakian origin and imported into this country by Selmer Musical Instruments. I had ordered mine from my local music shop Universal Music in Hatfield but was a little disappointed as the one they had sent was dark red and I had ordered a sunburst one. It didn't take too long to get over this and I took it straight home and plugged in and I was away. I was well pleased that it had finally arrived as in three days I was off to Butlins again and wanted to make a concerted effort in "The People National Talent Contest".

George Harrison played a Futurama Guitar in his early days with the Beatles.

Saturday 12th August 1961 - Saturday 19th August

It was back to Butlins Holiday Camp at Clacton for the annual holiday, and the car was packed with Mum and Dad, Nigel, our suit cases and most importantly my brand new Futurama guitar and amplifier.

On the first night I went up to the Rock and Calypso Ballroom (the music press were keen to have a rival style of music to Rock n' Roll, first it was Traditional Jazz and then Calypso music took over for a short time, hence the rather quaint name) I found a group called Terry Young and the Young Stars who were really good. They had a guy called Bruce Baxter on lead guitar, who would go on to join Swedish group the Spotniks followed by a spell producing all of the Top of the Pops albums. On bass was a guy called John Rostil who was only two years away from joining The Shadows. John was tragically electrocuted in his recording studio on 26th November 1973

I worked my way through the heats of the People National Talent Competition and on Thursday night won the 'speciality' section of the weekly final. I performed Lonnie Donegan's "Grand Coulee Dam" in front of 500 people in the Gaiety Theatre. My prize was £3 plus a free week's holiday at Butlins to take part in the end of season finals. Second prize was two weeks holiday ---. Sorry, I couldn't resist it.

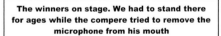

| The winners on stage. We had to stand there for ages while the compere tried to remove the microphone from his mouth | Looking rather smug as I'd just won £3.00 |

On the Friday afternoon I appeared in the final of the Players Bachelor Pop Singing contest backed by Terry Young and the Young Stars which was the first time I had ever sung with a full group. I was still in Lonnie mode so I sang "Have a Drink on Me", and was placed first winning £5 and 100 Players Bachelor cigarettes, which made Mum and Dad happy as I didn't smoke and they did.

Terry Young asked me to go back in the evening and sing a couple of songs with the band which I did, and later performed a short spot in the South Seas Bar. I travelled home the following day on cloud nine thinking that I had already made it in show business, and when I read the People newspaper on Sunday and found my name as one of the talent contest winners I was a legend in my own mind.

In the dining room at Butlins, the chefs would prepare the food in full view of the diners and one of these chefs was to cross my path many times during the coming years. I didn't know it at the time but his name was Tony Rivers.

Friday 1st September 1961

Today I went to the Radio and Television Exhibition at Earls Court in London, which I would try to visit every year. It was basically an exhibition for the radio and television trade, but I spent most of my time at the BBC and ITV stands where celebrities would make personal appearances, and some television programmes were even broadcast live. There was a group playing on the BBC stand called the Malcolm Mitchell Trio, who were asking people to get up and sing with them. Of course I had to get up and sing a couple of numbers obviously thinking that as it was the BBC someone would hear me and be very impressed and make me a star, but not today.

Tuesday 5th September 1961

Today I received my GCE results, not great, three passes, maths and metalwork grade 6 which was a minimum pass and music grade 4 (which was more to do with the aural paper, rather than any understanding I had of "Handel's Messiah"). I had already decided to stay on in the sixth form to do A level maths and physics, but I hadn't even passed O level Physics. I really wasn't bothered too much as all I could think about was returning to Butlins in a few days winning the talent contest and on to fame and fortune. How wrong was my thinking?

I had phoned Cyril and he had given permission to miss the first week of term.

Saturday 9th - Saturday 16th September 1961

It was back to Clacton by train (Butlins paid) but when I arrived, it was a bit of a shock, it was the very last week of the season and lots of things in the camp had closed down. Terry Young and the Young Stars had finished and gone home, it was a bit depressing. There had been four winners in the talent contest each week, one male singer, one female singer, one comedian and a speciality act, so there were 52 acts fighting for four places in the Grand Final. There were heats, a semi final and a final. I reached the final but didn't make it through. At the time it was a huge disappointment, and the compere, told me that I had missed out by three points but invited me to appear on his cabaret show on the Friday.

I sang few songs at the cabaret show and then the compere announced to the audience that I had made such an impression that he was going to personally get me an audition with the BBC. Bullshit, I never ever heard from him again.

Monday 18th September 1961

It was down to earth with a crash, and back to school to take on the complexities of Pure and Applied Maths, Physics, and to knuckle down and try to retake some of the O levels that I screwed up in the summer. We had a teacher, Mr. Madden who taught Pure Maths and I can honestly say that I didn't understand one thing he was talking about during the whole year that I suffered this intolerable subject. I didn't see the point in it, but Madden was responsible for one memorable comment to me when I was sitting in class day dreaming about Fender and Gibson guitars, "Griggs, you may be a virtuoso on the guitar but Pure Maths will get you much further in life."

Friday 1st December 1961

I had decided to have some singing lessons at the Maurice Burman School of Pop Singing. I'm not exactly sure of my reasons for doing this but from memory it may have been because Helen Shapiro had been to this school and been "discovered" there. This might have been my ulterior motive. The school was in Bickenhall Mansions just off Baker Street in London and cost £1.2s.6d for a 30 minute lesson. I had chosen Friday afternoons as I had no lessons and Cyril had given me permission, once again, to have the time off school.

I felt full of self importance as walked into the rather posh block of flats, climbed the stairs and rang the door bell. I was introduced to my teacher Jack Ball and in the first lesson; he recorded my voice on a very professional looking tape machine, and gave me some vocal exercises to practise at home.

Saturday 2nd December 1961

Today I had a letter to say that I had been chosen as the outright season's winner of "The Players Bachelor Pop Singing Contest" at Butlins and had won a recording test for Filmusic Publishing Company. This had been judged by Terry Young and the Young Stars, to whom I was very grateful. My hopes for instant stardom rose once again.

Wednesday 27th December 1961

I taught Nigel, now aged eleven, a few basic things on guitar. It was the first time he'd shown an interest, although it would be 1963 before he took up the bass guitar seriously, and further fourteen years before he would join New Zealand band "Split Enz".

1962

Monday 1st January 1962

Although not many people outside of Liverpool knew of the Beatles, on this day they were in London having a recording test for Decca Records. They recorded mostly songs from their stage act plus a few originals for Decca A & R manager Mike Smith. They subsequently failed the audition and Mike Smith would be forever known as the man who turned down the Beatles, although listening to these tracks today, they were OK, but there wasn't much hint of what was to come. They were, however, only ten months away from releasing their first single "Love Me Do".

In the top ten this first week of 1962 were two "trad jazz" records, Acker Bilk at No.1 with "Stranger on the Shore" and Kenny Ball at No.6 with "Midnight in Moscow". Also in the top ten were Frankie Vaughan with "Tower of Strength", Petula Clark with "My Friend the Sea", and Billy Fury keeping the Rock n' Roll flag flying with "I'll Never Find another you" although this was more of a ballad.

Tuesday 9th January 1962

My first day back at school after the Christmas holidays was always hard to take, but I'd only been there an hour when Dad arrived to tell met there had been a call from my singing school and that I should get there as soon as possible as the BBC were filming a piece for their "Tonight" programme and they wanted me to take part. I (reluctantly?) left Mr. Madden's pure maths class and headed off to catch a train. I spent the day at the Maurice Burman School, with several of the other pupils, where the BBC filmed me singing one song before I was interviewed by a guy called Trevor Philpot.

Friday 12th January 1962

I had told the whole world that I was going to be on television this evening but when the piece came on it lasted about a minute and they did not show my song or my interview, just a quick glimpse of me sitting in the background. I was devastated and I knew I had some explaining to do.

Saturday 27th January 1962

Entertaining the kids at Saturday Morning Pictures whether they liked it or not.

I sang a few songs at the Hatfield Odeon, for the kids at Saturday morning pictures. The manager, Mr. Firman, had asked me to perform after reading an article about me in the local paper. Ten unfortunate boys were required to hold the letters that spelled out my name across the stage, which I found extremely embarrassing, but singing on a proper stage with stage lights was incredible.

Mr. Firman said that he would like me to come back again in a couple of week's time when the new Cliff Richard film "The Young Ones" would be shown.

Friday 16th February 1962

My first time in a studio. Nice guitar lousy tie.

It was the day of my recording test. I had to get a taxi to take me, my amplifier and guitar to the station, then a taxi the other end to Oriole Records, in Bond Street, London. I performed two songs with just my guitar for backing; they were "Grand Coulee Dam" and "Sea of Heartbreak" a recent hit for Don Gibson. When I heard the playback I was pleased as they had used reverberation (a type of echo), and this was the first time I had heard this effect on my voice, which probably needed all the help it could get.

The people at Film Music Publishing Company said they would let me have a copy of the recording and also send it off to record companies, but once again nothing would come of this venture.

Friday 2nd March 1962

We had our mid term A level exam results today and I came twelfth out of thirteen in both physics and pure maths and was amazed that there was one person worse than me. I did achieve two more O level passes making the total now five.

In the evening I did a repeat performance at Hatfield Odeon playing a short set before the showing of Cliff Richard's film "The Young Ones". I was horrified when Mr. Firman the cinema manager asked me specifically to sing Cliff's song "The Young Ones", but I reluctantly agreed. I was not a Cliff Richard fan.

Thursday 22nd March 1962

Dad had received another call from the Maurice Burman Singing School. ITV were doing a piece on the school in a fifteen minute daily magazine programme called "Here and Now" and they wanted me to appear in it. Rehearsals were today at ATV Studios in Wembley. Dad drove me to the school to meet everyone and then it was off to Wembley for rehearsals. Because I missed out last time I was asked to sing a song and be interviewed. The programme would be recorded next Tuesday and broadcast the same day. I was quite excited by this but decided not to tell too many people after the disappointment of last time.

Tuesday 27th March 1962

I struggled to the train with my guitar and amplifier, on my way to Associated Rediffusion Studios in Kingsway, London, to record the TV programme "Here and Now". We rehearsed throughout the day and the programme was recorded at 5.45 and went out on air one hour later at 6.45pm. There were several of the pupils on the show and Jack Ball, the teacher, was interviewed just before my spot.

I was interviewed by a guy called Michael Ingrams:

MI. "Paul do you think you've learned a lot from this school"
PG "Yes, er, I think my breathing has improved and also my voice production"
MI "Do you think you are ready to turn professional yet"
PG "Well I'd like to---
MI "Do you think you could wow them at The Palladium"
PG. "Oh I don't know about that"
MI "Well wow us now.

I then sang "The Comancheros" another song of Lonnie's although it was the beginning of the end of my Lonnie Donegan era. When the show was over we went upstairs to a viewing lounge for drinks and to see the programme transmitted live on air. It was strange seeing myself on television for the first time, don't forget this was 1962, we were years away from home videos, and it wasn't even in colour.

I said my goodbyes and then this new found star of television struggled with his guitar and amplifier back to the underground and then onto the train and home to Hatfield. I was paid seven guineas (£7.35p) for my performance.

Wednesday 28th March 1962
At school, Cyril mentioned in assembly that I had been on television the previous evening and I wallowed in the glory of people coming up to me and saying that they had seen it. After morning lessons I was a legend in my own lunchtime.

Thursday 31st May 1962
It was obvious to everyone including myself that I was never going to pass any GCE A levels and that I would be leaving school in the summer, and as I hadn't yet achieved fortune and fame in the pop music business, the reality was to find some "honest" employment. I had already been for a few interviews at banks and for the civil service, but today I had an interview with the Westminster Bank Head Office in Lothbury London. The building looked as if it should have been a museum, and I didn't really want to be there, but after the interview "The Westminster Bank" was destined to become my employer, if only for eighteen months.

Monday 18th June 1962
I had answered an advert in the local paper from a group who were looking for a rhythm guitarist who could sing and today I auditioned for them. I sang a few songs and got the job. It was a five piece band, two guitars, bass and drums, and a lead singer. The group was to be called Bobby Hale and the Halestones (great name?) and it was run by the lead guitarist a guy called Roy Staughton.

Thursday 21st June 1962

Today I bought my last ever Lonnie Donegan single. I had become increasingly disillusioned with Lonnie as he had started to record a lot of material with orchestras and this was not what I wanted to hear. His last single had been "The Party's Over" coupled with "Somewhere over the Rainbow". This latest one was a song he had co-written with his ex. guitarist Jimmy Currie and was called "I'll Never Fall in Love Again". It was the first single of Lonnie's that failed to make the charts, although it would become a hit for Tom Jones some years later.

I wasn't just a fan of Lonnie, it was seeing him as part of a group that was the attraction, but it was obvious that he wanted to branch out and be an all round entertainer, which didn't please his hard core fans. Lonnie would only have one more chart hit "Pick a Bale of Cotton" that was destined to reach number eleven in August 1962.

Joe Brown and the Bruvvers (a great act but they couldn't spell) had just enjoyed a huge hit with "A Picture of You" and my allegiance had shifted. Joe was a great guitarist and once again it was a band situation. "A Picture of You" had been co-written by Peter Oakman who would go on to be Lonnie Donegan's bass player and would play with Lonnie at his last ever show in Nottingham a few days before he died in 2002.

Friday 27th July 1962

My last day at school, and I can't say I was sorry. I had wasted a year of my life studying things that would be of no use to me in my life ahead. The only thing I learned in the sixth form was how to swim. Because of my kidney complaint I hadn't been allowed in the water until last year, so when I was awarded my 25 yards certificate in assembly I was the lone sixth former amongst a sea of juniors.

I now had six weeks before I was due to start work. In the evening I sang at one of my local pubs, the Hilltop in Hatfield and had two of my new band mates backing me.

Monday 3rd September 1962

Today I got on my bike and cycled to the Westminster Bank in Hatfield for my first day's work. I nervously went in and was introduced to my boss, the bank's chief clerk Mr.McCombie. I was put to work doing 'sort away', a job I would have to endure for the next two months. All cheques written by customers were eventually returned to the bank and my job was to file them. In 1962 there were no customers names printed on the cheques, so I had to read their names from the signatures, many of which were illegible. It was mind numbing, and as new boy I was bottom of the pile when it came to choosing holiday dates, still I could pick any date in January or February. My salary was £310 per year.

As I lived only ten minutes away from the bank, at lunchtime I would cycle home, grab a quick sandwich and spend thirty minutes playing my guitar. It was much needed therapy.

Friday 5th October 1962

The Beatles record "Love Me Do" was released today but it passed me by and it would be another six months before they made an impact on me.

Saturday 20th October 1962

Bobby Hale and the Halestones on stage.

Me showing off.

It was the first booking for Bobby Hale and the Halestones at St. Mary's Church Hall, in Welwyn. We had been rehearsing for the last couple of months and now we were ready to go. I had a spot where I sang a couple of Joe Brown Songs and played a couple of instrumentals. Joe Brown would perform "Hava Nagila", playing the last section with his guitar behind his head, and I had been practising this for the last few weeks and managed to get through it without making a prat of myself. I also did "Orange Blossom Special" a very fast instrumental recorded by Swedish group "The Spotniks" which was quite impressive if you didn't cock it up. Our opening song was Cliff Richard's "It'll Be Me".

We all wore matching blue cardigans with an "H" badge which looked as though it should have been on a school cap, while Jock our lead singer wore a suit and a bow tie. The gig went well, there was only one fight, and we were paid £2.00 each.

Sunday 28th October 1962

The whole world was worried about the Cuban crisis. We were in the middle of the cold war and the USA and the USSR both had a large stockpile of nuclear weapons and were playing cat and mouse with each other. The USA had evidence that the Soviets was building missile launching sites in Cuba and when a fleet of Soviet ships was seen heading towards Cuba with nuclear weapons on board, President Kennedy ordered American ships to stop them. It was a really frightening time as there was a strong possibility that the world would be plunged into a nuclear war. In the end The Soviet ships turned back and on this day President Khruschev agreed to dismantle the Cuban missile sites. The world breathed a sigh of relief.

Friday 9th November 1962

This evening was Bobby Hale and the Halestones second booking but first I had a day at work hoping that I would not be kept too late. The Westminster Bank in Hatfield was a very busy branch and the staff could not leave until the days work was finished i.e. when the tills and the books balanced. After 5.00pm we were paid overtime and generally this was everyday with Fridays being exceptionally busy. Sometimes on a Friday we would work as late as 8.00pm, which was great for the extra money, but not a lot of good for a young man of seventeen with outside commitments.

We got out at 7.15 and Dad was waiting in his car with my guitar and amplifier, and my "naff" blue cardigan, and we drove straight to the Market Hall, St. Albans as we were due to be on stage at 8.30. I made it OK although rather smelly and hungry, as there was no time for a bath or food. The gig went well; we supported the top local group of the time, the Bluetones. One of their members was Jim Rodford who would later play with the Kinks and Argent.

Tuesday 27th November 1962

This evening I went to the Odeon Cinema St. Albans to see "Larry Parnes Mammoth Star Show 1962." Larry Parnes was a concert promoter and artist manager. He gave his artists quite aggressive names like Billy Fury, Marty Wilde, Vince Eager and Dickie Pride and would promote pop shows that featured them. Tonight Billy Fury was top of the bill backed by the Tornadoes and supported by Joe Brown, Marty Wilde, Mike Sarne, The Karl Denver Trio, Jimmy Justice, Mark Wynter and Peter Jay and the Jaywalkers. Joe Brown was great as expected, but I also enjoyed Peter Jay and the Jay Walkers who were a seven piece instrumental band who played matching Vox Phantom guitars and each member wore a different coloured suit. There was also a light inside the bass drum that flashed when it was hit. Pretty impressive stuff in 1962. They would go on to tour quite extensively with the Beatles but only had one small hit "Can Can 62". Today Peter Jay is one of Europe's top circus directors and runs the Hippodrome circus in Great Yarmouth.

Sunday 9th December 1962

Lonnie Donegan appeared on Sunday Night at The London Palladium, the first that I had seen him on television in a while. Denny Wright had rejoined on lead guitar after an absence of five years.

Denny Wright is considered by most people, me included, to be the best guitarist ever to play with Lonnie. He had joined Lonnie in 1956 and although his first stint lasted barely a year, before he handed over to Jimmy Currie, Denny made a big impact playing on the early hits. He played memorable guitar solos on "Don't you Rock me Daddy O" and "Cumberland Gap" (that last note was unique) and also played great blues piano on "How Long How Long Blues". He inspired many guitarists who were starting out around that time.

A few years ago I was asked to sing a few of Lonnie's songs in a charity show arranged by top session drummer Bobby Graham, and had the honour of Big Jim Sullivan playing lead guitar with me. We had a chat about Lonnie (Big Jim had recently played with him in concert) and he enthused about the huge influence Denny Wright had been to him when he first took up the guitar. Denny also played with Jazz violinist Stephane Grappelli and Johnny Duncan and the Blue Grass Boys. He sadly died from cancer in 1992.

1963

Thursday 3rd January 1963

Last month the Beatles had struggled to Number seventeen in the charts with "Love Me Do" with little hint of the amazing impact that they would have in just a few months time. Top of the Charts this first week in 1963 was Cliff Richard with one of his now customary ballads, "The Next Time", Elvis was at Number two with "Return to Sender", Frank Ifield at three with "Lovesick Blues" and Rolf Harris at four with "Sun Arise".

Bobby Hale and the Halestones had been rehearsing at the Breaks Youth Centre in Hatfield, for the past few months. It was run by Bill (Skip) Salmon, and every Thursday night he would put on a dance and tonight I saw Brian Poole and the Tremeloes for the first time. They were very professional and had top class Fender equipment, both guitars and amps. They put on a great show and I was really impressed, and I walked home wishing the Halestones could replace their, hotchpotch, gear with some top of the range equipment.

After Brian Poole and the Tremeloes had signed to Decca Records, a story emerged claiming that when the Beatles had been turned down by Decca, it was because the preferred act had been Brian Poole. I have always suspected that a publicist was responsible for that one.

Wednesday 13th March 1963

Today I went to St. Albans Odeon to see another one of Larry Parnes package shows called, "Your Lucky Stars". This time Joe Brown topped the bill supported by, Rolf Harris, Shane Fenton, The Tornados, Peter Jay and The Jaywalkers, Jess Conrad, Susan Maughan, and Eden Kane.

In the 1970s Shane Fenton would change his name to Alvin Stardust and become a fellow artist on Magnet Records when Guys n' Dolls signed to the same label in 1974

Thursday 11th April 1963

Bobby Hale and the Halestones appeared for the first time at the Community Centre in Welwyn Garden City, known as the Hop. We had a bad gig and afterwards there was a huge row. Cracks had been appearing in the band and I felt its days were numbered. It was the usual type of group arguments everybody blaming everybody else for the bad gig; it was very Spinal Tap. "This is Spinal Tap" was a spoof documentary made in 1984 about a fictitious Rock Band and all the trials and tribulations associated with it. It is one of my favourite films and brilliantly funny especially to anybody who has been involved with a band. There had been tensions in the group for some time. Jock our lead singer was often absent from rehearsals, so in his absence we would learn instrumentals or songs that Roy or I would sing. Jock would then argue that he was not singing enough. Catch 22. I only had two months left.

On this day the Beatles" released "From Me to You" which as a song knocked me out completely. Probably in hindsight, with all their great songs that followed this is not a classic, but at the time it was so uniquely different to anything that had gone before. There was so much energy and musically the chord changes were different. It was in the key of C and instead of the middle eight bars going to the obvious F, it went to G minor. Not only that there was a diminished chord as well. Brilliant! Roy and I were soon singing this in The Halestones one of the songs we learnt in Jock's absence.

Thursday 2nd May 1963

Tony Rivers & the Castaways with the Beatles. 21/4/1963

(Photo courtesy of Tony Rivers)

This evening I went to "The Breaks Youth Centre" to see a group called Tony Rivers and the Castaways. When the curtains opened I suddenly realised that the lead singer, Tony Rivers, had been my chef at Butlins way back in 1961. After they had finished I went to have a chat with Tony and he remembered me from appearing in the talent competitions at Butlins and our paths would be destined to cross many times in the years to come. The group were great, they specialised in doing a fair number of Beach Boys songs and the harmonies were spot on.

I only found out years later but ten days prior to our meeting, Tony Rivers and the Castaways had supported the Beatles at the "Pigalle Club" in London on Sunday 21st April 1963.

Thursday 9th May 1963

A week later I was back at the Breaks for the Thursday dance and this week it was Nero and the Gladiators who were a four piece band led by Mike O'Neil (aka Nero) who wore a toga and laurel leaves on stage. The other three musicians wore roman/gladiator type costumes and for 1963 it was visually impressive. They had made several records one of which was a complicated instrumental called "Czardas". This was on old Hungarian folk dance that was fast and difficult to learn how to play, which I knew as I was still labouring with it.

I requested Czardas and was told that Colin Green the guitarist on the record had left the band and the new guitarist couldn't play it. Colin Green had joined Georgie Fame and the Blue Flames.

Friday 10th May 1963

The amplifier that Dad built me had served me well, but it was time to upgrade and I had my heart set on a Vox, which is what all the top bands including the Shadows and the Beatles were using. I had been saving every penny I could since I started work and today spent £142.16s.0d (£142.80p) on a brand new Vox AC30 super twin amplifier. It looked and sounded great and it was loud, very loud.

Monday 13th May 1963

The Halestones had a meeting this evening, and like most of our meetings it deteriorated into a row over some minor point, and tonight was no exception. Roy had recently bought a van and was using it to transport the group and the equipment to and from gigs. Tonight he decided that to make life easier, all the gear should be kept in the van at his house, it would be locked in a garage and safe (so he said). I objected to this strongly as there was no way I would let my pride and joy, my three day old Vox AC30 amplifier out of my site let alone leave it in a van four miles away. It provoked a major argument between Roy and I but there was no way I was going to budge.

Monday 20th May 1963

By now the Beatles had made a huge impact on me and having bought their first album "Please Please Me" I had persuaded the group to learn a couple of their numbers. We learned "Twist and Shout" which was fast becoming a major performance number for the Beatles, although they never released it as a single.

Brian Poole and the Tremeloes recorded a very fast emotionless version of the song, which I wasn't keen on, but it would give them their first hit reaching number four in the charts.

Monday 10th June 1963

In the evening we had group practise after which there was a huge row between Roy and me, which culminated in me throwing my toys out of the pram and quitting the group. Roy and I had got on well, until the argument about leaving the equipment in his van, since then the relationship had been strained.

Tuesday 11th June 1963

I had wanted my own band for sometime and had a friend called Roger Cook who was a drummer and I'd jammed with him a few times. I called him and said that I was starting my own group and he said "I'm in". I then placed an advert in the local paper looking for a singer, a bass player and rhythm guitarist.

Thursday 20th June 1963

Johnny Kidd
and the
Pirates.

I had a reply to the advert from a guy called Barry Banks who was a rhythm guitarist and his girl friend, a singer called Pat Heley. They were to become members of my new band, but finding a bass guitarist would prove more difficult.

In the evening I went to the Breaks and saw Johnny Kidd and the Pirates who were great. They'd had several hits in the past few years including "Shakin' all Over" which reached number one, and was one of the great early British rock records. They had a raw edge and aggression on stage and dressed in pirate costumes and had a back drop of a pirate's ship. Their lead guitarist was Mick Green, who went on to join Billy J. Kramer's Dakotas and would play with Paul McCartney, on his "Run Devil Run" album.

Johnny Kidd was killed in a car crash near Bury on Friday 7th October 1966. The Pirates still perform to this day.

Friday 16th August 1963

I was by now completely hooked on the Beatles and had bought everything that had been released, which were three singles and one album. I was fascinated by their image and their instruments. I had never seen a Hofner Violin Bass, or a Rickenbacker guitar before. George played a Gretsch Country Gentleman and although I'd seen Duane Eddy and Eddie Cochran with Gretsch guitars I had never seen a Country Gent. I wanted to see the Beatles live and had heard that they would be playing at the California Ballroom in Dunstable. This was a huge venue with two stages, and although almost every top act from that time, including the Rolling Stones, performed there, despite the rumours the Beatles never did.

I had read that the Beatles would be at Luton Odeon on Friday 6th September, so I had sent a postal order and a stamped address envelope to the box office and requested three tickets. The tickets landed on my doormat this morning.

I had been practising with my new band since June and we had decided to call ourselves Shelayne and the Cortinas, (Shelayne was Pat's idea).but we were still short of a bass guitarist. We had tried a couple but they were hopeless so we continued for now with two guitars, drums and a lead singer.

The bass guitar was still quite a recent phenomenon, as the very first one, the Fender Precision, had only been introduced in 1951. In the fifties, the upright double bass had been used by people like Elvis Presley, Bill Haley and of course Lonnie Donegan but with amplified guitars getting louder it couldn't cope.

Friday 6th September 1963

Flyer from "The Beatles" at Luton Which shows "Freddie Starr & the Midnighters" who were replaced by "The Fourmost

"She Loves You" had been released two weeks ago and was already top of the charts, and today I as going to see the Beatles play live for the first time but first I had to endure a day's work at the Westminster Bank. I almost had a nervous breakdown wondering if I would get out in time to see the show. As I've already said, we left the bank when the days work was done, and the books were balanced and Friday was always the busiest day.

I was especially worried as there had been some rather late nights recently and a couple of times we hadn't left until 9.00pm. I rushed around all day probably driving the rest of the staff mad trying to make sure they weren't slacking. I was just too conscientious in those days; I should have called in sick.

I eventually got away at 8.00pm, my two mates were waiting outside and we drove straight to Luton for the 8.45pm performance. I remember queuing outside and behind us were the Zombies, a local group that I knew as Colin Blunstone the lead singer lived around the corner from me. The Zombies were still a year away from having their first hit with "She's Not There" which was helped when George Harrison gave it a favourable review as a member of the panel on a programme called Juke Box Jury.

We had pretty good seats about fifteen rows from the front and had to endure four other acts before the Beatles. No matter how good they were there was only one act the audience had come to see.

A group called Rockin' Henry and the Hayseeds had just finished their act and there was one more name in the programme before the Beatles, and that was Patrick Dane's Quiet Five. I hadn't read the small print under their name which said that they were only on selected dates and not Luton. Suddenly the compere, Ted King, announced, "Ladies and Gentlemen, THE BEATLES!", and there they were. There were no curtains at the Odeon, the group just ran on stage wearing their famous grey collarless suits, plugged in, and went straight into "Roll Over Beethoven" followed by "Thank You Girl", "A Taste of Honey", "She Loves You", "Baby It's You", "From Me To You", "Boys", "I Saw Her Standing There", and finally "Twist and Shout", and they were gone. The PA system was two small speakers, one each side of the stage and you could just about make out which songs they were singing above the continual screams, but it was fantastic. We drove home from Luton planning when we would see them again.

Today the Odeon Luton is a church called "The COGIC Centre."

Saturday 7th September 1963
The Westminster Bank opened on a Saturday morning and today I had to work. My body was in the bank but my mind was still at Luton Odeon.

Tuesday 17th September 1963
I had an idea how to resolve our bass player problem. I had been trying to get my brother Nigel interested in playing bass. His musical background was similar to mine i.e. forced piano lessons with Mrs. Johnson, but he was also a dab hand on the recorder. We had done some harmony singing together and I had finally persuaded (or conned) him into buying a bass guitar. He was more interested in football and still is.

Today we collected his brand new cherry red Framus Star Bass from Universal Music in

Hatfield. It cost around £65 and as Nigel was still only 14 years old, the bass was almost as big as him. Bill Whyman from the Rolling Stones played one of these basses and the 'Stones' were just beginning to make an impact.

I began teaching Nigel easy bass lines and one of the first songs was "Thank You Girl" by the Beatles. You could play this song using virtually all open strings and very little fingering. He soon began to be able to pick out bass lines on his own. He needed an amplifier so good old Dad came to the rescue and built him one.

Saturday 28th September 1963

Over my right shoulder is a future Rolling Stone	Barry & I share a microphone	Roger Cook & his petrol powered drums.

Today Shelayne and the Cortinas had their first booking, at Onslow School Fete in Hatfield. The fete was opened by local actor Philip Madoc who over the years has appeared in many television productions, but is probably best known for that classic moment in "Dad's Army" when he played a captured German Officer, who was annoyed by Corporal Pike making fun of Hitler. The German officer said "What is your name boy" and Captain Mainwaring says "Don't tell him Pike."

Nigel had not yet got an amplifier and wasn't ready to play live, so we performed without a bass guitar. We had two Vox AC30 amplifiers and because we didn't have our own PA system, the two microphones went through these as well as the guitars. It seemed to work OK and we went down well, with Shelayne singing things like "It's My Party" and I sang, surprise, surprise, a few Beatles songs. In the crowd watching was a future Rolling Stone, a young Mick Taylor, who had been in the same class as Nigel at school.

Sunday 13th October 1963

Beatlemania was officially born on Sunday 13th October 1963 when the Beatles appeared on the top variety show of the time, Sunday Night at The London Palladium which was introduced by Bruce Forsyth. The show normally opened with a dance group called the Tiller Girls, but on this night, the curtains opened and there were the Beatles singing just the opening verse of "Please Please Me". The audience went wild with girls screaming at the tops of their voices. The curtains closed and for the next forty odd minutes Bruce Forsyth had a tough job trying to keep the audience from screaming during the other acts which consisted of a singer called Brook Benton and Des O'Connor.

Finally Bruce appeared on stage dressed in a "Beatles" collarless suit and a wig and said "I thought I'd be a dead ringer for Ringo,--- are you ready---are you steady--- 5, 4, 3, 2, 1, the Beatles". Cue for pandemonium as they sang "From Me To You", "I'll Get You", "She Loves You" and finally "Twist and Shout". The papers the following day reported the scenes of screaming fans inside and outside The Palladium and one of the papers coined the phrase, "Beatlemania". I still have my original reel to reel tape of the show, recorded with a microphone in front of the TV. It was just a year since the release of their first record "Love Me Do" (5/10/1962) and yet with only eighteen songs commercially available the Beatles were already the biggest pop act this country had ever seen, and nobody, and I'm sure, not even the Beatles themselves realised that the best was yet to come.

One thing the Beatles suffered from this evening was something that would often occur when they performed live on television, and that was bad sound balancing. Whoever was balancing the sound would often assume that there had to be a lead singer which wasn't always the case. The Beatles would use only two microphones on stage and when they sang songs like "From Me to You", and "She Loves You", John and Paul used separate mikes but would both be singing the lead line and occasionally breaking off into a harmony, sometimes with George joining them. At the beginning of their first number "From Me to You", Paul's microphone was hardly on so the sound was a bit odd. What should have happened was the two mikes should have been left at the same volume leaving the Beatles to balance themselves vocally, which is what they had been used to doing after playing up to six hours a night in German clubs.

Saturday 19th October 1963

The Cortinas had decided on what to wear on stage. It was to be pink shirts with tab collars, knitted ties, blue leather waistcoats, black trousers and Cuban heeled Beatle Boots. The Beatles had been wearing this style of boot from the beginning and they were fast becoming the "must have" footwear. Many shoe companies had latched on to this and were producing their own Cuban heeled boots, but the genuine ones that the Beatles wore came from a theatrical footwear retailer called Anello and Davide who had shops in London's Charing Cross Road, and Covent Garden.

There was such a demand for these boots that Anello and Davide found it hard to keep up, so they only sold them at their Covent Garden branch on a Saturday morning, until that day's supply had gone. I went with Roger Cook our drummer and joined the queue outside the shop. They let in four customers at a time and after an hour Roger and I managed to get in and buy our boots (£3.7s.6d if I remember correctly)

Tuesday 29th October 1963

I was becoming increasingly frustrated working at the bank. Although I was making extra money from the overtime, I hated never knowing what time I'd finish; and when I had a gig in the evening it was a nightmare. I had graduated to working as a cashier at the counter which I didn't mind as I got to meet the customers, like the girl who brought the cash in from the chemist and the girl from the bakers, both of whom I fancied.

Today was probably my worst day. After the bank closed each cashier had to balance his till and today my till was £100 over. £100 was a lot of money in 1963 and it meant that somewhere a customer was £100 short which the bank found totally unacceptable. Everything was checked and double checked and despite staying very late (my name was mud with the rest of the staff) we could not find it. At 8.00pm (and three hours overtime) we called it a day.

The mistake was rectified a few weeks later, when a local store found that a credit they had paid in had been added up incorrectly by £100 i.e. £130 + £230 = £260. It was as simple as that. I hadn't noticed the customer's mistake.

Wednesday 30th October 1963

Today I went to St. Albans Odeon to see a touring show that had an amazing line up of acts. Top of the bill were the Everly Brothers supported by the Rolling Stones, Bo Diddley and Little Richard. I liked the Everly Brothers but having them top of the bill was probably a mistake as there was so much excitement with the other acts, it was a bit of a come down in atmosphere having them close the show. Although they were excellent it was Little Richard who stole the show.

There was a local character called Cuddles, and anybody who went to local dances knew him as he would always ask the bands to let him get up and sing Little Richard numbers, the problem being once he was up there you could never get him off. He would dress as a "Teddy Boy" and wasn't really the full ticket, if you know what I mean. When the compere announced Little Richard the whole audience saw Cuddles leap from his seat, turn to the crowd with his arms in the air, and then turn towards Little Richard on stage and bow in homage. He then began dancing in the only way he knew how, mind and body in perfect un-coordination. What a sight.

The "Stones" were great, and I preferred them in those early days, they'd had a small hit with "Come on" and had just released the Beatles song "I Wanna Be Your Man". They had so much attitude and aggression. Opening the show was Mickie Most who would go on to be a top record producer and have his own successful record label RAK. The show was promoted by Don Arden, who had a reputation of being a hard man in the pop world (he allegedly dangled business rival Robert Stigwood out of a third floor window) and was Sharon Osbourne's Dad.

Saturday 2ⁿᵈ November 1963

"Shelayne and The Cortinas" featuring Nigel and his Giant Framus Bass (far right)

We had started to have problems with Shelayne. We had done a few gigs and she had started to get a bit temperamental and diva like. Today we played a local gig at De Havillands, Hatfield, our first with Nigel playing bass. The gig went well but afterwards Pat had rather too much to drink and became a little embarrassing.

Saturday 10ᵗʰ November 1963

The Beatles had appeared on the Royal Variety Performance last Monday 4ᵗʰ November and today it was shown on television. The sound was much better than their recent Palladium show; there was no screaming from the audience, who wore posh frocks and dinner jackets, just polite but enthusiastic applause at the end of each number. They sang "From Me To You", "She Loves You", "Til There Was You" and after John Lennon's now famous "rattle your jewellery" comment they ended with Twist and Shout.

Watching the recording again I was amused to see that immediately after John had said "would the people in the cheaper seats clap your hands, and the rest of you just rattle your jewellery" the TV people cut to a quick shot of the Queen Mother standing waving. This was obviously taken from the end of the show when she was about to leave, but I guess the producer thought it a good idea to have the Queen Mum appear to acknowledge John's now legendary comment.

Another amusing incident was when they'd finished their spot. In perfect unison they pulled their microphones back, unplugged their guitars, Ringo hopped off his drum stool, they all walked to the front, bowed to The Royal Box and then to the audience. While this was going on the orchestra was playing the most appalling, "lift music" version of "Twist and Shout".

Monday 18th November 1963

Things came to a head with Shelayne today. We had played at Sherrardswood Spastic Centre in Welwyn Garden City two days ago and Shelayne had been so emotional, having been confronted with a room full of disabled people that she could hardly sing. She kept bursting into tears so I did most of the singing, but they were a great audience and really knew how to enjoy themselves.

Tonight we had a group meeting which got rather heated and ended with Shelayne leaving the group. I cannot remember whether she was pushed or if she walked, but it meant we lost her boyfriend Barry too. We decided to look for a replacement guitarist while I would become lead singer, and as a four piece we would simply be called The Cortinas.

Friday 22nd November 1963

Today I heard the new Beatles single "I Wanna Hold Your Hand" and even on first hearing it sounded awesome.

In the evening while watching television there was a news flash and at that moment it seemed the whole world went into shock. The American President John F Kennedy had been brutally assassinated in Texas.

Sunday 24ᵗʰ November 1963

"THE JUNIORS"
(left to right)
John Glascock,
Mick Taylor,
Brian Glascock,
Malcolm Collins,
Alan Shacklock.

(Photo courtesy of Malcolm Collins)

Mick Taylor, who would eventually replace Brian Jones in the Rolling Stones, called round with his dad, and said that he was thinking of leaving his group the Juniors, and was interested in joining us. Mick was 15 years old, the same age as Nigel and was already a good guitarist. We had a chat and he said he would go away and think things over. Unfortunately a few days later he called to say that he had decided to stay with the Juniors, so we were still a guitarist short.

Sunday 8ᵗʰ December 1963

This evening I went to The Odeon Cinema in Watford and saw a show that featured Gerry and the Pacemakers topping the bill supported by, among others, the Rolling Stones.

It seems incredible today that the 'Stones' would be a support act, but at that time Gerry and the Pacemakers were hugely popular. They achieved their success mainly thanks to the Beatles manager Brian Epstein, who at this time could do no wrong. Their first three record releases had reached number one in the charts, the first time any act had achieved this. It was quite a short lived chart success as they would have their last ever hit in 1965.

Saturday 28ᵗʰ December 1963

I didn't have to wait very long to see the Beatles perform live again, as they were to perform a Christmas Show at the Finsbury Park Astoria (later to become the Rainbow) from Christmas Eve 1963 up to January 11th 1964. A friend and I managed to get two tickets (7/6d or 37p each) for the show on Saturday 28th December 1963. This show featured, Billy J. Kramer, the Fourmost, Tommy Quickly and Cilla Black who were all Brian Epstein's artists. The Barron Knights were also on the show and the whole thing was compered by Rolf Harris.

At the beginning of the show a large cardboard helicopter was lowered to the stage and one by one each act pretended to climb out and then be introduced by Rolf Harris. Everybody was off except the Beatles and the audience was teased by the helicopter taking off and hovering. Eventually it landed again and out came the Beatles to the loudest screams imaginable. They took part in several sketches during the evening until it was time for their closing spot which included tracks from their second album "With The Beatles", released a few weeks before on November 22nd. Once again they opened with "Roll over Beethoven" followed by "All My Loving", "This Boy", "I Wanna Be Your Man", "She Loves You", "Til There Was You", "I Wanna Hold Your Hand", "Money", and finally "Twist and Shout". Once again it was a great show.

1964

Saturday 4th January 1964

A few months ago I had ordered a Gibson 335 semi acoustic guitar from my local music shop Universal Music in Hatfield. Claude Childs the owner had told me it would take twelve weeks, but it had been nearer sixteen weeks since the order went in and there was still no sign.

The shop used to be a meeting place for musicians and we often popped in to see if Claude had anything new of interest. One of the musicians who I would often meet there was Donovan. Donovan (Leitch) lived in Hatfield and if you walked around South Hatfield on a summer's evening you would probably hear the strains of an acoustic guitar. That would be Donovan sitting on a wall somewhere. He was a year away from three consecutive weeks appearing on the top music show of the day Ready Steady Go, followed by a string of hits.

Today I went into the shop and from Claude I heard the usual story that there was no sign of my guitar, but he said he had just taken delivery of a brand new Gretsch Tennessean guitar that I might like to try. My thinking was George Harrison played a Gretsch so they must be OK. I tried it out for about thirty minutes, loved it and bought it. When I got it home I kept taking it out of the case every fifteen minutes just to look at it.

To make my day complete, a friend came round and said that he had got a couple of tickets spare for the Beatles Christmas Show next Friday, and did I want them? Did I want them!!!!!!?

Friday 10th January 1964

Tonight it was back to the Finsbury Park Astoria to see the Beatles Christmas show again. This time the seats weren't very good as we were right up high at the back, in the Gods, and because of the screaming I could hardly hear a thing.

Sunday 12th January 1964

The Beatles appeared for the second time on Sunday Night at the London Palladium and for the first time ever George Harrison was playing a Gretsch Tennessean Guitar like the one I had bought a week ago. I was rather chuffed.

Once again the opening of the show was different. Instead of the Tiller girls the curtains opened and in the dimmed lighting could be seen the outline of four people, three who seemed to be holding guitars. The audience thought is was the Beatles and went ballistic, the screams were deafening. The lights came up and there was Bruce Forsyth and three guys dressed as stage hands with brooms in their hands sweeping the stage.

Years later Bruce Forsyth would tell me the story of how they had wanted to do something different with the Beatles on that particular show, and their manager Brian Epstein had invited him to one of their Christmas dates. Bruce couldn't believe the volume of the girls screaming, so they came up with the idea of doing a sort of interview with no speaking. Bruce and the Beatles talked to each other, holding up cards with the words on them. It culminated with the four Beatles each holding up a card telling Bruce to "GET OFF YOU NIT".

Friday 24th January 1964

THE CORTINAS
(back) Nigel Griggs
Paul Crowland
(front) Roger Cook
Paul Griggs
Posing in front of our
Bedford Dormobile
Van

We had been auditioning rhythm guitarists for the past few weeks and decided on a guy called Paul Crowland, who lived locally. He had a Burns guitar which was OK.but was just about to get a Gibson 335 and a Vox amplifier. Roger Cook had just taken delivery of a brand new set of gleaming red "Trixon" drums so all in all the group had really good gear, much better than the Halestones. I've always been a self confessed snob when it comes to group equipment. Over the years when we've had changes of personnel and people ring for auditions, one of the first questions from me would be, "what gear have you got?"

Dad had recently bought a Bedford Dormobile van with the express purpose of driving us and our gear around. My Mum was the group's manager so with my brother Nigel on bass guitar the Cortinas were a bit of a Griggs monopoly. Nigel would get to find out a bit of what it's like in that sort of situation, when years later he joined Split Enz where two of the members would be brothers Tim and Neil Finn.

Thursday 30th January 1964

I was getting to really hate working at the bank with the stress of never knowing what time I was going to leave. The chief clerk was a tyrant and if any of the staff made a mistake, i.e. my £100 till difference, they would be shouted at and given a long lecture and as it was an 'open plan' bank it would be in front of customers which I found totally unprofessional.

A friend, who knew I was unsettled at the bank, had told me of a job that was available in an accounts department of a, made to measure, corset factory called Barclay Corsets, in Welwyn Garden City. "Made to measure corsets?" you might ask. This company specialised in customised corsets for the larger woman, the women would be measured up and a corset made to their specifications. Mind boggling, and difficult to comprehend in the twenty first century.

I had an interview and was offered a job at £475 per year and the hours were 9.00am to 5.30pm and 1.00pm finish on Fridays. I knew I was going to have a problem telling people I worked at a corset factory but I took the job.

Tuesday 4th February 1964

I had handed in my notice at the bank, the chief clerk Mr. McCombie was not amused and today I was summoned to The Westminster Bank head office for a meeting. I sat with a bank official and it was a bit like an interrogation with him wanting to know the reasons for me wanting to leave such a 'good' job. He went onto explain what a fine career banking was and that if I worked hard I could be a bank manager within twenty years, (what a scary thought), and said there were many good financial reasons why I should stay. All this fell on deaf ears, I was amazed that they had taken all this trouble and hadn't realised that the Westminster Bank thought I was such a "valuable" asset. I hoped that they would be able to struggle on without me.

Saturday 22nd February 1964

The Beatles had returned from their first trip to America today having spent two weeks there with incredible success. On the 8th February they had appeared for the first time on the Ed Sullivan Show and it was estimated that over seventy million people watched it. This show is now available on DVD and the performance was great, but they still suffered microphone balancing problem with John's mike not being loud enough.

Today they returned home and it was classed as being such an important news event that the afternoon sports programme Grandstand was interrupted while we watched the Beatles arrive at London Airport.

The Cortinas had been rehearsing hard for the last few weeks and this evening we performed our first gig with the new line up at the Cavendish Hall in Hatfield. It went well except that Nigel broke a bass string. There were a few girls screaming and throwing jelly babies, which was a sign of affection not a criticism. We performed covers of recent chart hits of the time, and closed with "Twist and Shout".

Monday 2nd March 1964

Three days ago I had said a joyful goodbye to the Westminster Bank and was given a

Chet Atkins LP as a leaving present. Today I reported for work at Barclay Corsets (but don't tell anyone), in Welwyn Garden City. From the outside it was quite an impressive Art Deco building that was built in the 1930s, but inside it was a bit old and jaded. I began work in the accounts department just me and five girls which was a bit of a bonus.

Sunday 22nd March 1964

Today the Cortinas performed at the Hilltop pub (now called the Harrier) in Hatfield and this would be the beginning of a residency that would last until the end of the year. The Hilltop had a large function room and they had begun to hold Sunday night entertainment which consisted of , the Cortinas opening and closing the show with a few numbers, a compere/comedian and a couple of different acts each week. It did us as a group, a lot of good as it made us learn new material all the time so the numbers weren't the same each week. On this first night we sang the brand new Beatles single "Can't Buy Me Love" which had only been released two days ago and which we had been frantically learning this morning.

Sunday 26th April 1964

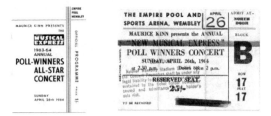

By the next time that I saw the Beatles live, they had conquered America and completed their first film "A Hard Day's Night", but today they took to the stage at the Empire Pool in Wembley for the annual New Musical Express Poll Winners Concert. I hadn't been to the Poll Winners Concert since 1961 and was there mainly to see the Beatles, but I was also keen to see the Rolling Stones who were by now becoming a major act and in a short time would be rivalling the Beatles.

These concerts tended to reflect the current climate of the British Pop Music industry and apart from Cliff Richard and the Shadows it was a completely different line up to the show that I had seen in 1961. Although the Beatles were by now the biggest thing since sliced bread, strictly there was no top of the bill, as all of the artists were listed in alphabetical order, and the line up was amazing:-.

Beatles, Joe Brown, Dave Clark Five, Freddie and the Dreamers, Gerry and the Pacemakers, Jet Harris, Hollies, Frank Ifield, Big Dee Irwin, Kathy Kirby, Billy J. Kramer and the Dakotas, Joe Loss Orchestra, Manfred Mann, Merseybeats, Brian Poole and the Tremeloes, Cliff Richard, Rolling Stones, Searchers, the Shadows, Swinging Blue Jeans.

The equipment for each band was on small individual stages, which were wheeled to the front of the main stage by stage hands who wore white coats. At last a small stage was wheeled out with Ringo's drums and that all too familiar Beatles logo, 10,000 people went crazy. Of all the places I saw the Beatles play live, Wembley's Empire Pool was the worst for sound. There was the four of them with three small amps and a drum kit, using the PA system that was used for the ice shows with a few small speakers in the roof and nothing at ground level. With 10,000 kids screaming, you really could hardly hear a thing. They sang "She Loves You", "You Can't Do That", "Twist and Shout", "Long Tall Sally" and finished with "Can't Buy Me Love". The Beatles were not the last act on, so when they had finished the Merseybeats came on stage to sing a couple of their hits to an audience who were coming down to earth after the mass hysteria of seeing the Beatles and I felt quite sorry for them. The reason for this was that while the Merseybeats were singing, the Beatles were making their exit from Wembley before 10,000 people made their escape impossible.

The concert was recorded by ABC Television and shown in two parts and the sound quality and balance in general was awful. There was only about a minute between each act to reset the stage and set up microphones so I wasn't really surprised. The stage was built specially for the show out of planks which wobbled and made the vocal microphones sway. One of the mikes was loose in the stand and about every thirty seconds gradually swivelled until it was at a 90 degree angle to the performer who then had to push it back to face him. At no time in the whole show did one of the white coated stage hands think to just tighten the mike holder.

The Beatles suffered badly with the TV sound. John had a bit of a mental block and sang a wrong verse in "She Loves You", Paul and George obviously couldn't hear him, and hadn't noticed, as they sang the correct verse over the top so it was a bit of a shambles. Ringo's drums could barely be heard.

Saturday 9th May 1964

The Cortinas had performed quite a few gigs in and around Hatfield in the past three months and we noticed that we had started to build a bit of a fan base from girls, a lot of whom thought Nigel was quite cute (he was still only fourteen years old). We started to get messages written in lipstick on the van and soon it was completely covered, mostly with declarations of love for my brother. This was a phenomenon that happened to most bands at all levels of popularity. Every band travelled to gigs in a van and it became a bit of a status symbol as to which band had the most messages. Some bands (without a sex god like my brother) were known to write their own messages, if they didn't get enough by natural means.

It was time to try our hand in the recording studio, so today we recorded two tracks at Regent Sound in Denmark Street, London, (Tin Pan Alley). It was the same studio that the Rolling Stones had recorded all their early hits and their first album, which quite impressed us, but when we got there we found a small dingy room with egg boxes on the ceiling to deaden the sound. However we were more than pleased with the results. We recorded two songs that the Beatles had sung on their radio shows "Pop Go the Beatles" but had never committed to vinyl. The first was "Clarabella" originally recorded by American group the Jodimars and the second the Carl Perkins song "I'm sure to Fall" and with Bill Farley, who engineered the Rolling Stones sessions, in charge, they sounded great.

Tuesday 12th May 1964

Roger Cook, the Cortinas drummer called in at Regent Sound to collect copies of the demo that we had made last Saturday. He saw the Rolling Stones there, who were recording a couple of new tracks..

Thursday 18th June 1964

This evening we had our first booking at one of the Breaks Youth Club Thursday night dances that were promoted by a guy called Stanley Dale. We supported Tony Rivers and the Castaways who were great as always. We had a bit of a jam session with them afterwards.

Saturday 27th June 1964

THE CORTINAS
On stage at "The
Westminster
Lodge".
There's nothing
like industrial
pipes and
brickwork to make
you feel like stars.

The Cortinas took part in a beat group competition that was held at the Westminster Lodge in St.Albans, with local groups like the Trekkas and the King Bees. In the afternoon they held heats and we got through. The final was held in the evening and was judged by the Barron Knights; the Cortinas were placed first and won £25. We had to play another short set before the Barron Nights closed the evening.

Sunday 12th July 1964

The Beatles new single "A Hard Day's Night" had been released a couple of days ago and this morning the Cortinas were frantically learning the song ready for tonight's gig at Hatfield's Hilltop pub. I had recently bought a fairly cheap Hawk acoustic 12 string guitar with a pick up and was trying to find the opening chord, something which has puzzled guitarists up to this day. It was played on George's Rickenbacker 12 string guitar.

I think George Harrison may have forgotten what he played because I heard an interview with Guitarist Gary Moore, who had asked George to show him the chord. It didn't sound quite right and Gary Moore said to him "are you sure" and apparently George gave him a look and said "I was there".

My own way of playing it is G.D.C.F.C.G. on a twelve string guitar. Is it right? Answers on a postcard.

Wednesday 29th July 1964

**Far right
A young
cricketing
Colin
Blunstone**

Travelling on a bus to St.Albans I met Colin Blunstone the lead singer with the Zombies. We had a chat and he was quite excited as their first record "She's Not There" had just been released and had been voted a hit on Juke Box Jury last week when George Harrison was a member of the panel. George had said that he liked the record and having the endorsement of a Beatle could do nothing but good. It was already selling well and would stay in the charts for eleven weeks peaking at number eleven. I was pleased for him but more than a little envious and wondered how long it would be before the Cortinas released a single.

Way back in the early fifties when I first got my Brownie 127 camera, I took a photograph of a group of friends who had been playing cricket. One of them was a very young Colin Blunstone.

Monday 10th August 1964

I was on holiday in Llandudno with a couple of mates and we decided to drive to Liverpool and visit the famous Cavern Club where the Beatles had played almost 300 times before they were famous. We parked the car and walked up Mathew Street and found the entrance. We went in, down the stairs that we had seen so many times on TV into this dark dank cellar, with bare brick walls. My first impression was how small and cramped it was. We bought a bowl of soup and a roll and sat down on rather uncomfortable wooden chairs and watched a Liverpool band called Earl Preston and the Realms perform a lunchtime session. It was only half full but I could just imagine the atmosphere that there must have been when it was packed, and the Beatles were playing on the rather small stage. Before we left I bought a Cavern badge as a souvenir.

Wednesday 2nd September 1964

The Cortinas had been invited to take part in a beat group contest at The Radio and Television Exhibition at Earls Court and having won the previous contest in June we fancied our chances. The group had quite a following in the Hatfield area by now, and we decided to try and take a coach load of fans up to Earls Court to give us support. We managed to fill a 44 seat coach and set off for London. I had managed to get the afternoon off from the corset factory.

We performed three songs, the fans that had come along with us gave us magnificent vocal support, and we were slightly pissed off as we were placed third behind the Nomads and the Bow Street Runners. The Bow Street Runners would shortly win television's Ready Steady Win, which was a bit like a sixties X-Factor for Pop Groups.

One of the people organising things was Peter Huggett who had been Lonnie Donegan's bass player back in 1960. He invited us to come back and perform a complete set on the following Saturday.

Saturday 5th September 1964

The Cortinas played at Earls Court again and some of our local fans came up again to give us support. We did our set just after there had been a personal appearance by the Yardbirds. We got talking to them in the dressing room and one of them seemed much quieter than the others. His name was Eric Clapton, and he was soon to leave the Yardbirds and join John Mayall's Bluesbreakers.

Sunday 11th October 1964

A guy called Mickey Willett, who had been the Kinks original drummer, phoned to say that he would like to bring Tommy Bruce along to see us this evening. Tommy had a number three hit in 1960 with "Ain't Misbehavin'" .

After our regular Sunday spot at the Hilltop in Hatfield, Mickey brought Tommy Bruce backstage to meet us and I remember being rather impressed that a real pop star was visiting us. He said that he had written a couple of songs and would we be interested in recording them. We said yes and Tommy said he would come to our rehearsals and teach them to us.

Wednesday 28th October 1964

Tommy Bruce had been down to the Breaks Youth Centre a couple of times to teach us his songs. It caused a bit of a stir as it wasn't often a "pop star" visited the Breaks. This evening the Cortinas were back in Denmark Street, London at Southern Music's Recording Studio, to record Tommy's songs. The session went well, one song was called "I'm Thinking" which was quite melodic and Beatles like. The other was called "Tennessee" and was much R n'B and a bit Rolling Stones. We were able to double track our voices, and for those who don't know, that means singing the same thing twice, so it sounds as if there are two of you singing. It thickens out the vocals especially where there are harmonies.

Mickey and Tommy were both pleased with the results and said they would see if they could get any interest from record companies.

Tommy Bruce passed away in 2006 and I put a tribute on his web site mentioning the songs that we recorded all those years ago. I was contacted by his manager who knew nothing about Tommy writing these songs so I was able to send a copy for him and Tommy's family.

Wednesday 4th November 1964

It was Beatles time again. the Beatles were nearing the end of their 1964 British tour and this evening they were back in Luton at the Ritz Cinema. I had managed to get three tickets for myself, Nigel and a friend with a car (which was important as I didn't drive).

Between 1963 and 1966 I managed to see the Beatles live on stage ten times (the restraining order has now been lifted) and I can honestly say I never had much problem getting tickets. These days it can be difficult getting tickets for major acts either on the phone or on the internet, but in the sixties all I had to do was find out from the venue when tickets were to go on sale, I would then send a cheque or postal order and a stamped addressed envelope. Only once did I have my cheque returned because they had sold out.

Once again we had to sit through six acts before the Beatles came on. One of the acts was Mary Wells an American singer that the Beatles admired and she was good. The Liverpool band the Remo Four were also good, but the rest of the bill I found a bit hard going.

Finally they were on stage and it was the best I'd seen them and despite the screaming girls I could hear them well. They opened with a shortened version of "Twist and Shout", followed by:- "Money", "Can't Buy Me Love", "Things We Said Today", "I'm Happy Just To Dance With You", "I Should Have Known Better", "If I Fell", "I Wanna Be Your Man", "A Hard Day's Night" and finished with "Long Tall Sally".

Thursday 26th November 1964
Today I heard that "She's Not There" by the Zombies had reached number one in the charts in America. I was pleased for Colin Blunstone as he was a Hatfield boy, but not ashamed to admit that once again I was a little jealous.

Monday 7th December 1964
Yesterday I had read in the paper that Tony Rivers and the Castaways had been involved in a serious road crash in their van, and drummer Brian Talbot know as "Shirt" had been killed. The paper said that three other members of the band were in a critical state. It was a huge shock as we knew them all well. We had been support band to them only a few months ago.

 I rang Tony's manager, who told me that Tony was OK but at that point Ray Brown the bass guitarist was in a bad way. He and the rest of the band would eventually make a complete recovery and be back on stage.

Saturday 19th December 1964
Tonight the Cortinas appeared at the Hermitage Ballroom in Hitchin, supporting Steve Marriott's Moments. In a few months Steve Marriott would form the Small Faces, and my only memory of him that night was that he was a bit cocky, and told us that their guitarist had been injured in a car accident and tonight he was going to have to play lead guitar for the first time.

1965

Thursday 7th January 1965

The Beatles performed a series of Christmas concerts for the second year running calling them "Another Beatles Christmas Show" which ran from Christmas Eve 1964 to Saturday January 16th 1965. This time it was at Hammersmith Odeon in London and I had sent away for tickets a couple of months ago and managed to get two seats for this evening in the third row of the circle at £1.00 each.

Nigel and I travelled up to London by train, and made our way to Hammersmith. When we reached the theatre we were greeted by an amazing sight. There were crowds of girls outside screaming at anything that moved inside the building. If a person's shadow was seen at an upstairs window, it must have been made by a Beatle, so the girls erupted, it was mayhem. We eventually made our way inside, found our seats, and waited for the curtain to rise.

On the show with the Beatles were Freddie and the Dreamers, Sounds Incorporated, Elkie Brooks, The Yardbirds, Michael Haslem, The Mike Cotton Sound, and Ray Fell. The show was compered by DJ Jimmy Saville. The Beatles appeared in a couple of sketches, but in my diary I wrote that the show, in general, was a bit boring until it was time for the main attraction.

The sound was good with the Beatles performing a great set, even better than at Luton, last November, and they were now including tracks from their latest album "Beatles For Sale" which had been released a month earlier. They opened with a shortened version of "Twist and Shout" followed by, "I'm a Loser", "Baby's in Black", "Everybody's Trying To Be My Baby", "Can't Buy Me Love", "Honey Don't", "I Feel Fine", "She's a Woman", A Hard Day's Night", "Rock n' Roll Music", and finally "Long Tall Sally".

One thing I found a little odd was that during the Beatles set; Jimmy Saville found it necessary to watch the show from the side of the stage, not behind the curtains but in full view of the audience. This I found rather annoying but I guess he was just trying to show everyone that he was close to the Beatles; they were now so big that it gave great kudos if one was seen to be their friend.

Eric Clapton was still playing guitar with the Yardbirds and it was probably at this show that he and George Harrison met for the first time, in a friendship that would last until George died in 2001.

GUITAR FACT. I noticed that John Lennon was playing a Rickenbacker "Fireglow" 1996 guitar tonight instead of his custom built "Jetglow" 325 model. This was apparently because he had damaged his 325 by dropping it. The 1996 was one of the first series of Rickenbacker Guitars imported into this country by Rose Morris.

.

Saturday 30th January 1965
Sir Winston Churchill had died on 24th January and today was his state funeral which dominated our television screens.

In the evening the Cortinas paid one of their now regular visits to the Community Centre (The Hop) in Welwyn Garden City, Hertfordshire. The hall was packed and we had a great gig.

Monday 1st February 1965
I went back to "The Community Centre" in Welwyn Garden City to see Tony Rivers and the Castaways play. It was the first time I had seen them since their tragic accident of a couple of months ago and bass player Ray Brown had still not recovered sufficiently to return. They had a new drummer called Brian Hudson and put on a great show as usual. After the show Tony told me that lead guitarist Steve Scott was leaving and asked if I'd be interested in joining them. I was very flattered and said I would think about it and let him know, and I mulled things over for a few days. I was happy with the way things were going with my own band the Cortinas and eventually decided that I wasn't yet ready to turn fully professional. How could I possibly leave my job at the corset factory? I phoned Tony and told him that it would have to be a reluctant "No".

Thursday 11th February 1965
Once again I had sent away for tickets for the annual New Musical Express Poll Winners Concert at Wembley on Sunday April 11th. There was only one show and it was always over subscribed, especially as the Beatles and the Rolling Stones would be appearing. Once again I was lucky, very lucky. This morning the tickets arrived and they were for the second row.

Today Ringo Starr married Maureen Cox.

Friday 12th - Saturday 13th February 1965

St Valentine Pyjama Dance

Georgie Fame and the Blue Flames

Keith Smiths Climax Jazz Band — The Cortinas

FEBRUARY 12-13 ★ 11pm-5am

SEVEN SHILLINGS & SIXPENCE ★ BAR

This evening the Cortinas supported a big name act for the first time, and made their London debut. We were booked at Battersea College in London for a St. Valentine's Day, all night Pyjama Dance. We played with Georgie Fame and the Blue Flames, who had recently reached the number one spot in the charts with "Yeh Yeh" toppling the Beatles song "I Feel Fine". We had a great night Georgie Fame performed an excellent set, and we finished our last spot at 3.45am on Saturday morning, and eventually arrived home as the sun was rising, completely knackered.

Friday 26th February 1965

A few weeks ago I had applied to buy shares in the Beatles music publishing company Northern Songs. John Lennon and Paul McCartney's songs were published by a guy called Dick James who had set up their own company in which he had the controlling interest. They had now decided to change Northern Songs from a private company to a public company that would be listed at the Stock Exchange. This meant that anyone could apply for shares, and it was an opportunity I couldn't miss.

The buying price was 7/3d (36p) and I had sent a cheque for £72 for the minimum amount of 200 shares, and today I found out that I had been successful and my share certificate arrived. I now owned a little piece of the Beatles.

This in a way was the start of a long and bitter struggle over any Beatle's composition assigned to Northern Songs. In a few years time amid much acrimony, Dick James would sell Northern Songs, against the Beatles wishes, to Lew Grade and his ATV Music company and it would eventually be owned by Michael Jackson and Sony. This would effectively mean that Michael Jackson would earn more from each Lennon / McCartney song than either Paul McCartney or John Lennon's estate.

Saturday 6th March 1965

Today the Cortinas travelled to London to audition for Opportunity Knocks, a television talent show hosted by Hughie Green. When we arrived we were told that we couldn't use our own equipment, we had to use the equipment that was supplied and it was awful. Roger Cook had to hastily rearrange an unfamiliar drum kit as he was left handed. Consequently our performance suffered and it was obvious to us that we had failed the audition.

Thursday 11th March 1965

This evening we turned up for a group rehearsal and Paul Crowland our rhythm guitarist dropped a bombshell by saying that he was leaving the group, but would stay until we found a replacement. Paul wasn't a natural musician and his heart wasn't completely into playing in a band. He now had a steady girlfriend who would eventually become his wife, and girlfriends had a tendency not to want their boyfriends travelling around in bands without them being there to keep an eye on them.

Today my shares in "Northern Songs" dropped to 6/- (30p). Shock Horror!

Sunday 21st March 1965

We auditioned a new rhythm guitarist called Cliff Franklyn who had been in a local group called the Stalagmites (they're the ones that go up). He played well and had a Levin Goliath acoustic guitar fitted with a De Armond pickup along with a Fender Tremolux amplifier, so he passed my "is his gear good enough?" test. We asked him to join and Paul Crowland agreed to stay until Cliff was ready.

I had failed my driving test and was at present getting around on a crappy, second hand moped, which had a top speed (downhill) of about 25mph. This afternoon I was stopped by the police and warned for dangerous driving.

Monday 29th March 1965

This evening the Cortinas appeared at the Hermitage Ballroom in Hitchin, supporting Screaming Lord Sutch and the Savages. This was a horror act, many years before Alice Cooper did something similar. Sutch would come on stage dressed as "Jack the Ripper" and proceed to run around the stage wielding a large knife and then pretend to cut up one of his band members who was dressed as a woman. There were lots of fake blood and body parts. All good tasteful stuff and politically incorrect. He never made the top forty with any of the records he released but his stage act was legendary.

Screaming Lord Sutch had many well known musicians that passed through his band, and his guitarist this evening was Ritchie Blackmore who would go on to become a guitar hero in bands like Deep Purple, and Rainbow. When we arrived at the Hermitage, Ritchie Blackmore was jamming with the bass player and drummer playing "Czardas" the instrumental recorded by Nero and the Gladiators that I've already mentioned.

We found "Sutch" a bit intimidating and kept well out of his way. In the years leading up to his death in 1999 Lord (David) Sutch was more famous for being the leader of the

Monster Raving Loony Party and he would stand for parliament in each general election, although he never managed to get more than a few hundred votes.

Tuesday 30thth March 1965

The Melody Maker was running a Beat Group Contest at the Wimbledon Palais in London, and The Cortinas had applied to enter. This morning a letter arrived to say we had been chosen to take part, and our heat would be n Sunday 2nd May. It would be judged by the members of the audience as there was a voting slip with each ticket, so they were encouraging bands to bring their own supporters with them to increase their chances of winning.

We had a good local following and as we had managed a coach load for last year's Earls Court competition, decided to advertise locally for support. Posters were placed in shops and we made up flyers that were given out at our gigs. Things were looking promising so we provisionally booked a 44 seater coach.

Sunday 11th April 1965

Nigel and I travelled to Wembley by bus and underground for the annual New Musical Express Poll Winners Concert, and as I've already said we were in the second row.

The complete line up for the show was:- the Animals, the Beatles, Cilla Black, Donovan, Dusty Springfield, Freddie and the Dreamers, Georgie Fame and the Blue Flames, Hermans Hermits, the Ivy League, the Kinks, the Moody Blues, the Rolling Stones, the Searchers, the Seekers, Sounds Incorporated, Them (featuring Van Morrison), and Wayne Fontana.

Once again the line up reflected the changing face of Pop music with quite a few new acts in the line up, and quite a few missing from last year. Ahead of the pack in popularity were the Beatles with the Rolling Stones not that far behind.

This was the first time the Beatles had sung live since they had finished their Christmas shows in January and at present they were in the middle of filming their second film "Help". Despite the Wembley sound system they sounded good and for the first time were wearing their beige military jackets that would feature in their momentous, Shea

Stadium Concert in America in a few months time.

Our seats were on George Harrison's side of the stage which meant I could get a good close up of his playing but I was a bit disappointed that he wasn't using his Rickenbacker 12 string guitar. They performed "I Feel Fine", "She's a Woman", "Baby's in Black", their latest single "Ticket to Ride" and finished with "Long Tall Sally".

When the TV broadcast of the concert was shown a week later the sound was much better than last year with the screams of the crowd not swamping their music. "The Beatles" did suffer one of the usual problems, as Paul and George's microphone wasn't turned on until about a minute into "I Feel Fine".

Public transport eventually got us home at around 9.00pm but we were in time to see the Beatles appear live on TV. They were all interviewed, and then sang their latest record "Ticket to Ride", on the Eamon Andrews Show.

Monday 12ᵗʰ April 1965

After only three weeks of frantic rehearsal, it was Cliff Franklyn's first gig this evening, when the Cortinas supported Tony Rivers and the Castaways at the
Hop in Welwyn Garden City.

Cliff had inherited Paul Crowland's blue leather waistcoat, which fortunately fitted him, and he played well. It was a good gig for the group and we even attempted a version of a Beach Boys song called, "Hushabye". This had a very complex four part harmony, and considering we were appearing with Tony Rivers (Mr. Harmony) we were either very brave or extremely foolhardy.

Saturday 1ˢᵗ May 1965

Nigel and I watched the FA Cup Final on television and saw Liverpool win the trophy for the first time. They beat Leeds 2-1 after extra time with goals from Roger Hunt and Ian St. John. At this time Nigel was still a bigger Liverpool fan than me, but I was getting there.

Sunday 2nd May 1965

The Cortinas.
On stage at
Wimbledon
Palais.

It was the day of our heat in the "Melody Maker National Beat Contest" (beat was a much used word in the sixties, today it seems quaint) and in the morning we checked on the final arrangements for the coach carrying our supporters. It was due to leave from our local pub the Hopfields, then pick up people at various points and off to Wimbledon. We travelled up in our new van which my father had just bought. It was an Austin J4 van which replaced our old Bedford Dormobile. The only problem was that all the declarations of love, written in lipstick had to be cleaned from The Dormobile before we sold it, and now we had a new van and no lipstick messages.

It was a great night, the Cortinas were drawn number four and each group performed three songs (I can't recall what we sang), our fans did us proud screaming and cheering, and then it was down to the audience to fill in their voting cards and put them in the ballot boxes. We actually came second but that was OK as the first two acts went through to the semi finals.

After the show we got to our van and found that our fans had been busy as it was already adorned with brand new messages of love and affection, still mostly directed at Nigel.

Saturday 15th May 1965

The Cortinas
With
Billy J. Kramer

Another London gig for the Cortinas, this time at the Porchester Hall in Bayswater. We played for a local Hertfordshire firm called Rodex and supported Billy J. Kramer and the Dakotas. They had achieved their success in the "Merseybeat" boom of 1963 and were managed by the Beatles manager Brian Epstein. Their current hit was a song called, "Trains and Boats and Planes" which was destined to be their last. Mick Green, who I had last seen playing with Johnny Kidd and the Pirates a couple of years ago, was now one of their guitarists.

Sunday 30th May 1965

My Gran and My Mum at "The Melody Maker Beat Contest".
My Gran has her voting slip tucked safely in her hat.
Every vote was valuable.

For the Cortinas it was semi final day in the Melody Maker National Beat Contest, and once again we had a coach load of fans making the trip. A couple of nights ago we had received a phone call from the organisers asking if we wanted any more tickets, and when we said we were probably OK, they told us that some of the bands had taken more tickets than us which meant we were at a disadvantage as each ticket was a vote. What they were saying was, did we want to buy some more votes. We thought about it and in the end bought some more tickets even though it was doubtful that we would sell them at this late stage.

We arrived at Wimbledon Palais with about twenty tickets unsold. We were drawn number ten and didn't go on until 10.30pm the fans were great as usual. Talking to some of the other groups it was apparent that they had all received calls about extra tickets and some had bought them. Everybody voted including us with our extra twenty votes, and we were placed third which meant we went through to the final. We were pleased to be in the final but with the way votes were being bought it was a bit of a hollow victory. We were told that the final would have proper judges.

Sunday 27th June 1965

I had recently traded in my crappy moped for a green Vespa Sportique scooter. This was the era of Mods and Rockers where Mods rode scooters, wore smart suits and listened to the Who and Rockers rode motor bikes, wore leathers and were into Rock n' Roll. Both factions hated each other and it lead to massive confrontations and fights at seaside resorts in the sixties.

I suppose I was never a proper Mod as I never owned a Parka which was a necessary part of the uniform but I did manage to put a lot of chrome on my scooter i.e. bumpers, and front and rear luggage racks (although they were never used for luggage as it would ruin the look). It was also deemed to be "cool" to have as many headlights as possible, (they didn't have to work) but I didn't go that far.

Today my scooter was parked outside a friend's house when suddenly we heard a loud crash. I rushed outside to see a car disappearing around the corner and my scooter lying quite badly mangled in the road. We called the police but unfortunately nobody saw the car's number plate, so there was very little they could do.

Friday 2nd July 1965

Pop singer victim of hit and run

A member of the 'Cortinas', the local pop group currently making a name for themselves in the 'Melody Maker' national beat contest; suffered a minor set-back this week when an 'unknown vehicle' struck his motor-scooter.

The group member was Paul David Griggs, of Chelwood Ave, Hatfield, and the vehicle which collided with his scooter, which was stationary at the time, did not stop.

It must have been a very quiet week for local news as there was a piece in the Hatfield Herald about my scooter being hit.

Wednesday 14th July 1965

The Mecca ballroom in Stevenage held dances every Wednesday featuring top acts of the day and tonight I rode over on my newly repaired scooter to see the Who. They'd had two top ten hits so far, with "I Can't Explain" and "Anyway Anyhow Anywhere" but were still a few months away from releasing the song that became a bit of a 60s anthem, "My Generation". They had become very popular with Mods and the place was packed. I thought they were great it was a very dynamic show and at the end Keith Moon kicked his drums over and Pete Townsend pushed the neck of his guitar through the cloth that covered his amplifier. This was relatively tame by comparison to the next time I saw them.

GUITAR FACT. Pete Townsend was playing one of two Rickenbacker 1993 12 string guitars that he owned and it is possible that it was the one I was to buy in a few years time.

Wednesday 28th July 1965

Today we heard that one of the judges for The Melody Maker National Beat Contest final in August was going to be Graham Nash of the Hollies there was also a rumour that some of the Rolling Stones would be joining him.

We had received a letter from the organisers that in the final, each act would perform three songs, one of which would have to be an original composition. Nigel and I had both been dabbling at song writing and after looking at what we had, it was decided to perform a song of Nigel's called "Magic in a Word".

Saturday 31st July - Saturday 7th August 1965

The Griggs brothers must have received sweaters from a relative last christmas

It was back to Butlins for a week, but this time it was Bognor Regis and this time I went with Nigel. We had a great week and while we were there we entered the People's National Talent Competition as a duo.

We had taken our guitars and my Vox amplifier with us, and sang the Beatles song "If I Fell". We got through the heats and on the Thursday won the speciality section which meant a week's holiday and £3.00 (the prize money hadn't risen since 1961). With my job and Cortinas gigs we were not certain if we were going to be able to return.

Sunday 15th August 1965

Today was the final of the Melody Maker National Beat Contest once again we took a coach full of fans to Wimbledon Palais this time purely for vocal support as the contest was to be judged by among others, Graham Nash of the Hollies, TV producer Muriel Young and DJ Kenny Everett. Despite the rumours there were no Rolling Stones.

We played our three songs and had a bit of a nightmare, as we didn't play well. I guess the occasion got to us as we knew when we left the stage that we had blown it.

In first place was a group called St Louis Union who won a recording contract with Decca records, some group equipment, and an appearance on one of the top music shows of the day "Thank Your Lucky Stars". To make matters worse, our fragile egos were dented even further by a rival Hatfield group called the Tudors and the Carolines being placed third.

St. Louis Union had one top twenty record, when they covered the Beatles song "Girl" in 1966. The only act in the whole of the contest who achieved real fame and fortune, was a then unknown group who were beaten by St Louis Union in their heat of June 26th, and they were called Pink Floyd.

We licked our wounds placed our tails firmly between our legs and headed back home to Hatfield.

Sunday 15th August 1965

This evening I went on one of my now regular trips to the Mecca ballroom in Stevenage, this time it was to see the Hollies who were really good live. The Hollies had an amazing run of 17 top ten hits between 1963 and 1974 but only reached the coveted number one spot once with "I'm Alive" in May 1965.

GUITAR FACT. Graham Nash was playing a Danelectro Longhorn solid body guitar, but it wasn't plugged in to an amplifier during the whole show and I've always wondered why.

Saturday 25th September 1965

There was a well known joke shop in Shaftsbury Avenue, London, quite near to Drum City if I remember. It was a small narrow shop run by a guy who sat behind the counter all day with a dagger through his head. We had recently been in and bought a horror mask with fangs and long straggly hair, along with a large fake hairy hand (I don't know why we only bought one). The idea was to spice up our stage act and add a touch of Screaming Lord Sutch, and I'll take complete blame for the whole idea.

Tonight the Cortinas performed at the Rhodes Centre in Bishops Stortford, and tried out the new part of the act for the first time. We had built a cardboard coffin and while the rest of the band played "Monster Mash" I dressed up in the mask, the hand, and a long green cape and was pushed on stage inside the coffin. I then slowly opened the lid and climbed out and proceeded to terrorise the audience, at least that was the idea. In fact the audience just stared at me with a look of "what the f--- does he think he's doing" and the whole thing went down like a lead balloon. We tried it a couple of more times to a similar reaction and gave up on the idea.

Sunday 3rd October - Saturday 9th October 1965

GOLDIE & THE GINGRBREADS
(bottom left) Carol McDonald (Guitar)
(top left) Margo Lewis (Organ)
(centre) Goldie (Genya Ravan)
(right) Ginger Bianco (Drums)

(Photo thanks to Genya Ravan)

It was back to Butlins Bognor Regis today for Nigel and me for the end of season finals of the Peoples National Talent contest. We must have been gluttons for punishment as we knew they were only going to pick four acts out of around fifty, so our chances were slim. Dad took us down in the van as I wanted to take my scooter.

A couple of months ago we had seen a brilliant all girl group called Goldie and the Gingerbreads at Stevenage Mecca Ballroom, and on Sunday 3rd October they were due to perform their last ever gig before breaking up at a place called Hassocks which was about thirty miles from Bognor Regis and I wanted to go. Nigel came with me and we travelled to Hassocks on my scooter to see a great last show in quite a small club. Goldie (Genya Ravan) had a strong soulful voice, and after the group broke up she was part of Ten Wheel Drive and still gigs to this day.

Goldie and the Gingerbreads were discovered in New York's Peppermint Lounge by the Animals and their manager Mike Jeffries who brought them over to England where Alan Price produced their one and only hit "Can't You Hear My Heartbeat". This reached number twenty five in the charts and was far superior to Herman's Hermits version that was a hit in the USA. They had toured with the Rolling Stones, the Kinks, and the Animals and to me although they were greatly admired by fellow musicians they were in general vastly underrated.

We had a good Holiday for the rest of the week, we failed to get placed in the talent contest and were not really bothered until they put all the marks up and we discovered that we had come fifth with four going through to the Grand Final. Oh well!

Monday 11th October 1965

I should have gone back to work at Barclay Corsets but during the night I had been violently sick so I took the day off. I had a call from my boss to say that he was sacking me as he didn't think my heart was in the job and outside interests seemed much more important to me (really?). He sent me a months pay (£79) and my cards. So for a while I would be a professional musician.

Tuesday 26th October 1965

A friend and I decided to make one of our regular visits to London's Charing Cross Road to look at the guitar shops (something I still enjoy doing to this day). It was the day the Beatles were at Buckingham Palace to receive their MBE awards from the Queen, so we decided to make a detour to The Palace and see what was going on.

When we arrived it was mayhem, the Beatles were already inside and there was a crowd of several hundred girls going crazy outside trying to climb the gates. We stood for a while by the Victoria and Albert Memorial watching a handful of police trying to cope, and then a black limousine drove through the gates and we caught a glimpse of Ringo waving.

Wednesday 24th November 1965

The Juniors were looking for songs to record and this afternoon I went to Alan Shacklock's house and taught them a song I had written. I said I was going to see "The Animals" in the evening and Mick Taylor said he'd like to go, so we hopped on my scooter and went to the Stevenage Mecca Ballroom and saw a great show.

Sunday 31st October 1965

I was in a queue at the Finsbury Park Astoria to get tickets for what would be the last ever British Tour by the Beatles. There were only about ten dates on this tour and at Finsbury Park there were no postal applications, so we got there quite early as tickets went on sale at 11.00am. Despite being in a long queue I managed to get two tickets for the first performance.

Saturday 11th December 1965

The Beatles last tour programme & the autograph of Roadie Mal Evans

It was back to the Finsbury Park Astoria to see the Beatles on their last British tour. It was a great show which featured several tracks from their new album "Rubber Soul". This had been released a few days earlier on 3rd December, and would become my favourite "Beatles" album. They sang:- "I Feel Fine", "She's a Woman", "If I Needed Someone", "Act Naturally", "Nowhere Man", "Baby's in Black", "Help", "We Can Work it Out",

"Yesterday", "Day Tripper" and finally "I'm Down".

We saw the first show and when we came out we found a ticket tout selling two tickets for the second show at double the list price, which we bought and went back inside and saw them again. The following day they played two shows in Cardiff and that was the end of British tours for the Beatles. In 1966 they would perform only once in this country and in August they would make their last ever live appearance, (apart from the Apple roof top show on January 30th 1969) in America.

We bumped into the Beatles road manager Mal Evans outside the Theatre and I got his autograph. (Mal Evans was shot dead by police in an incident at his Los Angeles home on 4th January 1976).

Throughout their touring years the total entourage of the Beatles was just eight people: The four Beatles, their driver Alf Bicknell, roadies Mal Evans and Neil Aspinall and manager Brian Epstein. How different things are today.

Tuesday 21st December 1965

On a day out shopping in London I visited Anello and Davide, the shop that sold the Beatle Boots. There was a lady being served and when she turned round I realised that it was Diana Rigg the actress. She was currently playing Emma Peel in "The Avengers" on television and wore a black leather cat suit that made her every man's fantasy. She had no make up on and still looked great.

Wednesday 29th December 1965

I had been on the dole since I was sacked from Barclay Corsets, and a couple of weeks ago I was told by the unemployment office that there may be a suitable job for me, right next door at Hatfield's Income Tax Office. Today I was informed that I had the job and could start in a few days time, although I must admit I didn't really relish the thought of going back into an office.

1966

Monday 3rd January 1966

Another year begins and today I set off on my scooter, for my first day's work at the Tax Office, taking my brother with me. This was because he had been working at the Social Security Office, which was in the same building, since he left school last summer. Nigel had managed to scrape together three GCE O levels, Maths, English, and Music and had drifted into a Civil Service job as a Clerical Assistant. After a short while he had taken an exam, which in his words was, as easy as the eleven plus, and was promoted to Clerical Officer for which five GCE O levels was the standard requirement.

My first day was OK, it was a bright modern office and the staff were friendly and we finished work at 5.00pm, which suited me fine. I had a meeting with my boss who had discovered that I had five GCE O level passes to my name which meant that although I had started as a Clerical Officer I could be upgraded to a Tax Officer immediately, which meant more money. Promotion on my first day can't be bad.

Friday 21st January 1966

George Harrison married Patti Boyd whom he had met while filming the Beatles first film "A Hard Day's Night". Patti had played a school girl in the film and had one word to say, "Prisoners"?

Tuesday 25th January 1966

Today I passed my driving test at the third attempt. I still had my scooter and had managed to pass my motor cycle test on that a few months ago.

Thursday 3rd February 1966

1966 would turn out to be a year of changes for the Cortinas and today was the first one when Cliff Franklyn our Rhythm Guitarist informed us that he would be moving out of the area and would therefore be leaving the group. Here we go again.

Thursday 17th February 1966

I bought my first car a 1963 Mini Deluxe which was red with a black roof and looked very cool. The registration was 65 UUR and it cost me £385, and now I had something warm to go to work in on these cold winter mornings, and hopefully improve my own pulling power, if you know what I mean.

In the evening we auditioned a rhythm guitarist but he wasn't very good. When auditioning new musicians, it was immediately obvious if they were not what we were looking for, but if someone has taken the trouble to come for a try out you felt compelled to give them a fair amount of time to audition, even though it was pointless.

Saturday 12ᵗʰ March 1966

New line up for The Cortinas. (left to right) Roger Cook, Paul Griggs, Nigel Griggs, Mick King.

I have naturally curly hair and here can be seen one of my sad attempts at a Beatle Hairstyle.

We had chosen our new rhythm guitarist and his name was Mick King, who lived in London Colney, near St. Albans. We had been rehearsing with him for the past three weeks and tonight was his first gig.

We performed at the Rhodes Centre in Bishops Stortford, with Dave Dee, Dozy, Beaky, Mick and Titch, who only a week ago had peaked at number four in the charts with their first top ten hit "Hold Tight". They were a good live act and had a novel line in stage costumes. Each of their trouser legs were a different colour.

Monday 18ᵗʰ April 1966

Tonight while the Cortinas were having an awful night, gigging at the Barn Cellar in St. Albans, to people who thought we were too loud and wanted to hear waltzes and foxtrots, a little piece of pop history was being made a few miles away at the Hop in Welwyn Garden City.

Mick Taylor had gone along to the Hop with his colleague Alan Shacklock from their band the Juniors and drummer friend Danny Bacon, to see John Mayall's Bluesbreakers featuring Eric Clapton, who had become, probably, the first guitar hero. Eric's gear was on stage along with his Gibson Les Paul Guitar but unfortunately there was no Eric.

 The band performed the first set and in the interval Seth Rees, the promoter at the Hop asked several local guitarists that were in the audience if they would like to get up for the second half. Everybody declined, except Mick Taylor who said that he would have a go and promptly got up and did an amazing job with Eric Clapton's gear. Even his mates hadn't realised that Mick had been at home playing the blues for hours on end. In the Juniors he was only the rhythm guitarist.

In 1967 following the departure of Eric Clapton and Peter Green, John Mayall put an advert in the music press to find a new guitarist. Mick answered the advert and joined the band and it was on John Mayall's recommendation that, when Brian Jones left the Rolling Stones, his replacement was Mick Taylor.

I knew Mick as one of a group of local musicians, from rival group the Juniors. He was in Nigel's class at Primary School and was an excellent footballer. Mick was always very quiet and shy and would normally never push himself forward, so who knows what would have happened to him if Eric Clapton hadn't missed the gig at the Hop.

Thursday 28th April 1966

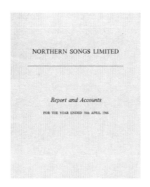

Today was the annual general meeting for shareholders of Northern Songs, the Beatles publishing company, and I being a holder of 200 shares was invited. I was full of self importance as I drove up to London expecting, at the very least, John Lennon and Paul McCartney to be at the meeting.

The meeting was held in a small room in a hotel, there were about thirty shareholders in attendance, and chairing the meeting was Dick James with not a "Beatle" in sight. It lasted a full ten minutes as Dick James read out a few facts and figures and that was it.

A few weeks later I received the Northern Songs report and accounts for the year ended 30th April 1966, and noticed that there were four names on the list of directors and not one of them was a "Beatle". I remember thinking that considering it was supposed to be the Beatles' own company it was a little odd.

Sunday 1st May 1966

On 1st May 1966, Nigel and I went back to the Empire Pool Wembley to what was now our regular pilgrimage to the New Musical Express Poll Winners Concert, and although we didn't know it at the time, this would to be the last time (apart from the Apple rooftop show) that the Beatles appeared live on stage in Great Britain. They hadn't played a live concert since their short UK tour of December 1965 and were in the middle of recording their next album, the ground breaking "Revolver".

The Beatles could never do anything wrong in my eyes, but today they were not very good. They sang just five songs "I Feel Fine", "Nowhere Man", "Day Tripper", "If I Needed Someone" and "I'm Down", and from what I could hear, with the diabolical Wembley sound, they seemed under rehearsed, and looked as if they didn't want to be there. In fact they were completely fed up with playing live, and not being able to hear what they were playing above the screaming of the audiences, which never stopped. They were also starting to write and record more complex songs, which were very hard to perform in a live situation given the technology that was available in 1966. They were only three months away from their last ever show at Candlestick Park in San Francisco on Monday 29th August 1966.

We walked away from Wembley feeling a bit deflated at the Beatles performance but in reality it was a transition stage for them. In 1966 they had stopped being "Fab", and moved on to a phase where they would change the way records were made for ever. There was so much more to come, and my favourite "Beatles" song was still two years away from being written.

Once again the concert was recorded for television, every act that is except the Beatles and the Rolling Stones, both acts not allowing their performance to be filmed. Subsequently not all of the ITV regions showed the concert, and that included the London area, as it was felt that without the two biggest acts the audience would be limited.

Wednesday 11th May 1966
The Cortinas were back trying their hand in the recording studio again, this time at

Jackson Recording Studios near Rickmansworth. It was run by two brothers whose father was Jack Jackson a radio and television DJ from the late fifties and early sixties.

We recorded two songs "Soldier of Love", a song that the Beatles performed on Radio but never recorded and one of my early, quite lame, attempts at song writing, "Trust Your Luck". We liked the sound when we heard it back in the studio but were disappointed with what we heard on the actual discs.

Monday 23rd May 1966

My friend Alan Shacklock had been lead guitarist with local group the Juniors, but when they disbanded he formed a new soul band with brass called Harlem Shuffle. Tonight I had a call from a friend to tell me that our drummer Roger Cook was rehearsing with this new line-up. We never mentioned to Roger that we knew, and he never told us, and nothing came of it, but the relationship between Roger and I was becoming a little strained and he seemed to be losing interest in the group.

Saturday 11th June - Tuesday 14th June 1966

The Cortinas had played several times at the Rhodes Centre in Bishops Stortford for a promoter called Alan Goldsmith. Alan had recently started running gigs at the Supreme Ballroom in Ramsgate and he had booked us for two gigs over this particular weekend which meant we would have to stay over. Alan said we could sleep in the ballroom, which we thought was a great idea.

The journey to Ramsgate from Hatfield took four and a half hours. This was 1966, there was no M25 and there was always a long queue at the Dartford Tunnel which at that time was just one tunnel with single lane traffic in each direction. We eventually arrived at the venue which was on the sea front, and it was to be a new experience for us playing at the seaside and staying over.

We performed on the Saturday night and then set up camp on the upstairs balcony with sleeping bags and pillows. Alan had a large Alsatian guard dog called Tumble which he left downstairs and we were all a bit nervous of him. We barricaded ourselves in with chairs and my Dad, who was with us as roadie, found an old chair leg which he kept by his side and his words were, "just in case that bugger comes near me".

We had a day off on the Sunday and we had been relaxing on the beach when Alan asked us if we fancied playing an afternoon gig on the roof of the ballroom. We set the gear up and started playing and soon attracted a crowd. We managed to play for about forty minutes before her majesty's finest, arrived saying that we were causing a disturbance and would have to stop. The Cortinas preceded the Beatles' Apple roof top concert by two and a half years.

During the night Roger Cook our drummer had answered a call of nature and been bitten by "Tumble", which he didn't find at all amusing. First thing in the morning, it was off to the local hospital for an anti tetanus injection.

On Monday evening we played with the Alan Price Set, before spending our last night camped in the ballroom and travelling home. These few days had been our first taste of life on the road and I really enjoyed it

.

Tuesday 21st June 1966

Tonight the Cortinas performed at Sandridge Youth Club near St. Albans and afterwards our drummer Roger Cook said that he wanted to leave but would stay until we found a suitable replacement.

It had been obvious that Roger had been losing interest in the group and it is possible he may have felt overpowered by the "Griggs" domination in the Cortinas. This is something that Nigel and I hadn't recognised, or thought about at the time, but something we have considered in recent years.

Monday 18th July 1966

We had seen a drummer that we were interested in called Dave Cooper, but he was already playing with another local band called Op Scene. We approached him on the quiet and asked if he was interested. Today in football terms this would be called "tapping up".

He had thought about it then came down for a try out, and this evening I had a call to say he would like to join. This meant another few weeks practicing all of our material with Dave which was very necessary but a bit of a chore.

Friday 22nd July 1966

The Beatles new album "Revolver" was due to be released on Friday 5th August, six days after that historic moment when England lifted football's World Cup, but I managed to get my copy two weeks before.

The Cortinas were playing one of their regular gigs at the Bees Club which was the social club for Brentford F.C. While we were there a guy was selling copies of Revolver for 25 shillings (£1.25p). Obviously he shouldn't have been doing this and as we were only a few miles from Hayes in Middlesex where they were pressed, they were probably stolen, but couldn't resist being one of the first people to have the latest Beatles Album, so I bought a copy.

Tuesday 16ᵗʰ August 1966

Once again the group was thrown into disarray as rhythm Guitarist Mick King told us after tonight's gig, that he had joined a group called the Trespassers which was more of a soul band. To make things worse he was leaving immediately and didn't have the decency to stay until we found a replacement, which meant cancelling bookings. There was no hint of this coming and I got on well with Mick socially during his five months with the group so I was understandably annoyed. We had only just started gigs with our new drummer.

Friday 24ᵗʰ August 1966

I had approached Alan Shacklock about standing in for us until we found a permanent replacement. We had known each other for several years and he had seen us play many times so he knew most of our numbers. He said he would stand in unless he had a commitment with his own band Harlem Shuffle. Tonight was our first booking with Alan and it was fine.

Alan Shacklock would go on to form the band Babe Ruth in the early 70s, and they released two successful albums on the Harvest label. Alan then turned his hand to production, producing artists like It Bites and Roger Daltrey and he was behind the desk for the Chesney Hawks number one hit. "I am the one and only". Today he lives in Nashville and records Christian music.

Friday 9ᵗʰ September 1966

Today I took my Gretsch guitar to Selmer Musical Instruments in Charing Cross Road, as I needed some adjustments and there was a guy who worked there who had a great reputation for "setting up" guitars.

While I was waiting the actor David Kossoff came in with his son, who was looking at the guitars and I remember his son saying, "That's the one I want it's called a Les Paul". This was fifteen year old Paul Kossoff who I didn't know of at the time but in a few years the whole world would know him when he became a member of Free and would play that very recognisable guitar solo on their hit, "Alright Now".

He died from drug related heart problems in 1976.

Sunday 2ⁿᵈ October 1966

There were a few gigs coming up that Alan would not be available for, so today I went to see Mick Taylor who said he would help out when he could and we arranged to have a rehearsal. Mick knew most of our numbers so it didn't take long.

Over the next few weeks Alan Shacklock and Mick Taylor helped us out until we found a permanent replacement, and we even did a couple of gigs as a three piece. I actually asked Mick if he would join us on a permanent basis but he declined. Looking back it's a bit embarrassing that I asked him to be our rhythm guitarist when in less than three years time he would be lead guitarist with the Rolling Stones.

Wednesday 2nd November 1966

Tonight the Cortinas had been booked to support one of the first super groups, Cream (Eric Clapton, Jack Bruce and Ginger Baker) at the Hemel Hempstead Pavilion, which we were quite excited about but it turned out to be the gig from hell. The audience had obviously come to see Cream, so we played our one hour set to calls of "get off" and "we want Cream" (and they were the polite ones). Eventually we finished and walked off the stage only to be met by the manager saying, "sorry boys Ginger Baker is in no fit state to play at the moment, so you'll have to go back and play another half an hour". It was terrible to have to go back and explain to the audience and it was the longest half hour of our lives. Eventually they were ready so with a big sigh of relief we finished. As we walked down stairs to the dressing room we passed Eric Clapton and Jack Bruce walking up followed by two guys virtually carrying Ginger Baker who was mumbling "Where's the fucking stage man". They sat him on his drum stool and they were off and I have to say they were brilliant.

Thursday 10th November 1966

I bought the Record Mirror today and there was a small piece in the gossip column that said "Hatfield's Cortinas are a group to watch."

Sunday 27th November 1966

We had found our new guitarist a few weeks earlier, his name was Rick Williams, but he was still playing for a St.Albans group called the In Sect (using the word "Sect" when naming groups had become quite fashionable.) He had practiced with us a few times and today we decided to offer him the job and he accepted. Hopefully we now had a stable line up.

Saturday 17th December 1966

Billy Fury and
the Gamblers.
Plus
The Cortinas.
Worth 8/11d of
anyone's money.

Tonight we supported Billy Fury for the second time. On 23rd October 1965 we had supported him at the California Ballroom in Dunstable, tonight it was at the Rhodes Centre in Bishops Stortford. The place was packed and Billy put on a great show.

We were packing the gear away as Billy Fury was leaving. He passed my Dad in the corridor who came out with a very casual, "Goodnight Bill" as if Billy Fury was his best friend. It may not seem particularly funny but at the time it was hillarious and Nigel and I never forgot it or allowed him to.

Dad passed away in 2006 and at his cremation I put the words "Goodnight Bill" with his flowers as it was such an endearing memory for both Nigel and I.

1967

Monday 2nd January - Friday 6th January 1967

I spent the first week of 1967 at the Civil Service Training School in London, and it was one of the most mind numbingly boring weeks of my life.

Thursday 12th January 1967

Nigel and I were both really fed up with our day jobs and tonight we discussed the possibility of becoming full time professional musicians with the Cortinas. It would mean we would be able to travel further a field, and there appeared to be enough work available to make a living.

At the time it seemed such a big deal giving up our jobs but we both liked the idea and decided to put it to the others. Even though Rick Williams hadn't been with us for very long, he agreed immediately. Rick had joined the Cortinas almost straight from school and at the time was totally enthusiastic about being in the group. Dave Cooper wanted to give it some thought as he had quite a good job with an insurance company.

It was hoped that if everyone agreed we would try to be fully professional by August or September.

Sunday 22nd January 1967

Tonight I saw the Rolling Stones appearance on the prime time television show, Sunday Night at The London Palladium amid much controversy. They were having a hit with "Let's Spend the Night Together" and strange as it may seem today, they were being criticised for it being in bad taste. The problem was with the word "Night", and I believe the record had been banned by the BBC Light Programme. The BBC Light Programme was the only BBC Radio Station on which you could hear Pop Music, even then only occasionally, and it was the forerunner to Radio One.

There was much speculation as to whether they would sing this song on the show and in the end they did, preceded by Mick Jagger's comment "This is the dirty one", and although they sang live the backing was pre-recorded, which was also quite controversial at the time. At the end of the show all the artists would appear on the revolving stage, standing behind letters that spelt out Sunday Night at the Palladium, and waving to the audience. The Stones refused to do this, and the following day they received a lot of negative press, which I guess helped to perpetuate the image they were creating.

The Rolling Stones were not far behind the Beatles in popularity and were selling bundles of records, but whereas the Beatles were much loved by almost everyone, young and old alike, the Stones were in general hated by parents and the establishment, who thought they were dirty, scruffy, and a bad influence on the young. 1967 would turn out to be a troubled year for the Stones.

Today Sir Mick Jagger is part of the establishment that he was trying to alienate in the sixties.

Friday 27th January 1967

Nigel with Liverpool Captain Ron Yeates

Nigel gives Ian St. John a few tips on how to avoid the offside trap.

Nigel and I both had a day off work so we decided to go to London and look round the music shops. Liverpool FC were playing Watford in the F.A.Cup and as we drove through Hendon we noticed a football team, all wearing red track suits, training in a nearby field. We drove over and to our amazement, there was the whole Liverpool team with Bill Shankly, having a training session. We stopped to watch and I took some photos. The following day Liverpool drew the match 0-0 but eventually won the replay at Anfield 3-1.

Sunday 29th January 1967

The Beatles manager Brian Epstein had leased the Saville theatre in London's Shaftsbury

Avenue, and began putting on Sunday Pop concerts. On Sunday 29th January 1967 I went along to the Saville to see the Who topping the bill supported by Jimi Hendrix. As we waited outside the theatre a green Aston Martin sports car screeched to a halt and out leapt Paul McCartney and John Lennon who rushed straight inside before anyone realised what was happening. The Saville was quite a small theatre and I had tickets in the second row of the balcony. To my right Brian Epstein had his own personal box and with him in the box were: John Lennon, Paul McCartney and George Harrison, who by now had all grown moustaches. In the other box to our left, were Eric Clapton, Jack Bruce and Spencer Davis.

It was the first time I had seen Jimi Hendrix who was just beginning to make an impact and he was amazing. At one point in the act he used a strobe light, which at that time I had never seen before. My abiding memory of the Who is of Roger Daltrey, Pete Townsend, and Keith Moon thrashing around wildly, and a motionless John Entwhistle standing there just moving his fingers. Suddenly a small flashing toy robot appeared from the wings and slowly made its way across the stage. As it passed John Entwhistle he just moved his right leg and kicked it into the audience.

Monday 30th January 1967
Today our drummer Dave Cooper said he had talked things over with his parents and was agreeable to turn fully professional later on in the year. I decided to grow a moustache.

Friday 17th February 1967
I always had to have a Beatles record on the day it was released (sometimes before) and today I bought the double A sided "Penny Lane" and "Strawberry Fields Forever", and both songs were about places in Liverpool. "Strawberry Fields Forever" was a complete departure in style for the Beatles and many people think it's one of their best of all time, but I preferred "Penny Lane" and still do. The musical structure of "Penny Lane" is unique (here he goes again). Sometimes when you want to build up a song or piece of music, modulation is used. That is changing key, and you normally move up a tone or a semi-tone to give it a lift. In "Penny Lane" the verse is in C and the chorus modulates down a tone to B flat but the song still seems to have lifted. Very clever Mr. McCartney.

Despite both songs being credited as having been written by Lennon and McCartney it is widely know that "Strawberry Fields Forever" was written by John and "Penny Lane" by Paul. Although they helped each other out with the occasional idea and odd lyric, they had written separately since around the time of "I Want to Hold Your Hand".

Tuesday 22nd February 1967
Tonight it was off to the Mecca Ballroom in Stevenage to see rock legend, Chuck Berry. I was standing at the bar waiting to be served and looked up to see Chuck Berry standing almost next to me, having a drink on his own. The bar area was crowded but nobody else

seemed to notice that he was there.

The show was disappointing; Chuck Berry has a reputation for not rehearsing with his backing band. He just starts a song and expects the band to be there with him, and to be honest, although I've always loved his records, on stage it was a bit of a shambles. There is a great documentary called "Hail Hail Rock n' Roll" where Rolling Stone, Keith Richard tried to get a bunch of musicians together to rehearse and back Chuck Berry for a special show. Much to Keith's annoyance Chuck Berry was quite difficult and did his best to sabotage things.

Sunday 12th March 1967
We had a group rehearsal today and received some bad news. Our drummer Dave Cooper had changed his mind and did not want to turn professional. He now had a steady girlfriend and with his steady job he had decided he did not want to risk everything for the uncertainty of the music business. We decided that for the rest of us there was no turning back, and so we would look for another drummer, although the thought of going through the audition process again really did not have much appeal.

Wednesday 12th April 1967
Working at the tax office was becoming unbearable, especially with the thought of turning professional in a few months time, but today I received a bit of a shock.

A notification came into the office regarding the Cortinas, which listed all the gigs we had performed at the Hermitage Ballroom in Hitchin. This was to check we had been paying the correct amount of income tax and this was something none of us had thought about and I was really worried. I thought that I'd probably be locked up for tax evasion, and was genuinely scared stiff. I thought about it for a while, before going to my boss to explain the situation. She sat down with me and asked what the outgoings of the group were, and explained all of the things that could be claimed against tax, like our equipment, stage clothes, the van, and petrol. Even the music papers that I bought could be set aside against income tax. We had only been performing a couple of gigs a week and with all of our expenditure there was absolutely no tax liability, although we would still need to submit accounts. I breathed a huge sigh of relief and went back to work.

Saturday 15th April 1967
We had advertised for a new drummer in the Melody Maker and had been auditioning for the past few weeks. Today we decided on a guy called Nigel Whinyates who came from Birkenhead. He was now living in St. John's Wood in London and was currently with a professional group who were on the verge of splitting. He had a Ludwig drum kit, just like Ringo's, so he easily passed the equipment test, and as we already had a Nigel in the group it was agreed that he would be called by his second name, Gary.

Thursday 27th April 1967

Tonight we were driving to Gary's house in St. John's Wood for a rehearsal, and as we passed Abbey Road recording studios we saw a crowd of girls standing outside going crazy. The reason for this was that John Lennon, Paul McCartney, and George Harrison could be seen getting out of their limo and heading into the studio. I always wondered what they were recording on that particular night that we saw them. Years later I discovered a book that listed all of the Beatles recording sessions, and on 27/4/1967 they were recording the lead and backing vocals on "Magical Mystery Tour". (I'm such an anorak.)

Wednesday 3rd May 1967

Rod Argent and Chris White, who were both members of the Zombies, had been to see the Cortinas a few weeks ago and Rod had suggested that we recorded a song he had written. Tonight we were at Central Sound studios in Denmark Street in London with Rod and Chris to record the song which was called "I want Her She Wants Me". It was a great song but it didn't really suit us and I was unhappy with my own vocal performance. The song would eventually resurface on the Zombies album, "Odessey and Oracle"

Friday 12th May 1967

Pirate radio stations had appeared in the mid sixties, these were stations that broadcast illegally from ships anchored outside the three mile zone around Britain. The best reception from where I lived was Radio London which broadcast on 266 medium wave. Radio London was the first radio station in the world to play the Beatles new and revolutionary album "Sgt. Pepper's Lonely Hearts Club Band" on Friday 12th May 1967, three weeks before its release on 2nd June 1967.

I arrived home from work just after 5.00pm and switched on. The DJ, Kenny Everett, said the boat carrying the new album was on its way. There was a huge build up as the boat got nearer and eventually the album was on board and played from beginning to the end. I sat recording it with my little Grundig tape recorder trying to take in the complexities of what I was hearing. Even on first hearing I knew it was something special and when it got to the last track "A Day in The Life" and that final chord I was completely blown away.

Wednesday 24th May 1967

We had been rehearsing with Gary for the past few weeks and he was now ready, so tonight was Dave Cooper's last booking as a member of the Cortinas. We played at Stevenage Mecca Ballroom and supported the Move, who already had two top ten hits to their name, but were more known for their stage act. They had become notorious for chopping up televisions, cars, and bust's of Adolf Hitler on stage. Tonight they were much more restrained.

They had just returned from Europe and although the group were there, their equipment had been held up at customs. We had finished our spot and their gear eventually arrived and after some frantic setting up they performed a great set. We shared a dressing room with them and although we found them to be good blokes we also found them to be a little "nuts".

Dave Cooper packed his drums away for the last time. He had been with us for ten months and would be remembered mainly for his dreadful driving. You took your life in your hands when you went out with him in his car. He was also very short sighted and wore glasses which he was quite self conscious about. If he was at a dance he would take his glasses out of his pocket, spot a girl he wanted to dance with, work out the distance, put his glasses away and blindly make his way over to her.

Sunday 4th June 1967

Today Nigel and I went to see Jimi Hendrix top the bill at Brian Epstein's Saville Theatre. He opened his set with his version of "Sgt. Pepper's Lonely Hearts Club Band", only two days after the Beatles album had been released. It was a great show and sitting in Brian Epstein's private box were George Harrison and his wife Patti Boyd. Also on the bill were Denny Laine and his Electric String Band. Denny Laine had been the lead singer with the Moody Blues on their 1964 number one hit "Go Now". He now had the usual, guitar bass and drums line up augmented with an amplified string quartet, which was ground breaking stuff in 1967, and they were excellent. Denny Laine would go on to be a founder member of Paul McCartney's "Wings" after "The Beatles" had disbanded.

I have read interviews where Paul McCartney says that he was there on this particular night but he may be mistaken. I went to the Saville several times and any Beatle in attendance always sat in Brian Epstein's private box, if they had sat anywhere else in the theatre they would have been hassled by fans. According to my diary only George and Patti were present. I have a fairly good memory for events but writing this book I have been surprised how the memory plays tricks and things I thought happened in a particular way, didn't.

Thursday 8th June 1967

Today Nigel and I took the plunge and handed in our notice to quit to our respective offices, giving the date of our leaving as Nigel's eighteenth birthday, Friday 18th August. I was finding life in the tax office unbearable, the other members of staff were OK but it was a large office, about twenty people, and I remember it as being so quiet and serious all day long. I have only one memory that raised a smile, and that was when a letter was received addressed to, "Her Majesty's Thieving Bastards" and instead of a stamp, a Swastika had been drawn.

Thursday 29th June 1967

Last February there had been a drugs raid at the home of Rolling Stone Keith Richards and four amphetamine tablets had been found on Mick Jagger's person. Today Mick Jagger was sentenced to three months imprisonment for possession of illegal drugs, and Keith Richards sentenced to one year in prison for allowing his home to be used for drug purposes. They spent one night in prison before being released on bail pending their appeal.

It was widely thought that the sentences were harsh, unfair, and that the two were being victimised. A week later Keith Richards would have his sentence quashed and Mick Jagger given a conditional discharge.

A busy day for news as it was announced that actress Jayne Mansfield had been killed in a car crash in America.

Thursday 6th July 1967

This evening I paid my first ever visit to the world famous Marquee Club in Wardour Street, London with our new drummer Gary and saw Marmalade who had a weekly residency. They were excellent musicians and did a great set of songs. We would get to see them quite often over the next few months and I have to admit we stole some of their ideas. They would perform some great versions of Temptations and Four Tops songs and some of these would find their way into the Cortinas set.

In August 1967 Marmalade released a great single called "I See the Rain", which was a bit like Jimi Hendrix with harmonies. This failed to make any impression on the charts and they would have to wait until August 1968 for chart success. They reached number six with the, rather bland, "Loving Things". Their version of "I See the Rain" was heard in a "Gap" commercial a few years ago and still sounds good today.

Thursday 8th June 1967

I had decided that as I was turning professional I needed a new amplifier. My Vox AC30 had served me well for the past four years but I wanted one of the new Top of the Range Vox Supreme solid state amplifiers. I reluctantly decided to sell the little piece of the Beatles that I owned, and traded in my shares in Northern Songs. They had by now doubled in price, and today went to London and bought my new amplifier for £254.00. It was one of the first guitar amplifiers to have built in echo, and distortion effects, and had a chrome stand which looked pretty impressive.

Although I used this amplifier for the next few years, in retrospect it wasn't as good as the AC30. Most guitarists went through a phase of trying out the new solid state technology but would ultimately return to valve amps, which are still favoured today. I returned to a VOX AC30 in the eighties, and today play through a small Fender Blues Junior valve amp because at 63 years of age (me not the amp) the AC30 is just too bloody heavy.

Sunday 13th August 1967

Mick Taylor had joined John Mayall's Bluesbreakers a couple of months ago, replacing Peter Green. Today I went to the Windsor Jazz and Blues Festival and saw them perform, and it goes without saying that Mick played really well. Topping the bill were Cream supported by among others Peter Green's new band Fleetwood Mac.

Monday 14th August 1967

I had been listening to the pirate station Radio London (Big L) since it began broadcasting in 1964. It introduced the world to DJs like Kenny Everett, Tony Blackburn, and John Peel, who would go on to become household names. Radio London and other pirate stations broadcast non stop pop music which was not available anywhere else at that time, with the exception of Radio Luxemburg, for which reception in The United Kingdom was very patchy.

Today the Marine Offences Act came into force which meant Radio London was closing down for good, and it was like losing an old friend. I listened to the final hour with a lump in my throat, there were many personal messages from stars of the day, including the Beatles, and then came the last track, the Beatles "A Day in the Life". Paul Kaye announced, "Big L. Time is three o'clock, and Radio London is now closing down". The Radio London theme was played and then, silence -----

Later that day the disc jockeys arrived back by train at Liverpool Street Station in London to a hero's welcome. In just over one month's time some of them would be joining the brand new, BBC Radio One.

Wednesday 16th August 1967

Tonight the Cortinas auditioned for the Clayman Agency in London. We passed the audition and were immediately offered three months work in Germany and Switzerland, playing for four and a half hours a night, seven days a week and the money was poor. We turned it down.

Friday 18th August 1967

The Woodhall Community Centre, (The Hop) Welwyn Garden City. The Cortinas first professional gig.

(*Photo Thanks to David Barber*)

It was Nigel's eighteenth birthday, and for both of us, our last day at work. As I have already said, it seemed quite a big deal at the time giving up a regular income for the unknown pitfalls of the music business. I remember having a feeling of anticipation and fear. Needless to say I didn't do much work and at the end of the day I was given £3.5s.0d (£3.25p) worth of record tokens as a leaving present. Nigel and I drove home hoping the civil service wouldn't collapse without the Griggs brothers.

In the evening, the Cortinas performed their first ever professional gig at one of the regular venues the Community Centre (The Hop), in Welwyn Garden City.

Monday 21st August 1967

Today was my first Monday as a professional musician so I did what most professional musicians did, I stayed in bed all of the morning. Later on I went to the Breaks Youth Centre to discuss with the Youth Leader, Bill Salmon, whether we could practise there regularly during the day.

Sunday 27th August 1967

Today it was announced that the Beatles manager Brian Epstein had been found dead of a drug overdose at his flat in London. There would be much speculation about possible suicide but it was officially ruled as accidental death. All four Beatles were adamant that it wasn't suicide and they were closer to him than most.

This evening Nigel went to the Saville Theatre, to see Jimi Hendrix in concert. When he arrived he found that the concert had been cancelled as a mark of respect for Brian Epstein.

Monday 18th September 1967

We had been trying to find a new and bigger group van, which would take all our gear and which we could fit with comfortable seats. We had been looking at old ambulances and today attended an auction in Wandsworth, South London and successfully bid for an ex. London Austin Ambulance No. YLD 269 and paid one hundred and thirty five guineas. A guinea was one pound and one shilling. i.e. £1.05p, so we paid £141.75p.

Over the next few weeks we would all work on the ambulance, we repainted it, inside and out and then eventually found some old aircraft seats which we fitted. The main problem was that it was made of fibre glass and was very draughty. The heater was quite inadequate in cold weather so we would have to take sleeping bags with us to keep warm in winter.

Tuesday 26th September 1967

The Cortinas had been approached by a guy called Mike Swain, who owned a recording studio called Studio Sound in Hitchin. He was looking for a band to produce, and wanted to record a couple of tracks with us and then approach record companies. He already had a contact with Decca Records. This evening we made a start on a song that he had found called "In the Park".

The image of the Cortinas was changing, it was the era of Psychedelia and a strong Eastern influence had emerged, so we all went out and bought brightly coloured kaftans to wear on stage. There was no uniform anymore, everyone wore whatever they wanted.

Saturday 30th September 1967

This morning Tony Blackburn uttered these immortal words, "-- and, good morning everyone. Welcome to the exciting new sound of Radio One". He then played "Flowers in the Rain" by the Move and BBC Radio One was up and running. I listened to it on and off throughout the day and thought it was OK, but I was still mourning the loss of Radio London.

Sunday 1st October 1967

Broadcast this evening was the first episode of a new television series called "The Prisoner" starring, and created by, Patrick McGoohan. It was a bit off the wall but thoroughly thought provoking and basically told the story of a guy who had been involved with some sort of intelligence service who suddenly resigned only to be kidnapped by unknown forces and imprisoned in a strange village where his captors tried to extract "information". It became one of my favourite programmes and years later I would start my own entertainment agency called "Village Entertainments" using a Penny Farthing logo in homage to the show.

Wednesday 11ᵗʰ October 1967

The Cortinas set off to audition for Mecca at their Lyceum Ballroom in The Strand, London. Mecca had ballrooms all over the United Kingdom and they also had their own booking agency so we were keen to be involved with them. We performed a few songs in front of a guy called Phil Tate, who was an ex. band leader and now ran the Mecca Agency. He said he could offer us a residency at one of their ballrooms, which we were not sure about. Playing at the same venue seven nights a week was not what we really wanted to do.

As we were packing our gear away we were approached by a guy who we had seen hanging around in the background while we were playing. His name was Graham Dee, he had a terrible stutter and seemed slightly mad. He told us that he was from Polydor records and said that he had liked what he had heard and would we be interested in having a recording test. We thought about it seriously for about a second and said "Yes". We exchanged telephone numbers and he said that he would be in touch. We tried not to get too excited by this as we had been promised many things over the years, by people from whom we had never heard from again.

Saturday 14ᵗʰ October 1967

Today we had a phone call from Graham Dee who said that he had arranged a recording test at Polydor records for the following Tuesday and we would need to perform four songs from our stage act. We were still in the middle of recording tracks for Mike Swain at Hitchin, so we phoned him and explained the situation. He was fine about it and didn't want to stand in our way, and in fact asked if he could come with us to our recording test.

Tuesday 17ᵗʰ October 1967

This morning we drove to Polydor Records which was in Stratford Place just off Oxford Street in London's West End. We met Graham Dee before unloading our equipment and set up in Polydor's own four track studio. The tracks that we had decided to record were "Baby I Need Your Loving", "Back in my Arms Again", "Happy Together", and "By Bye Baby". "Bye Bye Baby" would be released by the Bay City Rollers in 1975 and would prevent me getting a number one hit with Guys n' Dolls.

The backing was recorded first on two of the tracks, we then double tracked the vocals on the remaining two tracks. We were pleased with the results, it was a good studio and it was the best we had ever sounded on a recording. Graham Dee, who was a very excitable person, was well pleased with the results and started jumping about saying that he was sure he could get his bosses at Polydor to give us a recording deal and he wanted us to sign with him as a manager.

Graham had to submit the recordings to a Polydor A&R meeting and it would be a few weeks before we knew the result.

Monday 23rd October 1967

We were keen to work in London Clubs and today we auditioned at the Whiskey a Go Go in London's Wardour Street. As our manager, my mother, came with us and succeeded in getting several bookings there. She also went to see John Gee who was the manager of the Marquee Club," just down the road, and it seemed promising. The Marquee Club was a place that we really wanted to play.

Sunday 19th November 1967

Despite the death of Brian Epstein, The Saville Theatre, in the West End of London, continued to put on Sunday concerts, and this evening Nigel and I went along to see the Bee Gees, supported by the Bonzo Dog Doo Dah Band, the Flowerpot Men, and my old mate Tony Rivers. It was a good show and it was great to see Tony Rivers perform again and since the last time I saw him he had almost completely changed the line up of his band the Castaways.

In the late Brian Epstein's box this evening was Paul McCartney and Lulu, who at the time was engaged to "Bee Gee" Maurice Gibb. After the show we saw Paul McCartney drive away in his Vintage 1920 Hispano-Suiza Car.

Monday 20th November 1967

I spent the evening of my 23rd birthday at "The Cooks Ferry Inn" in Edmonton North London, watching "Marmalade".

Thursday 7th December 1967

The silk label
from my Apple
Jacket

Two days ago the Beatles had held a launch party for their new boutique Apple at 94, Baker Street in London and today it was open to the public for the first time. The Cortinas were on their way for a meeting with Grahame Dee at Polydor records, but we just had to stop at Apple to see what it was all about. The outside of the shop was painted with a huge mural, which after a short while, some of the neighbouring shops would object to and it would be painted over white, which I thought was a great shame as it looked amazing.

We went in and immediately were hit by a smell of Apples coming from the incense that was burning around the shop. There were rails full of brightly coloured hippy style clothes each with an embroidered silk "Apple" label. The clothes and the mural had been designed by three Dutch artists who called themselves "The Fool". There was colourful inflatable furniture scattered around the floor, relaxing music, coloured lighting, and an air of peace and tranquility. Nigel and I both bought jackets to wear on stage and it wasn't long before we were all wearing "Apple" clothes. I still have mine today.

We arrived for our meeting with Graham Dee, and he had some really good news for us. Polydor were offering us a five year recording deal and Graham would produce our records. To say we were pleased would be an understatement.

Sunday 10th December 1967

Today the Cortinas made their London, West End Debut, playing at the Whiskey a Go Go in Wardour Street. The Club was situated at the lower end of Wardour Street, which was a one way street, very narrow, and very difficult to park our Ambulance. We had to find a parking space as close as we could then carry the equipment up two flights of stairs to the club which was on the first floor. The stage was the size of a postage stamp, but despite all of the difficulties we had a good night and really enjoyed playing to a London crowd. We had been booked to return on Boxing Day, by the owner of the club, who at the end of the evening said he was interested in managing us.

Sunday 31st December 1967

The Cortinas finished 1967 with an enjoyable New Years Eve gig at their second home, the Breaks Youth Centre in Hatfield. It had been a good year and ended with us being full of optimism. We had turned fully professional and secured ourselves a record deal with a top label.

1968
Wednesday 17th January 1968

The Cortinas
Record Producer.
Graham Dee

We all went to Polydor Records to meet our record producer Graham Dee and rehearse songs that we hoped to record. While we were there we bumped into John Rostil, who I had first met at Butlins in 1963, and was now a member of the Shadows. I was a bit star struck as John was with fellow "Shadow", Bruce Welch. DJ John Peel was also there, and since the demise of Radio London, he was making a name for himself with a show called Top Gear on BBC Radio One.

Graham Dee wrote songs with a guy called Brian Potter and we listened, and tried out quite a few, before choosing a couple, one called "I Can Guarantee You Love", and the other "Poor Boy".

Brian Potter would eventually team up with top American writer/producer Dennis Lambert and have much success as the Lambert/Potter writing team.

Monday 22nd and Tuesday 23rd January 1968

We spent two days in the studio recording the tracks that we hoped would make up our first single. There were only two members of the Cortinas playing on these tracks and they were Gary (Drums) and Nigel (Bass). Graham Dee played Acoustic Rhythm guitar and he brought in a session piano player. I was a bit miffed at not playing on the tracks and I now knew how Ringo Starr felt when a session drummer was brought in for the Beatles first single "Love Me Do".

The practise of individual musicians, and sometimes the whole band not playing on records happened quite often, either when a musician wasn't thought to be good enough, or when the producer found it more convenient and time saving to use session musicians. the Love Affair were top of the charts this week with "Everlasting Love" and it had been reported that only Steve Ellis, the lead singer, featured on the record and this caused a bit of a stir in the press.

Sunday 4th February 1968

This evening we performed one of our regular gigs at the Breaks Youth Centre which meant I missed the final episode of The Prisoner. Everyone who had been following the series thought that questions posed by the programme were going to be answered tonight. Instead the episode created a furore with viewers jamming the switchboards, complaining. Patrick McGoohan, who had conceived the whole idea and in fact written the final chapter himself, was accosted in the streets by angry fans that could not make head nor tail of what went on. Due to the fact that this was 1968 and domestic video recorders were still a thing of the future I had to wait until the series was repeated before I saw the final episode entitled "Fallout". It was 'of it's time' and rather surreal, there was much psychedelic imagery, lots of music, but I thought it was OK.

Friday 9th February 1968

On trips into London we would often pop into to the Apple boutique in Baker Street to see what was new. Today I was there with Rick, and as we were leaving we met Donovan who, to my amazement, remembered me from the old days in Hatfield. He stopped for a chat and said that he was there on business with the Apple Publishing Company whose offices were upstairs above the boutique.

Donovan's latest record at that time was "Jennifer Juniper" which he had written about his, then, girlfriend Jenny Boyd. She was George Harrison's sister in law and actually worked in the Apple boutique.

Monday 12th February 1968

The Cortinas Wearing their "Apple" jackets standing by their draughty Ambulance.

(Photo by Dennis Williams)

I'd always wanted a Rickenbacker 12 string guitar like the one George Harrison played. On the 12th February 1968. I finally bought one from PAN Musical Instruments in Shaftsbury Avenue, London.

There were two advertised for sale and when I arrived at the shop the manager told me that they had both belonged to Pete Townsend of the Who which in those days didn't mean a great deal apart from the fact that they were a bit battered about. They were both 1993 models which were the first Rickenbacker 12 string guitars imported into this country by Rose Morris. I picked the better of the two, condition wise, paying £110, and using my old Vox AC30 in part exchange.

Thursday 15th February 1968

Today was not a good day. Graham Dee our record producer had said that he would like to come with us to our gig this evening we said OK. He travelled up to Hatfield by train and when we met him at the station he said that he had something to tell us. Polydor Records had just signed a group, and it had been decided that the song that we thought was to be our first single, "I Can Guarantee You Love" was going to be released by them. We asked who the group was and to our amazement Graham replied "Tony Rivers and the Castaways". I couldn't believe it, our paths had crossed so many times since I first met Tony at Butlins back in 1962 and now he'd pinched our song, something I never let Tony forget to this day. Although they had never had a hit record Tony Rivers and the Castaways were a highly respected band and in reality it was understandable that they would have preference over the Cortinas.

Graham said that he had a new song that he thought was right for us, it was about a flower seller that he passed everyday near Waterloo Station, the song was called "Phoebe's Flower Shop". This was 1968 and the height of "Flower Power" so it was quite fashionable to have the word "Flower" in the title.

Our gig this evening, was at the Penny Farthing Club in Leicester. We had a good night, but just as we had finished Graham got into fight with a member of the audience, which resulted in them crashing into one of our PA speakers and knocking it over, on to Gary's drums. It hit the tom tom that is fixed to the bass drum and there was the sickening sound of wood breaking as the bass drum split. Meanwhile writhing around on the floor was our record producer still trying to fight this other guy. Eventually the two were separated and Graham stood holding his eye, moaning "I can't see", with very little sympathy from the rest of us. We were all furious.

We eventually got the gear into the van and headed back down the M1 with nobody talking to Graham, who didn't stop complaining about his eye, saying that he should go to Hospital. We reached St. Albans and with a minimum amount of compassion took him to St. Albans City Hospital, where he was told there was no serious damage apart from a very black eye. It was now six o'clock in the morning, so we put him on a train for London, and to be honest were very glad to see the back of him.

Friday 16th February 1968

Problem! We had one broken bass drum and a gig this evening. Dad, who as I have already mentioned was a woodworker by trade told Gary to bring the broken bass drum to him and he would see what he could do. He spent a few hours working on it, repairing and strengthening the shell where it was damaged, and in the end you could not tell that there had ever been a problem. Good old Dad, he was always coming to the rescue with emergency repairs.

This evening we performed our first ever gig at the Cooks Ferry Inn in Edmonton.

Monday 26th February 1968

We had just about forgiven Graham for his misdemeanour at Leicester, as we had received several phone calls from him apologising for his behaviour and promising to pay for any damage. Today we were back at Polydor recording new tracks for our single. While we were there Graham did show another moment of madness as he had just bought himself a bow and some arrows, (real ones not toys) and he proceeded to fire an arrow across his office that pierced a radiator and caused a mini flood. (Rock n' Roll).

He taught us "Phoebe's Flower Shop" and the potential B. Side "Too Much in Love". We weren't too sure about "Phoebe" as the chorus was sung in falsetto and there was one line that drove me mad, "I could not resist her golden daffodils", which I thought was awful. Graham was very persuasive and was adamant that the song was a potential hit (all record producers say that) so we went along with it.

We had a meal break and then it was into the studio to record the backing tracks. Once again Graham played guitar, not me, and once again I was a bit miffed.

Wednesday 28th February 1968

This afternoon we had a quick vocal rehearsal in Graham Dee's office at Polydor. While we were there Frank Fenter, who was the boss at "Polydor Records", came in with Hank Marvin and Bruce Welch of the Shadows. They had two girls with them named Pat and Olivia who were a vocal duo. Frank Fenter asked Graham if he could leave the girls with him while he, Hank and Bruce had a short meeting. Graham said yes but was obviously annoyed at this intrusion and wasn't particularly sociable to the girls, one of whom was a young Olivia Newton John.

This evening we recorded the vocals on "Phoebe's Flower Shop" and the B. side "Too Much in Love". Graham now had to mix the record and submit it to the company to be accepted for possible future release.

Friday 22nd March 1968

The Cortinas had a strong local following in St. Albans and since the group began, we had performed at over twenty different venues in the town. Tonight was the opening of the brand new St. Albans City Hall (now called the Alban Arena) and we were the first performers ever to play there. We supported the Nashville Teens who had a couple of top ten hits in 1964. It was a great night with one of the best receptions we'd ever had.

Wednesday 24th April 1968

In the sixties if you wanted to see one of the top music acts o f the day, you either went to package shows, which played mainly in cinemas, or Dance Halls. Tonight I was back at the Mecca Ballroom in Stevenage to see the Ike and Tina Turner Show which was amazing. There was "Ike Turner's" ten piece band on stage with three girl backing singers called the Ikettes, and up front the incomparable Tina Turner.

Ike Turner co-wrote what is considered by some to be the first ever "Rock n' Roll" record back in 1951. It was called "Rocket 88" and recorded with Sam Phillips at the legendary Sun Studios in Memphis and credited to Jackie Brenston and his Delta Cats.

Saturday 20th April 1968

Marquee Advert and The Compere from the Marquee. John Gee

We had wanted to play at the prestigious Marquee Club in London's Wardour Street for some time, and my mother had finally managed to negotiate us a booking. Tonight we played there for the first time and supported Timebox. We had a great night, went down well with the audience, and were given more bookings.

It wasn't a very large club but had a great atmosphere and the sound was always good. In 1968 The Marquee Club had no license for drinks. It was run by a Guy called John Gee who was also the compere and always dressed very formally, i.e. suit and tie, and in reality preferred Frank Sinatra's music. 1968 was in the middle of the "Flower Power" era and it was quite odd that between acts, John Gee would come on stage in his suit and announce in a very posh voice to the audience, who were usually all dressed in hippy clothes, "There will now be a break between bands but if you go to the cafeteria at the back you can buy a Coca Cola and a Mars Bar". The dressing room at the Marquee was like a small corridor and the walls were covered in graffiti, with messages like, "Eric Clapton Loves Bert Weedon" and "Pete Townsend is a nose on legs".

When the show had finished John Gee said that he had received a call from a guy called Laurie Jay who needed a band at the Scotch of St. James, which was one of the fashionable clubs that the Beatles frequented, and would we like to go on and play there. We said yes, but when we got there the place was so packed that it would have been impossible to get our gear in, so we went home.

Saturday 27th April 1968

Tonight was the Cortinas first ever gig at the Starlight Rooms in Boston, Lincolnshire, also known as the Boston Gliderdrome. We went on stage, and right in front of us was a guy in a suit and bow tie, holding a conductors baton, who then proceeded to conduct us throughout our whole set. We played there many times and he was always there. I've spoken to many other musicians who played at the Starlight Rooms in the sixties and they all remember this guy. He was always on his own and never seemed to speak to anyone.

Wednesday 1st May 1968

Our record "Phoebe's Flower Shop" was due for release on 10th May and today Nigel and I went to Polydor to pick up thirty advance copies which we were to use for promotion purposes. As we were leaving I saw John Peel sitting in the reception area and started our promotion campaign by rather embarrassingly going up to him with a copy saying, "It may not be your sort of record but we are Liverpool supporters" (John Peel was a fanatical Liverpool fan). He gave us a rather bemused look and took the record, which obviously he never played.

Thursday 9th May 1968

Our record was reviewed in Record Mirror today saying "nice story line, pleasantly sung" which at the time we thought was a great review, but looking back I suppose it was a bit "on the fence". We had a gig at Marham in Norfolk that evening and as we were unloading the gear "Phoebe's Flower Shop" was played for the first time by Dave Cash on Radio One who said that it was nice to have a song about someone called "Phoebe".

Friday 10th May 1968

The big day had arrived, our record was released, and we spent all day by the radio to see how many plays we would get on Radio One. At the end of the day we added them all up and the total was nil. The only good news we received was that the Record Room in St. Albans, where we had a big following, had ordered thirty copies and had sold out.

Saturday 11th May 1968

Tonight we played in Grantham, Lincolnshire, with Chris Farlowe and the Thunderbirds, who had a number one hit in 1966 with "Out of Time" . The Thunderbirds were Vincent Crane (Organ), Carl Palmer (Drums), and Albert Lee (Guitar). I was looking forward to seeing Albert Lee as I rated him highly. Unfortunately he didn't turn up, and Chris Farlowe went into quite a rage, and yelled "that's it he's fired". That's a rough translation, in reality the language was somewhat stronger.

My friend Alan Shacklock, from the Juniors, had been greatly inspired by Albert Lee and had learned a lot of his guitar licks. I had a chat with Carl Palmer and told him that I knew a guitarist who would make a great replacement. We exchanged phone numbers and I put Alan in touch with him. A couple of weeks later Alan was the new guitarist with the Thunderbirds.

Carl Palmer went on to drum with Emerson, Lake and Palmer, and Vincent Crane joined the, hot headed, Arthur Brown. "Fire!" da da daaaa ---

Monday 13th May 1968

Today we phoned Polydor Records to see how many thousand copies of our new single had been sold over the first weekend. The answer came back three hundred and fifteen,---- copies not thousands.

Wednesday 15th May 1968

We listened to Radio One constantly waiting for our next radio play (which was a bit sad really). This finally happened today on a programme called "Late Night Extra", at around 10.15pm by which time everyone was probably watching television or gone to bed. We had phoned Polydor and found out that we'd sold another 76 copies of the record on

Monday. It was the last time we phoned as it was getting a little too disheartening.

Monday 20th May 1968

Today "Phoebe's Flower Shop" received its third and final play on Radio One. It was played on the David Symonds show at around 4.50pm. Radio one was the only Radio Station that mattered in 1968 (there were no local stations), and unless your record was given a lot of Radio coverage, it stood little chance of success. So after only ten days since it was released, we already had a strong feeling that the record had flopped.

Sunday 30th June 1968

Our gig this evening was at the, world famous, Playboy Club in Park Lane, London, which had been opened by Hugh Hefner in 1966. There were a lot of rules that we had to adhere to, the first being we had to have our equipment set up by 18.00pm when the club opened. We then had to leave the club floor and stay in the staff room (with the bunny girls) until 8.30pm when it was time for our first spot. The staff room was quite luxurious and there was a very good choice of food laid on that we could help ourselves to, and the girls were friendly but dressed in their Bunny clothes I found them a little intimidating but very sexy.

After we had finished our first set, our drummer Gary said that Brian Jones of the Rolling Stones had been sitting, with his arms around two girls, watching us. I was a little concerned as one of the songs that we had sung was the Stones, "Paint it Black". Gary said that he was sitting just by the staff door, so I went down to have a look. I opened the door a little, and peeped inside. It was quite dark and I couldn't see anything until Brian Jones turned around and went "Boo!". I made a hasty retreat.

Monday 8th July 1968

(far left) Nigel with his Rickenbacker.

(left 1979) Malcolm Green and Neil Finn from Split Enz search through the rubble at Waihi.

(Picture courtesy of Split Enz Archive)

For the past year Nigel had been playing a Burns Bison bass guitar. Today he bought a second hand Rickenbacker 1999 Bass Guitar which was the earliest Rickenbacker Bass to be introduced into this country.

Nigel kept this bass until 1979 when he was then a member of New Zealand band Split Enz. They had hired a hall in Waihi in New Zealand to rehearse for a festival and left the gear overnight. During the night there was a fire which completely destroyed the hall and they lost thirty thousand dollars worth of equipment, which included Nigel's Rickenbacker Bass. He searched through the rubble and all he could find was the metal bridge.

Wednesday 10th July 1968

The diversity of our gigs was quite amazing at times. Today we were booked to appear at Rampton Psychiatric Hospital in Nottinghamshire, home to some of the most hardened criminals and mental cases. Our gear was piled onto trolleys to be taken from our van to the theatre. We were escorted by warders and every time we went through a door it was locked behind us, until we reached the stage. Our gear was unloaded and all the doors leading to the stage were locked. We were playing for the patients and when the curtains opened for our performance the men were one side and the women the other with warders separating them standing in the centre aisle. At the end of each song a few people clapped and a few people made comments like "get yer hair cut". To say it was the oddest audience we had played to is an understatement. We were very glad to get out of there.

Tuesday 23rd July 1968

It was back to London's Marquee Club this evening supporting, would you believe, Tony Rivers and the Castaways. We hadn't seen Tony since he "stole" our song at Polydor so we gave him a bit of stick. His record had been released and unfortunately, like ours, had failed to make the charts.

It was an enjoyable gig and at the end the club's manager John Gee said that he had received a call from Blaises, another of the fashionable London clubs, and they needed a band and would we like to do it. We said "yes", and quickly packed up and headed off. Blaises was only a short drive from the Marquee and we were up and running by 1.00am. The club was quite full and in the audience already were, Noel Redding (Jimi Hendrix Experience), Hilton Valentine (Animals) and the infamous Jonathan King.

We were half way through our first set when in walked Jimi Hendrix accompanied by Eric Burdon of the Animals and Long John Baldry. By this time Jimi Hendrix was a legend and we were all quite gob smacked as he stood drinking at the bar a few feet from where we were playing and I have to confess I found it quite unnerving. He stayed for around thirty minutes and as he left gave us a friendly musician's nod.

Wednesday 31st July 1968

I read in the papers that yesterday the Beatles had closed down their Apple boutique in London and had given away all the remaining stock on a first come first served basis. I was rather annoyed as only a few days ago I had spent £10.00 (a lot of money in 1968) on a new jacket. I actually sat down and wrote an, "Angry from Hatfield", letter to Paul McCartney. So far he hasn't replied

Wednesday 28th August 1968

The Beatles new single "Hey Jude" had been released a couple of days ago and I hadn't yet heard it on the Radio. I went out, bought my copy, came home and played it for the first time on my little record player. I thought it was amazing definitely the best single they had recorded to date and I loved the long ending. It was unheard of at that time to bring out a single that was over seven minutes long, but as always the Beatles were re-writing the rules.

Monday 2nd September 1968

We had been contacted by the Ford Motor Company who said they were holding a Ford Cortina day at Mallory Park, Race Circuit, in Leicester and as we were called the Cortinas they would like us to perform. "Ford" had sent us a Transit Van and a Ford Cortina Car to travel in. We arrived early as we had to drive to the centre of the track to set up before the racing started. We performed between the racing, which was by formula three cars. One of the drivers was a young James Hunt who was just eight years away from becoming The Formula One World Champion. There was also an appearance by the car featured in the film Chitty Chitty Bang, driven by the racing driver Graham Hill.

We had a great day but unfortunately we had to return the Ford Transit van and go back to our slow and draughty ambulance.

Saturday 7th September 1968

Paul Crowland, the Cortinas first rhythm guitarist, was married this afternoon and we went along to try and talk him out of it, but failed, so we wished him well before going to our gig at the Marquee Club where we topped the bill for the first time. We were supported by Spice who would eventually change their name to Uriah Heep. They had a strong following and I have to say that on the night, received a better reception than we did.

Friday 13th September 1968

Today we received our first ever record royalty cheque from Polydor Records. Our first record, "Phoebe's Flower Shop", had earned the group a total of £7.1s.0d (£7.05p). We immediately wrote to the Financial Times for advice.

The Cortinas had recently been released from our five year contract with Polydor Records by mutual agreement. After our first record had failed we had a few meetings with Graham Dee and listened to more material, but then he suddenly left Polydor, leaving us a bit high and dry without a producer. Nothing seemed to be happening and our contract didn't state that they had to release a certain amount of records, so in reality we could have been stuck with them for five years with no further record releases.

Friday 4th October 1968

Today I bought myself a second hand Gibson ES335 cherry red guitar and tonight we gigged at the University College in London. On the bill were Geno Washington's Ram Jam Band, Cupids Inspiration and Blossom Toes which was quite a differing selection of styles. There was supposed to be a guy from CBS Records coming to see us but he didn't show up.

Thursday 24th October 1968

We had been considering changing the name of our band as the Cortinas was getting to be rather out of date. I can't remember who came up with the suggestion of Octopussy but I seem to remember that it was mentioned, and I think it came from that. We all agreed on Octopus and it was just a matter of arranging exactly when the change would occur, as we would have to notify venues and agents.

Wednesday 6th November 1968

Tonight was another appearance at St. Albans City Hall supporting Status Quo. Status Quo had their first top ten hits in 1968 with "Pictures of Matchstick Men" and "Ice in the Sun" so they were still in their "Psychedelic" period but were really good live. They had two columns of coloured lights, one each side of the stage which were controlled by their roadie. It was quite unusual at this time for bands to carry their own lights, but we thought it was a good idea and it wasn't long before we got my Dad to make us some.

Friday 15th November 1968

The Cortinas were doing a lot of work for an agency in Nottingham called Banner Productions and tonight we were at Nottingham University with Marmalade and the Nashville Teens. Marmalade were very excited as they said that they had been given an exclusive track from the Beatles new album (The White Album) to record, and the song was "Ob-la-di-ob-la-da". They had been told that only they were going to release it as a single, but as so often happens in this business the truth was very different and there were several versions released. Two versions of the song reached the top twenty but Marmalade reached the number one spot.

We were given the kitchen as a dressing room and we indulged in a little bit of "Rock n' Roll" behaviour by taking a giant tin of baked beans with us when we left. My father discovered this a few days later and was rather horrified that he had stolen goods on the premises. He dug a large hole in the garden and buried the tin of beans and to my knowledge they are still there.

Wednesday 20th November 1968

I celebrated my 24th birthday by getting the new Beatles album two days before the official release. I'd only heard a couple of tracks on the radio, so I just played it from beginning to end. One track stood out for me immediately and that was the George Harrison song "While My Guitar Gently Weeps" which was to become one of my all time favourite song. It was only later that I discovered that the beautiful guitar solo was played by Eric Clapton and it was the first time that a non "Beatle" had such a prominent role on a "Beatles" track.

In the evening I went to the Marquee Club in London to see Love Sculpture which featured Dave Edmunds. They were having a hit with a guitar version of "Sabre Dance" which was one of the first pieces of music to make an impact on me in my younger days, so the girl that I was with asked the band to dedicate it to me for my birthday.

Thursday 21st November 1968

Today was the first official day for the change of name to Octopus, and we played a very uninspiring gig at Baldock Working Men's Club.

Wednesday 18th December 1968

We were on the way back down the M1 after a gig in Sutton in Ashfield in Nottinghamshire and stopped at the Watford Gap service station also known as the Blue Boar. It was about an hour's drive from central London and was a favourite stopping off place for bands travelling home, who wanted a greasy fry up in the early hours. Some nights there could be up to half a dozen bands in there at the same time. Tonight as we pulled in Amen Corner were just leaving and the Bonzo Dog Doo Dah Band were inside. We knew it was them, because carefully positioned in one of their van's windows was a case with the words "Bonzo Dog Shit" written on it. Musicians were an impoverished lot and often an order of "sausage, egg and chips" would be reduced to just "egg and chips" by the time the check out was reached.

Saturday 21st December 1968

Plastic Penny were a group who had a number six hit earlier in the year, with a song called "Everything I Am". Tonight we supported them at RAF Benson in Oxfordshire. After the show two members of the group Tony Murray and Paul Raymond approached us and asked if we would be interested in going into the studio to record a couple of their songs, as they had a song writing deal with Dick James Music. We said "yes" and they said they would be in touch.

Tuesday 31st December 1968

We finished the year with an awful gig at a firm's New Years Eve Dance in Dunstable, Bedfordshire. There was a huge fight and our PA speakers were knocked over doing quite a bit of damage

1969

Wednesday 1st January 1969

MELODY MAKER, December 28, 1968—Page 17

We started off 1969 with Dad having to do a rapid repair job on the damage done to our PA speakers the previous evening, before we headed off for another date at the Marquee Club in London.

We supported Yes who were just beginning a Wednesday night residency at the club and at that time were virtually unknown and yet to make a record. The original line up of Yes was Jon Anderson (Vocals), Chris Squire (Bass), Peter Banks (Guitar), Tony Kaye (Organ), and Bill Bruford (Drums). They had a unique style with great original songs mixed in with a few covers like the Beatles "Every Little Thing" and 5th Dimension's "Paper Cup". We were really impressed and they would have a big influence on us over the next couple of years.

Friday 3rd January / Tuesday 7th January 1969

At 24 years of age I had never been outside of England. Cheap holidays abroad were still a thing of the future and I hadn't even been to Wales or Scotland, but this was about to change as Octopus had been booked for two dates in Ireland.

We only had to take guitars with us as the rest of the equipment was supplied by the promoter so we set off on the evening of Friday 3rd January in two cars, Nigel and me in one, Rick and Gary in the other. It was a very cold night with a full moon, and we listened to "The Doors" on Nigel's new cassette player, travelling through the, snow capped, Welsh mountains to catch the ferry at Holyhead. The ferry left Holyhead at 3.45am on the morning of Saturday 4th January and three hours later arrived at Dun Laoghaire, just south of Dublin, to be met by the promoter a Mr. Whitron. He took us to our digs at a boarding house run by a really nice lady called Mrs. Keaney, who gave us breakfast and we went to bed.

In the afternoon the promoter took us to the venue which was called the Stella Ballroom in Mount Merrion. We were not too impressed with the equipment but the PA was good and Mr. Whitron was very proud of this as he had designed it himself. He kept saying that it was 100 volt line.

We played two shows at the ballroom on the Saturday and Sunday and had a good reaction from the audience, and the promoter said he would have us back. I have heard that a young Bob Geldof lived in the area at the time and was a regular visitor to the Stella Ballroom and who knows, he could have been there on one of those nights.

The journey home was a nightmare. We had a rough crossing and arrived back at Holyhead around 1.00am on the Tuesday morning. We set off in our cars but had only gone a few miles when my engine boiled up. I discovered that it was leaking water and had to keep filling the radiator about every ten miles. How I didn't ruin the engine I'll never know. Travelling through Wales in the early hours was quite bleak, there were no garages open and we even hit a snow storm, and at one point I had to stop for a short sleep. We eventually arrived back in Hatfield around 11.00am absolutely knackered, the journey having taken ten hours.

Monday 13th January 1969

Today we drove to Dick James office in London to meet Tony Murray from "Plastic Penny and listen to some of his songs and we picked out two possibilities to record. While we were there Dick James asked another one of his writers if he had any songs. He was a short guy with glasses whose face was familiar, and we remembered we had seen him working in a record shop in Berwick Street, Soho. He said "you may be interested in this song that I've written" and he gave us a demo record and on the label was written "When I was Tealby Abbey" by Elton John.

 He was a couple of years away from his first big hit with "Your Song" and years later, would successfully sue Dick James over copyrights in a landmark court case. I kept the demo for quite a while, it featured him singing with a full orchestral backing and the song has never been released.

Friday 31st January 1969

I read in the Newspaper that yesterday the Beatles had performed an impromptu concert on the roof of their Apple headquarters in Saville Row. They were eventually stopped by the police for causing a disturbance. I was disappointed that I had missed what would turn out to be their last ever public performance together, but in reality they had told no one that they were going to do it.

Tuesday 4th February 1969

There was a rival local group called Mixed Bag who had recorded a single for Decca Records featuring two songs from the, then unknown, musical "Joseph and the Amazing Technicolor Dreamcoat" by the equally unknown Tim Rice and Andrew Lloyd Webber. The A side of the record was "Pottiphar" and tonight they appeared on the children's TV programme Magpie singing this song.

In 1970 their keyboard player John Cook would join Octopus.

Wednesday 12th February 1969

"Octopus" Roadie
Jerry Bishop

Tonight it was back to the Marquee, to support Yes once again. Since we had played with them at the beginning of the year we had been back to see them several times and were now fans.

Up until now we had always set up our equipment ourselves, but our income was now large enough for us to employ a full time road manager. His name was Jerry Bishop and he had taken the plunge to give up his job as an optician, and come on the road with us.

Wednesday 12th March 1969

An early start today and we were off to Dick James recording studio in London for a session with Tony Murray and Paul Raymond of Plastic Penny. We recorded two of their songs "Turning Night into Day" and "Call Me a Fool" and Paul Raymond joined us on piano. The songs were a bit deeper and less "Pop" than we had recorded up until now, and I thought they turned out really well. Tony said that he would now try to get some interest from record companies.

These tracks never saw the light of day until they were included as extra tracks when the Octopus album "Restless Night" was re-released in 2006.

Today was the day that Paul McCartney married Linda Eastman at Marylebone Registry office not far from where we were recording. I remember hearing some of the girls in the Dick James office being rather bitchy about Linda. "How dare she marry the only unmarried Beatle."

It was a difficult day for George Harrison as he and his wife Pattie were arrested for possession of cannabis. (Cannabis as you probably know is a Scotsman with a bladder problem.)

Saturday 5th April – Tuesday 8th April 1969
We made our second visit to Ireland and performed a couple of shows at the Stella Ballroom in Mount Merrion. This time we decided to take our own equipment so we travelled in our ambulance, and had an enjoyable few days.

Friday 11th April 1969
With the new found influence of Yes, Octopus were beginning to change their musical direction and become a little heavier and a little more "progressive". We even learned a couple of Yes songs.

Nigel had been writing for sometime now and today we started working on a song he had co-written with Rick, which was called "Girlfriend". This would eventually become the B. side of our next single.

Wednesday 16th April 1969
In the late sixties there was a rumour, which I believe started in America, that Paul McCartney was dead, and today, I nearly brought some truth to the rumour. I was driving up to London past Lords Cricket Ground and I think I must have been distracted for a second. Out of the corner of my eye I could see someone was crossing the road and I had to brake sharply. To my great surprise there walking in front of me was Paul and Linda McCartney with their Old English Sheep Dog, Martha. Paul raised his arm as if to say "thank you for not killing me" and continued on his way and into Regents Park. I drove a little way up the road, stopped, and the girl I was with ran back and got his autograph.

Monday 21ˢᵗ April 1969

This evening it was off to the Royal Albert Hall in London to see Yes who were supporting Janis Joplin. Yes were excellent and although Janis Joplin had a great voice she wasn't really my cup of tea.

Wednesday 23ʳᵈ April 1969

Tony Kaye, the keyboard player from Yes, had recently upgraded from a Vox Continental organ to a Hammond. We had been thinking about adding a keyboard to the group for some time, as it would add a new dimension and Rick could alternate between guitar and keyboard. Today we went to Yes guitarist Peter Banks' flat, and paid them £45 for their Vox Continental.

Monday 12ᵗʰ May 1969

We received a summons for parking our ambulance in Mansfield with no lights, an offence that is probably hardly ever bothered with today. We were eventually fined £5.00 which I thought was a little harsh.

Thursday 22ⁿᵈ May 1969

Gary Whinyates, our drummer, now had a steady girlfriend called Angela, and they were planning to get married. Today he gave us the news that he would be leaving the group in August or September as he wanted to find himself a "proper" job and settle down. Here we go again.

Tuesday 3ʳᵈ June 1969

Brian Glascock had been the drummer with the Juniors the local group that I have already mentioned. He was a great drummer and at present was not in a band. Tonight we were trying him out in the hope that we could bypass the normal mass audition process. Everything went well and Brian agreed to join us when Gary left.

Wednesday 25ᵗʰ June 1969

Brian was still in contact with Mick Taylor who he had played with in the Juniors. Brian told us that Mick had called him and said, "I've just been offered a job with the Rolling Stones do you think I should take it". Brian Jones had been sacked by the Rolling Stones and John Mayall had recommended Mick Taylor as a replacement. The fact that he was even hesitating was no surprise as he was quite a shy, introverted person.

Wednesday 2ⁿᵈ July 1969

Yes had their first album released today, which was just called Yes, and Octopus had been invited to the launch party which was held this afternoon at Ronnie Scott's Jazz Club in Soho. It was the first time any of us had been to an event like this, with free food and drink which we gratefully accepted. Yes played a short set and then packed their gear for the short journey around the corner to Wardour Street for an evening gig at the Marquee Club.

We followed on and since we had last been to the Marquee Club, there had been quite a major alteration, as there was now a licensed bar. This had been built to one side of the stage and I felt it rather detracted from the normal "Marquee" atmosphere.

Saturday 5th July 1969
Mick Taylor made his debut with the Rolling Stones at a large open air concert in Hyde Park, London. This was two days after his predecessor Brian Jones had been found drowned in his swimming pool.

Thursday 10th July 1969
I was getting petrol at Waters Garage in Hatfield, when I met Donovan doing the same thing. He said he was just off to appear on tonight's "Top of the Pops" with his latest, and what would turn out to be his last, hit single, "Goo Goo Barabajagal (Love is Hot)" which he had recorded with the Jeff Beck Group.

Sunday 20th July 1969
Octopus often played in the Sheffield area and the gigs were mostly at Working Men's Clubs which were starting to become a little unsuitable for the type of music we were performing. Today was due to be Gary's last gig with us and it was at Shire Green Working Men's Club. We played a lunchtime show with a stripper, who was so rough we felt like calling out "keep em' on".

Since playing regularly in Sheffield we'd got to know a guy called Joe Kerrigan who had helped to get us bookings. If we were doing a lunchtime show he would always ask us back to his house and his long suffering wife Mary would give us all a tremendous, traditional roast dinner.

After the evening show we received a call to ask if we would do a lunchtime show the following day at the Black Swan. This was a pub in the centre of Sheffield that was nicknamed the Mucky Duck and a good place to play. We decided to do it and quickly found a hotel for the night. Unfortunately there were no televisions in the rooms so we missed the live coverage of Neil Armstrong being the first man to walk on the moon.

Monday 21st July 1969
Gary's last day as a member of Octopus before he took the slippery slope to marriage and respectability. Lunchtime gigs were usually a bit difficult, as we had to be up and playing around midday, but we did like playing at the Black Swan and today was a good gig.

The Black Swan was a familiar gig on the circuit and was run by a larger than life character called Terry Steeples. He always had a tale to tell and once told us about Joe Cocker. Joe had lived in Sheffield, and used to play at the Black Swan quite regularly, but if he was playing a lunchtime gig, Terry had to go round to his house and literally drag him out of bed to get him on stage, on time.

We travelled home and said goodbye to Gary who had been our drummer for two years and had seen us through the first stage of our professional life.

Thursday 7th August 1969

DOMINIC GRANT
From the Television Show Master of Pop
Presented by Yorkshire Television.

This evening I watched a Jack Good TV special called "Master of Pop, Innocence Anarchy and Soul" which featured Lulu, Brian Auger and Julie Driscoll and a guy called Dominic Grant. Dominic sang "Sea Cruise" supported by Pans People. I didn't know it then, but in a few years time I would be joining Dominic in Guys n' Dolls and he would become one of my closest friends.

Tuesday 19th August 1969

New line up for
OCTOPUS
(left to right)
Nigel Griggs
Brian Glasscock
Paul Griggs
Rick Williams.

Brian Glasscock had been with us for a month and today we were playing the last gig in a short run of dates at the Lyceum Ballroom in London. We hadn't heard from Tony Murray for a while and in truth had almost given up on the idea that he would be able to help us find a new recording deal, but a couple of days ago he had phoned to say that he was bringing Larry Page to see us.

Larry Page was originally a singer, and I had seen him billed as "Larry Page the Teenage Rage" at a Lonnie Donegan concert twelve years previously. More recently he had been running Page One records and had been involved with both the Kinks and the Troggs, but was now starting a new label called "Penny Farthing Records".

After our performance, Tony brought Larry Page around to meet us and he went straight into his well rehearsed "Record Label Boss" chat, about wanting Octopus to sign to Penny Farthing and that he would manage us. We arranged to meet up at his office the following day.

Wednesday 20th August 1969

Today we met with Larry Page at the offices of Penny Farthing Records in Tilney Street, Mayfair. Mum came with us as the group's manager and we discussed at length our aims and direction before finally agreeing to sign with his label. Tony and Larry would be our producers and we also discussed Nigel's songs as he had been very productive over the last year or so, and we were keen to record original material.

Thursday 21st August 1969

We were back at Penny Farthing today and signed a five year contract, probably a little too quickly as we didn't take it to a solicitor to check over first. I suppose we were a bit green at the time and thought that all contracts were the same.

We met some of the staff including a guy called Terry Noone, who looked after "Page Full of Hits" the publishing side of things. We also bumped in to Reg Presley and Ronnie Bond of the Troggs. I had put down in my biography that I was interested in astronomy and Reg was quite amused by this. This was long before he got involved with crop circles.

Wednesday 27th August 1969

Because we were called, Octopus the record company thought it would be a good idea to have a photo session at the seaside. Today we packed our buckets and spades and headed off to Eastbourne with a photographer and a girl called Lisa, who looked after the publicity.

They took over two hundred photographs and we managed to have a paddle.

Friday 29th August 1969

Tonight we made our last ever, appearance at the City Hall in St. Albans, this time supporting Desmond Decker. In our efforts to improve the visual content of the band, we had started using a stage explosion to close our act. They were called maroons and were triggered electrically by our roadie, Jerry, from the lighting board that we now carried. We would close our act with a version of Eddie Cochran's "Summertime Blues" and end it with us running around, rather maniacally, in a strobe light, followed by the bang, which was deafening, and then a blackout. When I think back about this it now, it was probably "bloody dangerous"! We had to place the maroons in a dustbin which, due to the intensity of the explosion, usually lasted around a month before it was completely destroyed and had to be replaced. The first time we ever tried this, the bin was placed rather too near to my speaker cabinet and it blew out all the speaker cones.

Tonight the bin was at the back of the stage, and the explosion ripped a hole in the curtains. There was a huge row with the staff of the City Hall and we were told we would not be welcome back.

Thursday 4th September 1969

Tonight Octopus did their first recording session for Penny Farthing Records. We went to

Chappells Recording Studio in the west end of London and recorded two of Nigel's songs "Laugh at the Poor Man" and "Girl Friend" and a song that Larry had found, called Without Your Love. Tony Murray was producing, and the session turned out well.

Friday 5th September 1969
Things seem to be moving quickly, as Tony Murray phoned to say that Larry had picked "Without Your Love" as the A side of our next single, backed with "Girlfriend".

Tuesday 9th September 1969
I finally sold my Gretsch Tennessean guitar to the Carlsboro shop in Mansfield for £80.00. Today I regret selling any of my past guitars, but needs must, and I needed the cash.

Thursday 25th September 1969
I managed to buy the new Beatles album "Abbey Road", the day before it was officially released, and spent most of the day playing it over and over again and as usual thought it was brilliant. I especially liked the long segued section on side two, and George Harrison had two great songs, "Something" and "Here Comes the Sun". This would be the last album that they ever recorded and although they would release "Let it Be" in 1970, it was in fact recorded before "Abbey Road".

Thursday 2nd October 1969
Larry Page was having second thoughts about the A. side of our single. "Without Your Love" was OK but he liked Nigel's song "Laugh at the Poor Man" although he thought it should be re-recorded. Today we were in De Lane Lea studios in London and did a new version of "Laugh at the Poor Man" along with another new song of Nigel's called "Thief".

"Laugh at the Poor Man" was about a man who lived 400 years ago and due to being poor ended up in the stocks, and with our Yes influence, we had played a piece of Ravel's Bolero in the instrumental section. It sounded good in the studio and was destined to become our first single release for Penny Farthing Records.

Wednesday 29th October 1969
Fabulous 208 was a teenager's magazine, and today Nigel had to go to their offices for a photograph session. He had been nominated by the magazine as one of "The Face 0f 1969" contenders amid many derisory comments from the rest of us. He would eventually be beaten by a guy called Steve Greenfield from Nottingham band Sons and Lovers.

While he was in London Nigel picked up some advance copies of our single and when he returned we eagerly put it on the record player. I have to say we were a bit disappointed as it didn't sound as good as when we recorded it. We hadn't been there when the tracks were mixed and although "Laugh at the Poor Man" was OK, we felt it could have been mixed a lot better.

Friday 7th November 1969

"Laugh at the Poor Man" was released today, and we received favourable reviews in the New Musical Express and Melody Maker. We listened to Radio One all day and it was eventually played by Johnny Walker on "Newly Pressed" who was very complimentary about it.

Wednesday 26th November 1969

Our record had received a few plays on Radio One but not enough to make a major impact. Today the whole group should have been travelling down to Exeter for a live interview on Radio One Club. Unfortunately I had been ill in the night with a severe stomach pain and had to call for the doctor. I was in no fit state to travel to Exeter so the others went without me.

They travelled down by train and shared a compartment with three guys who were members of a group called Butterscotch and were also to be on the show. Their names were Geoff Morrow, David Martin and Chris Arnold and in five years time they would be my managers when I became a member of Guys n' Dolls. In May 1970, Butterscotch would have a number 17 hit with a song called "Don't You Know".

I sat at home in bed and listened to the show on the radio. The Octopus interview went well, the interviewer wished me a speedy recovery, and then the record was played.

Thursday 27th November 1969

Today the pain had gone, the doctor said it may have been a kidney stone, and this evening we played one of our usual uninspiring gigs at Baldock Working Mans Club.

They were never an inspiring audience at this venue, and to make matters worse it was low paid and the gear had to be carried up three flights of stairs. These were called "take the money and run" gigs.

I was beginning to feel that we may be about to start having problems with Brian. He didn't seem to be that content being in the group and I began wondering how long it would be before we would be looking for yet another drummer.

Monday 15th December 1969

Tonight there was a concert at the Lyceum Ballroom in London in aid of UNICEF and it had been rumoured in the press that John Lennon and Yoko Ono would be appearing. John had been going through what I call his "Crazy Yoko" period. He had met Yoko in 1966 and since that time they had been inseparable, embarking on many odd publicity stunts in pursuit of peace in the world. They had made a couple of unlistenable albums together, one of which was called "Two Virgins" where they had posed naked on the front cover, and John's antics had tested the loyalty of even the most hardened fan.

Nigel, Rick and I decided to go, although I don't think we really thought we were going to see John Lennon. There was no problem getting in as it was by no means a full house. We sat on the floor and watched acts like the Hot Chocolate Band, (before they became plain Hot Chocolate), the Rascals, Arrival, and the Pioneers. I found it rather dull, and the only thing that was entertaining up until that point was Peter Banks, the guitarist from Yes, who had been sitting up in one of the boxes, and managed to knock a pint of beer twenty feet on to the dance floor, fortunately causing no injuries.

Around 11.00pm the compere, who was Radio One DJ Emperor Rosco, announced "Ladies and Gentlemen, the Plastic Ono Band" and onto the stage walked John and Yoko, both dressed all in white, followed by a ten piece band which included, Eric Clapton, Billy Preston, Keith Moon, Klaus Voormann, Delaney and Bonnie, and a long haired guy who looked familiar. "Bloody Hell! it's George Harrison". It was the first time that two Beatles had been on stage together since they stopped touring in 1966. John and Yoko had fliers which they threw out to the audience, and on one side it said "Love and Peace John and Yoko", and on the other was the Hare Krishna Mantra, which had been hastily added. I managed to collect a few of these and still have them today. John sang an extended version of his latest record "Cold Turkey" which sounded awesome, then the band started playing a riff and Yoko started screaming. This was called "Don't Worry Kyoko Mummy's only looking for her hand in the snow". It went on for what seemed like ages, and we all sat there pretending that we were enjoying it. After she had finished the band left the stage and that was it. It was great seeing John Lennon live on stage again even if it was only for one song, but I wish he'd left Yoko in the dressing room. Both of these tracks were released on John Lennon's album, "Sometime in New York City".

Wednesday 31st December 1969

Our last booking in the sixties was at "The Mansfield Palais" in Nottinghamshire, it was an enjoyable New Years Eve gig and on the way home we met Tony Rivers in the Blue Boar.

What a decade the sixties had been for music, we had seen the rise of the Beatles who had taken the world by storm and changed the face of pop music forever. We had seen many groups having their fifteen minutes of fame and fade into obscurity. The acts that really achieved longevity were mostly those with strong song writers within their ranks like the Stones, the Who and the Kinks.

After all the great music we had experienced what could possible be the last number one of the sixties. It was "Two Little Boys" by Rolf Harris.

1970

Saturday 3rd January 1970

I had been suffering with a severe sore throat for the past two days, and tonight should have been our first booking of the seventies at the Streatham Ice Rink in South London. I could barely utter a sound so we had to cancel.

Tuesday 13th January 1970

Today we all went for a meeting, with Larry Page at Penny Farthing Records and despite the lack of success of our first single, Larry agreed to let us record an album of our original material. He also told us that he had booked us for a German Rock Festival in May for which we would be paid £200, the biggest fee we had ever received by a long way.

Monday 26th January 1970

Lisa from Penny Farthing phoned to say that Octopus had been booked to appear on Portuguese television in just over two week's time. This caused a bit of a panic as, apart from our two trips to Ireland, Nigel and I had not been abroad or ever flown before. We didn't even have passports.

Wednesday 11th February 1970

Our roadie Jerry drove us to Heathrow Airport where we met up with Lisa and another Penny Farthing artist called Samantha Jones. While we were checking in we bumped into a "British Airways" stewardess who I thought I recognized. It was Ilona Lloyd, the girl I had provided with guitar accompaniment, in the school production of "The Merchant of Venice", way back in 1960.

We flew to Lisbon, and sitting in front of us was Tommy Docherty who told us he was on his way to a new football management job at Porto. We were met at the airport by people from the television company, who took us, first of all to our Hotel, and then on a sight seeing tour of Lisbon. I don't think they'd seen hair as long as ours before and there were a few calls of Beatles!

Since arriving we had been treated like stars, and in the evening we were invited for a traditional Portuguese meal. This was all rather new to us and I remember thinking, "I could get used to this".

Thursday 12th February 1970

It was time do some work. We were taken to the TV studios where we mimed (lip synced) to all of the six tracks that we had so far recorded for Penny Farthing. This included our first single "Laugh at the Poor Man" which had just been released. We were shown a playback of our performance which was in black and white as colour television had yet to arrive in Portugal.

Colour television had only been introduced into Britain in December 1967, and even that was limited to BBC 2.

Friday 13th February 1970

Friday 13th but we flew back to Heathrow with no incident. Jerry met us and we went straight off to an evening gig in Cheshunt.

Wednesday 25th February 1970

Octopus were booked into Radio Luxembourg's recording studio in Mayfair. It was a small four track studio and this was where we would record the rest of our album. Yesterday we had learned a new song of Nigel's called "The River". It was quite a basic rock song which derived a certain amount of inspiration from Canned Heat. We recorded it quite quickly and we all played well, getting a really tight feel, with solid drumming from Brian.

We were pleased with the way it turned out and went straight round to the office and played it to Larry. He raved about it immediately and said that it was to be our next single and that he would go all out with the promotion campaign.

Later that evening there was a huge row/discussion with Rick about whether or not he was going to stay with us. I had sensed he had not been that settled recently, he simply wasn't content being just the rhythm guitarist ... he wanted to play lead.

Tuesday 24th March 1970

Octopus had experienced an uneasy month. First of all Rick decided he wanted to leave, and we approached keyboard player John Cook from local group "Mixed Bag" to replace him. Mixed Bag were fully professional and John was happy where he was, so at that point he turned us down. We advertised for a keyboard player in the music press, but then Rick changed his mind and said he wanted to stay. Against our better judgement we agreed.

Today Jerry our roadie told us that he was going back to being an optician and would be leaving us.

Friday 3rd April 1970

A new roadie called Albert (no one can remember his second name) joined us today. Albert was born to be a roadie, he was big, scruffy, reliable, had a huge appetite, and his conversation was normally limited to four by twelves, 2K rigs, and women.

To the non musician a four by twelve is a loud speaker cabinet containing four speakers each measuring twelve inches in diameter, and a 2K rig is a public address system with an output power of two thousand watts. I'm not going to try to explain women.

Friday 10th April 1970

Nigel called in at Penny Farthing and collected some advance copies of the new Octopus single "The River" which is due for release on Friday 1st May. We were happy with the way it sounded, but a little disappointed with how "Thief" had been mixed on the B. side

Today Paul McCartney officially announced that the Beatles had split up, which didn't really surprise anyone. John Lennon had already released four solo singles and Paul had a solo album due for release in a couple of weeks time. George and Ringo were both working on solo material and there had been many references in the press of the tensions within the group, so the split was inevitable. In a months time they would release their final studio album "Let it Be" which was actually recorded before "Abbey Road". This had been remixed by Phil Spector against Paul's wishes and would be followed by many years of legal wrangling.

Like many others I was sad at the demise of the Beatles who had been an important part of my life for the past seven years, but nothing lasts forever and the legacy they left behind was amazing. They would individually go on to make more music in the years to come. Some of it great, some not so great but their contribution to music in general would endure.

There have been millions of words written about the Beatles and I'm going to add a few more. Having digested books, read articles, and lived and breathed the Beatles for most of my life I have come to the conclusion that Paul McCartney was the key ingredient to the Beatles greatness. I am not saying that he wrote the best songs; John and Paul were pretty equal on that front. I'm saying that if John Lennon had not met Paul McCartney and invited him to join his group, at that time called the Quarrymen, the creativity that made the Beatles what they were, would not have happened. I think John would have emerged as a star in his own right whatever the outcome but he would have probably been content to sing Rock n' Roll if Paul hadn't steered him into a different direction of creativity. In the early days when they had to play for six hours a night in the clubs of Hamburg it was Paul who chose songs to perform that were far removed from Rock n' Roll. There were songs from films and musicals like "A Taste of Honey" and "Til There was You" which exposed them to non Rock n' Roll guitar chords and progressions which would later feature in their own compositions. Paul was the strongest musician in the group and as well as being a bass player could perform on piano, drums and was a fine lead guitarist all of which he played at different times during Beatles recording career.

It was Paul who came up with the concept of "Sgt Pepper's Lonely Hearts Club Band" one of the most iconic (not necessarily their best) albums ever, his drive and enthusiasm endured right to the end when the rest of the group had already reached breaking point. This could be seen in the film "Let it Be" when his enthusiasm was interpreted as being domineering and he was clearly pissing the others off.

This is no detriment to John Lennon whose greatness is undeniable and the Beatles would not have been what they were without him. I just believe that Paul McCartney was the catalyst to their genius.

Tuesday 28th April 1970

Three days before the release of our new single "The River", Nigel travelled by train to Taunton in Somerset, to be interviewed on Radio One Club. It was the first time the record had been played on Radio and it came across well.

Friday 1st May 1970

Our second single as Octopus was released today, and once again it was down to listening to Radio One hoping they would play it.

In the late afternoon Tommy Vance played "The River" on his "What's New" programme and gave it a favourable review.

Friday 15th May 1970

We heard that our record was being played every hour on Radio Luxembourg. This was great but, unfortunately the station suffered from really dodgy reception, and since Radio One had begun playing round the clock music, not many people listened to Radio Luxemburg anymore.

Once again due to limited Radio One plays we already knew that the record would not make the charts, which was a great pity as we believed in it.

Saturday 16th May 1970

We drove to Gatwick Airport on the first leg of our journey to appear at a German Rock

Festival. There was a special chartered flight to carry all the bands which included: Status Quo, Love Sculpture, Love Affair, Humble Pie and Ginger Baker's Airforce. We flew to Dusseldorf and were taken first, to our hotel and then on to the stadium for the concert.

We had been told that the equipment was to be supplied by the promoters but already had our doubts as we had seen roadies loading speaker cabinets onto the plane at Gatwick. Sure enough we were told that we should have brought our own gear. Lisa from Penny Farthing was with us and after a bit of negotiating, persuaded Status Quo to allow us to use theirs. The concert ran from around midday to midnight and we performed our spot in the early afternoon, and it was quite difficult to get much of a reaction from a bunch of stoned Germans at that time of the day. The act that went down best of all was Status Quo. They'd just had a hit with "Down the Dustpipe" and were changing into the "Rock Band" we all know and the Germans loved them.

Closing the show was Ginger Baker's Airforce, preceded by Humble Pie. There was a stage at each end of the stadium and Ginger Baker decided that Humble Pie were overrunning so while they were still playing at the far end, he got up on stage and began loudly tuning his drums. This brought out a bit of verbal abuse from Steve Marriott and for a few moments they traded insults.

Eventually Ginger Baker's Airforce took to the stage. They were a ten piece band that included Stevie Winwood, Denny Laine and saxophonist Graham Bond among the line up. Graham Bond was a huge guy and I remember him struggling to negotiate the rather small portable toilets that had been supplied for the bands. After the show the bands returned to the hotel and had a bit of a party.

Sunday 17th May 1970

We were collected from our hotel at 6.00am, an unearthly hour for musicians. It was a very quiet flight home with a large group of hung over musicians trying to catch up on sleep.

Tuesday 26th May 1970

There were storm clouds on the horizon once again. Nigel and I could sense that our drummer Brian's enthusiasm for the group was waning. Rick was being very moody and difficult, and I'm sure he felt that he deserved a more prominent role in the group. He had just bought a brand new black Les Paul Custom guitar, which almost cried out, "I'm not staying on rhythm guitar forever".

He wanted us to learn one of his songs today so we had a go. I didn't think it was strong enough but we persevered in rather a strained atmosphere, and it was a difficult rehearsal.

Sunday 31st May 1970

Tonight would be the last night Octopus played with their present line up. The gig was at Tiffanys, a club in Shaftsbury Avenue, London, which was part of the Mecca group. There was a bad vibe on stage and we didn't play well. Rick and Brian were just going through the motions, and it was a painful gig.

Brian's brother, John Glascock had just joined Cliff Bennett's band Toe Fat. I had heard they were looking for a drummer and guessed that Brian wanted to join, although at that stage he had said nothing to us. Rick was becoming impossible to work with so it was time for a drastic change.

Friday 5th June 1970

Yesterday Nigel and I had told our producer Tony Murray that there were about to be changes in the group and this morning Brian told us that he was leaving the band, and as expected would be joining Toefat. They had been offered an American tour, supporting Eric Clapton's new band Derek and the Dominoes, and Brian felt it was an offer he couldn't refuse. Nigel and I went to see Rick and after a long discussion it was mutually agreed that he too would leave. At that point Octopus consisted of Nigel and I, our roadie Albert, and one third of a recorded album. It was quite a depressing time but calling it a day didn't enter our heads.

In March we had approached John Cook to join us and at that time he had said "no". Since then his group Mixed Bag had split up so we decided to approach him again. He wasn't on the phone and when we called at his house his mother said that he had taken a part time job in a metalwork shop. We tracked him down and he agreed to have a try out to see how things went. We then put adverts in the music press looking for a drummer.

Wednesday 1st July 1970

Things worked out really well with John Cook who agreed to join us. He played a rather unique sounding Wurlitzer organ and we had been rehearsing with him for the past few weeks, as well as auditioning almost every out of work drummer in the country. I have always been very fussy about drummers and having played with Brian Glasscock, Nigel and I were finding it hard to hear one who came close. The drummer and bass guitarist are the engine room of every group and it is important they are compatible. Many of the drummers we had tried out were trying to impress with their technique, rather than try and fit in and others were just hopeless.

Today we auditioned a guy called Malcolm Green who hailed from Southgate in North London. From the start he seemed promising and after spending the afternoon going through our numbers, we decided to offer him the job.

Because of the upheaval we had cancelled a lot of work, so we decided to rehearse every day, and be back on the road in two weeks time.

Friday 3rd July 1970

Today I drove to Maidstone in Kent to see Yes live on stage. Pete Banks their guitarist had recently left the band and had been replaced by Steve Howe and this was his first gig. They had learned a lot of new material since I had last seen them and Steve Howe was a brilliant guitarist, a lot more controlled than Pete Banks, and it was a great show.

Tuesday 14th July 1970

It was three days before the first gig with the new line-up. We had been rehearsing solidly and today we ran through our complete set to see if we had ninety minutes. It was maybe a few minutes short, so at least we could get back on the road.

We had kept some of our old numbers but included a lot of new material and it tended to be a bit heavier than before. One thing we learned was our own version of the "Peer Gynt Suite", a popular piece of classical music by Grieg. We incorporated two pieces, "Morning" and "In the Hall of a Mountain King" and turned them into a six minute instrumental. It sounded a bit Emerson Lake and Palmer in parts, and would become one of our most requested numbers in the days to come. There were three songs by Yes which in retrospect was probably too many, a couple of Neil Young and Beatles covers, including "I am the Walrus" which would also become a "crowd pleaser", mixed in with some of our original songs. We were moving away from being a pop group.

Having a keyboard player had changed the dynamics of the band. John was an excellent player who could also sing, so with Nigel taking the occasional vocal we now had three lead vocalists.

Friday 17th July 1970

OCTOPUS
New Line Up
(back) Malcolm Green
Nigel Griggs.
(front) Paul Griggs
John Cook.

We travelled to the Dolphin Hotel at Botley near Southampton for the first gig with the new line up. It was a bit of a nervy performance with lots of room for improvement but we were well received, and drove home much relieved.

Tuesday 21st July 1970

Today we went into Luxembourg Studios for our first session with the new look Octopus. We recorded four backing tracks, but our producer Tony Murray was not impressed with our new drummer. Malcolm was having problems with his timing and it was a bit of an effort to get a usable performance from him. We were already thinking that maybe we had made the wrong choice even though he had stood out from all the other drummers we auditioned.

Saturday 15th August 1970

Octopus had been invited to attend a Radio Luxembourg Exravaganza in Carnaby Street at a boutique called John Stephen. It was a morning event so we enjoyed a champagne breakfast, and rubbed shoulders with, among others, Carl Wayne (The Move), Barry Gibb (Bee Gees) and Doctor Who actor Fraser Hines. Peter Wyngarde the actor who played a character called Jason King in "Department S" was presented with an award for the best dressed male. When all of the champagne had been consumed we travelled up to Newark for an evening gig.

Tuesday 18th August 1970

Nigel celebrated his twenty first birthday, and Octopus celebrated three years as a fully professional band.

Most of the day was spent in the studio recording a song written by Nigel and John called "Tide". We also attempted to record our version of the "Peer Gynt Suite" but try as we might it never worked successfully in the studio, although on stage it was fine. A live version would eventually surface on the re- released Octopus CD in 2006.

Friday 18th September 1970

It was reported that Jimi Hendrix had been found dead at a flat in London apparently choking on his own vomit after a heavy drinking session. It had been less than four years since his first record, Hey Joe, had been released but in that short space of time he had attained legendary status which continues to this day.

Tuesday 29th September 1970

I was twenty five year of age and still living at home, but today I was offered a council flat in South Hatfield which I accepted, so I was about to fly the nest.

Nigel and I headed off to Penny Farthing once more to meet with Larry who had some news for us. He had received some good sales figures and it looked as if we were going to have a hit record in Italy with "The River", which was great news. Then it was back to the studio with Tony Murray to start mixing our album. We felt the album was a little short time wise, but I think the cost of studio time was affecting some of the executive decisions.

Tuesday 27th October 1970

Just over two weeks after the death of Jimi Hendrix, American blues/rock singer Janis Joplin had been found dead after an overdose of heroin and booze. One of the last songs she ever recorded, only days before her death, was the a cappella, "Mercedes Benz" which many years later would be used in a Gap commercial.

Tuesday 27th October 1970

Nigel and I had been summoned to Larry Page's office again. He told us that he wasn't very keen on the album so far and felt it was rather slow. He also bluntly told us that he did not like Malcolm's drumming and said we should get rid of him.

Malcolm had only been with us for three months but we already had doubts about his suitability. He was inconsistent, some nights he was fine and on others his mind seemed to be elsewhere. In the recording studio it had been a struggle, and now Larry was telling us to replace him.

Wednesday 4th November 1970

Today I had a call from Larry Page who said that our single "The River" was number twenty two in the Italian charts and there was a possibility that we might be doing a television show there. He asked about the situation with Malcolm and I told him we were trying to sort something out.

This evening we should have played at Hatchetts, a club in the West End, but when we arrived they insisted we use the club's amplification, even though we had previously been told we could use our own. They were adamant, so we did a moody and went home.

Wednesday 18th November 1970

Mike Tate, the road manager from Yes phoned to ask if Steve Howe could borrow my Rickenbacker 12 string guitar for a recording session. I said OK and this evening drove up to Advision Studios in London and dropped it off.

Thursday 19th November 1970

This evening I drove back to Advision studios to collect my guitar. I asked if they minded if I stayed a while and they said it was OK. Yes were in the middle of recording, what would turn out to be their breakthrough LP, called "The Yes Album" and while I was there I saw John Anderson recording the lead vocals on a song called "Yours is no Disgrace" which had some amazing guitar playing from Steve Howe. I also saw them recording two guys from a group called Gnidrilog, who were playing treble recorders on a track called "Your Move".

Wednesday 2nd December 1970

Our draughty old ambulance, had served us well for the past three years but it was very slow and becoming rather unreliable and it was time to upgrade. Larry Page had loaned us the money and today we bought a 30 cwt long wheel based Ford Transit van. The difference was immediately noticeable. It was warm and we could drive at a respectable speed and not get overtaken by bicycles.

Larry called to say that we were booked to appear on an Italian television show on New Years Eve. He also said that he didn't want Malcolm to go, which immediately caused a problem.

 Unbeknown to Malcolm we had been looking for a new drummer by answering adverts in the music press. This was rather underhanded but we didn't want to have another long spell off the road as we were doing this for a living and finances were an important factor.

Tuesday 15th December 1970

Brian Glascock had played drums on "The River" before leaving us to join Toefat; he had just returned from an American tour and wasn't working for a few weeks. We asked him if he would come with us to Italy for the TV show, and he agreed. Larry was pleased although I couldn't understand why he was so adamant about not wanting Malcolm to go, as we would be miming and it wouldn't have mattered if my mum had been the drummer.

Wednesday 30th December 1970

Albert took us to Heathrow for the 9.00am flight to Milan, but because of bad weather the plane was diverted to Malpensa, some thirty miles from Milan. It caused us a few problems before eventually meeting up with Terry Noone from Penny Farthing on the connecting flight to Pisa.

The show was an all evening variety show which went through into the new year with Octopus due to perform their spot at around 1.00am

Thursday 31st December 1970

We spent most of the day hanging around waiting to rehearse before finally being allowed ten minutes to run through our two songs.

The studio was set out like a night club, but the audience seemed very snobby, all posh frocks and dinner jackets, with the guest of honour Italian film star Marcello Mastrioni. We felt a bit out of place in our hippy gear but spent the night eating and drinking champagne, and for Nigel it was the night he discovered 'vodka and caviar'. By the time we came to perform we were all pissed, and 1970 was history.

1971

Friday 1st January 1971

Due to it being New Years Day, plus the fact that the weather was bad, there were no connecting flights to Milan so we enjoyed a very pleasant train ride across snow covered northern Italy to catch the plane home. We boarded our plane during a heavy snow storm and found a couple of guys sweeping snow from the wings ready for take, off. This didn't do me a lot of good as I had already become quite nervous of flying, but the pilot seemed to know what he was doing and we returned to England safely.

Saturday 2nd January 1971

Octopus arrive at
Storthfield Country
Club, South
Normanton
Nottinghamshire

It was back to gigging at a Sheffield social club today and these were gigs that we really did not enjoy although I have to say that at some of them, the rather "heavy" material we were now playing went down surprisingly well. Today was made more difficult by the fact that Malcolm was with us, and as he didn't know about the trip to Italy we hade to be careful about what was said, which was rather underhanded. We were still looking for a new drummer and there was a chance that Brian Glascock might be returning, as his band "Toefat" had broken up.

After the gig we travelled back to Storthfield Country Club in South Normanton in Nottinghamshire. This was a club that we regularly played at and would stay there if we were in the area. It was run by Roy and Ina Haywood and I'm still in touch with Ina who now lives in Mallorca.

Storthfield Country Club had bands playing on Fridays and Saturdays and as there was accommodation available some of the bands would stay over. We often found ourselves sharing a roof with Sweet or Mud before either band achieved chart success. We became good mates with Mud.

Tuesday 16th February 1971

During the past few weeks Brian Glascock had briefly joined the Bee Gees. This hadn't worked out and he had now agreed to return to "Octopus", so today Nigel, (I think he volunteered) had the unenviable task of phoning Malcolm to tell him he was fired.

Wednesday 24th February 1971

Tonight Octopus supported the Kinks at the Top Rank Ballroom in Leicester. I'd always liked the Kinks on record but on stage I found them a bit shambolic and untogether.

Sunday 21st March 1971

Octopus was thrown into turmoil once again when, barely a month after he had rejoined us, Brian announced that he and his wife had decided to go and live in America and would be flying out on April 2nd.

It was quite depressing and I thought seriously that we should call it a day and disband the group. I couldn't bear the thought of auditioning drummers yet again. I had a long discussion with Nigel and John and eventually decided that we would continue if we could find a suitable drummer, and in the meantime we would go cap in hand to Malcolm Green to see if he would stand in. In retrospect we had quite a nerve to do this, but amazingly he agreed.

Brian Glascock lives in America to this day, and achieved success with the Motels who had two small UK hits in the early eighties.

Saturday 24th April 1971

Octopus final Line Up (left to right) John Cook Nigel Griggs Tim Reeves Paul Griggs.

Our first gig with our sixth and what would be our final drummer Tim Reeves. Tim had moved up to Hertfordshire from Brighton and had previously been in a band called the Fox.

Friday 7th May 1971

The Octopus album "Restless Night" was released today and we were not that happy about certain things. Without consulting us, Penny Farthing had removed two slower songs from the album and replaced them with the up tempo "Thief" which had been the b. side of our single, "The River". A lot of money had been spent on the album cover which none of us liked very much. It had a gatefold sleeve with paintings of a naked woman with tentacles instead of arms. There were no pictures of the band to be seen. Larry Page's words to us were "don't worry the cover will sell it." We were also concerned about value for money, as the album was barely thirty five minutes long.

Although I can be critical of Larry Page, on the positive side I have to say that he gave us complete freedom in the studio to record our own original material in the way that we wanted, and did not interfere with the artistic side of things. I am still in touch with Larry who now lives in Australia.

Looking back today I am proud of this album and strangely, the fact that the line up of Octopus changed completely after a few tracks makes it more varied. The earlier tracks are more Rock, the later tracks more complex and melodic and these differences give the album added dimensions. I'm still not crazy about the cover, (several people have said the inside picture looks like Kat Slater from Eastenders), but today an original copy of the vinyl album is worth between £150 - £200 on the collectors market, and the cover is probably largely responsible for this valuation.

The album has been released on CD several times both here and in Japan, where there is a huge market for "British Psychedelia", which the album has been labelled. In 2006 I collaborated with Revola records to release the definitive version. The two missing original tracks were reinstated and unreleased demo recordings were included, along with the Cortinas single. This new package probably best sums up the Cortinas and Octopus' brief recording career.

Saturday 8th May 1971

A bad day for Nigel and I. Liverpool were beaten by Arsenal in the FA Cup final 2-1 after extra time. The sight of Charlie George lying on his back celebrating after scoring the winning goal in extra time, still haunts me. To make matters worse it meant that Arsenal had achieved the league and cup double.

Saturday 5th June 1971

We had built up quite a following by regularly playing at three clubs in an area of Nottinghamshire and Derbyshire. These were, the already mentioned, Storthfield Counry Club in South Normanton, the Golden Diamond in Sutton in Ashfield, and the Grey Topper in Jacksdale. This following had built up in the last six months and we began to recognize people who would turn up to all of these venues when we were playing.

Tonight we were at the Grey Topper and the place was packed. We played well and went down a storm and it was one of the best nights we ever had as a band.

Wednesday 16th June 1971

Today I exchanged my Gibson 335 semi acoustic guitar for a 1967 Gibson SG standard.

Saturday 2nd October 1971

I sold my Rickenbacker 1993 12 string guitar to the Carlsbro shop in Mansfield for £110. You should never have regrets in life but my one regret today is selling that guitar. These particular models are worth a considerable amount as there were only around twenty five ever built. Add this to the fact that mine had belonged to Pete Townsend of the Who it would have been a major investment, as today instruments owned by high profile musicians often reach phenomenal prices at auction.

Friday 22nd October 1971

Slade were a week away from their very first number one hit with "Coz I Luv You" and were one of the hottest bands of the moment. Tonight they were honouring a long standing booking at Cuffley Youth Club near Potters Bar and I went along to see them. It was a very small hall, the place was packed and Slade were loud, raw and brilliant.

Saturday 6th November 1971

I had been going through a stage of being dissatisfied with the way things were going with Octopus. Our album had only sold around six hundred copies and most of them in the Nottingham and Derby areas. We were playing too many social clubs. There was nothing happening on the recording front as things had gone very quiet with Penny Farthing records. We were getting a little stale as a band and although Tim Reeves was a good drummer he had a lazy, couldn't care less attitude which was annoying me immensely.

Tonight after playing yet another Sheffield working mans club, we returned to Storthfield Country Club and had a long discussion about the band. We eventually agreed that Octopus should break up in January, which gave us two months to sort something out for the future.

Thursday 25th November 1971

I hadn't given much thought to what I wanted to do when Octopus finished but the other day I was contacted by Alan Shacklock. He had formed his own band, called Shacklock, and asked me if I would be interested in managing them. Tonight they were playing at London's Marquee Club and I went along to check them out. They were a bit nervous but played well and I liked what they were doing, their only problem was that they needed a strong lead vocalist.

I eventually decided that management was something I didn't want to become involved with. Shacklock eventually added vocalist Jenny Haan and became Babe Ruth.

Wednesday 29th December 1971

I had a call from one of our agents, Banner Productions in Nottingham who offered me a job in the Nottingham based band Sons and Lovers. They were a harmony/cabaret band, far removed from what I was doing in Octopus but said I would give it some thought.

Friday 31st December 1971

The last day of 1971 found Octopus performing their last gig at The Golden Diamond in Sutton in Ashfield. The place was packed with lots of our regular followers and people were genuinely sad that we were breaking up.

1972

Saturday 1st January 1972

We had stayed over at Storthfield Country Club and today a guy called Eddie Cook, the bass guitarist from Sons and Lovers, came round to discuss the possibility of me joining them. After he had gone I thought about the offer seriously, I needed to work for financial reasons but I wasn't sure I could cope with the music they were performing.

Saturday 8th January 1972

 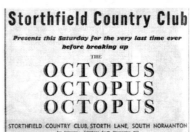

Tonight was our penultimate performance, and farewell gig at Storthfield Country Club. The club was small but packed to the rafters with over six hundred people including Mud, who had came along for support, and the atmosphere was electric.

We performed an emotionally charged set and played well. A few encores were required before I announced, with a lump in my throat, that this would be our last song. We finished with one of our most requested numbers, the Beatles, "I am the Walrus", and then left the stage to one of the most amazing ovations I would ever experience.

Tuesday 11th January 1972

I travelled to Burton on Trent to see a "Sons and Lovers" gig. They performed a lot of close harmony material by the likes of the Beach Boys and Four Seasons. I wasn't sure it was what I wanted to do but they said they would be disbanding in April so I agreed to join them until then.

Friday 14th January 1972

The last ever Octopus gig was at the St. Albans College of Further Education. Once again the hall was packed with a crowd that included many people we had got to know over the years, and even a coach load that had travelled down from the Nottingham area.

We played OK but it wasn't quite as good as Storthfield last week although still very emotional. The last number was Johnny B. Good with various ex. members coming on stage for a jam. It was probably a bit of a shambles as these things can be, but it finished off the evening well. Then it was over and for the first time in around eight years I no longer had a band.

Tuesday 18th January 1972

I was still feeling a little strange following the break up of Octopus, but today I had to drive to Nottingham for my first rehearsal with Sons and Lovers. It was odd not being in charge and having to learn things that I didn't particularly want to play and I found myself becoming increasingly bored.

Friday 21st January 1972

I had been staying with Eddie Cook in Nottingham and been rehearsing with Sons and Lovers during the day. I had been getting more depressed everyday and realized I should not have agreed to join them so soon after Octopus had finished. I told Eddie that I had to go home and would not be returning.

Wednesday 9th February 1972

Paul McCartney had formed a new band called Wings, and had decided to go out and play some gigs. He turned up unannounced at Nottingham University with his family and band and asked if he could play. The university charged 50p on the door to get in and they shared the takings with Wings. This was the first time Paul McCartney had played a scheduled gig in this country since that last Beatles show at Wembley in 1966. They did not perform one Beatles song. They continued doing this for a couple of weeks playing a total of eleven dates at various universities.

Friday 11th February 1972

I was twenty six years of age and had no idea what I was going to do next. I had been looking through the music press for jobs and had a couple of auditions, but today I decided it was time to sign on the dole.

Saturday 19th February 1972

Brian Glascock the ex. Octopus drummer had contacted Nigel to say that he was in a flamenco rock band called Carmen. They were based in Hollywood and needed a bass player. Brian had recommended Nigel, who had decided to take the job and today was flying out to Los Angeles.

I went with Mum and Dad to the airport to see him off, and thought he was very brave flying off to the unknown and I would miss him.

Monday 6th March 1972

I had answered an advert from a band that were looking for a lead guitarist and when I arrived at the audition discovered it was for the rock band UFO. I had a go but felt I was a bit out of my depth and did not get the job.

Saturday 25th March 1972

Since the demise of Octopus, drummer Tim Reeves had fallen on his feet and joined Mungo Jerry, and this evening I went to the St. Albans City Hall to see them.

Wednesday 12th April 1972

Today I managed to get myself an evening's work as a session singer at Decca recording studios. I sang on a cover version of the Beach Boys song "Disney Girls".

Friday 21st April 1972

I auditioned for an acoustic trio called Magna Carta run by a guy called Chris Simpson. I liked what they were doing and although I made the final short list, I did not get the job.

Thursday 8th June 1972

CARMEN
Featuring the
Glascock Brothers
(middle back) Brian
(front right) John

I went along with Mum and Dad to Luton airport to meet Nigel who had returned from Los Angeles having left Carmen.

Carmen was run by flamenco guitarist David Allen, his sister Angela danced with the band and their mother and father owned El Cid which was the only venue they played during Nigel's time there. He was having the time of his life in Hollywood, and although he was almost in awe of Carmen's music, something wasn't right. He said the band was over-rehearsed and had reached a standstill. I think he also became concerned at being so far from home. Brian Glascock's brother John came out to replace him.

After his stint with Carmen, John Glascock would return to England and join Jethro Tull where he remained until his untimely death in 1979.

Tuesday 20th June 1972

The Haywood family were selling Storthfield Country Club in South Normanton and moving to Mallorca. They had phoned and asked if Octopus would reform for the last night and now that Nigel was home from America this was possible.

We had a couple of days rehearsal and decided to do the show. The place was pretty packed but not as many people as our farewell performance in January, and the band was a bit under rehearsed. In retrospect it would have been better not to have done it and leave the memory as it was.

Monday 14th August 1972

I was going through a bad patch, I had been offered a few jobs and turned them down and now I'd stopped going to auditions as I wasn't sure what I really wanted to do. I was on the dole and today asked them to try and find me a job in a music shop.

Nigel was still going to auditions and today decided to join a band called Khan, fronted by a guy called Steve Hillage.

Saturday 7th October 1972

Today I started work at Hammonds of Watford, my first proper job since 1967. Hammonds was a large two storey music shop that sold musical instruments, records and sheet music. I was in the musical instrument section working with a fellow musician called Paul Green.

Tuesday 31st October 1972

Dave Mount the drummer from Mud came round for a meal and to discuss the possibility of me joining them. I can't remember if their guitarist Rob Davis wanted to leave at that time or if they wanted to add another guitar, but the outcome was I turned down the offer. Mud were five months away from reaching number twelve in the charts with "Crazy", the first of a string of hits.

I'm not sure why I said "no", they were a professional group and we got on well, and considering I would say "yes" to joining Guys n' Dolls in two years time, this was a strange decision.

Monday 20th November 1972

Today was my twenty eighth birthday and I felt that life was passing me by.

One of our regular customers at Hammonds was Kenny Baker who at that time was in a comedy harmonica group called the Mini Tones and would go on to star as R2D2 in Star Wars. Many years later Guys and Dolls would stay at the same hotel as Dave Prowse who became the original Darth Vader.

I find it rather cool to say I've shared a hotel with Darth Vader and sold a harmonica to R2D2.

Monday 11ᵗʰ December 1972

Out of the blue I received a phone call from Terry Noone of Penny Farthing records with a proposition. The label had a record called "Dreams are Ten a Penny" under the name of Kincade and it was becoming a hit in Europe. The record was made with session musicians by a guy called John Carter who was an original member of sixties chart group the Ivy League. John had sung the lead vocals but did not want to go out on the road again so Terry Noone asked if I could put together a group to become Kincade and mime to the record on Dutch television in about a week's time.

I phoned Nigel who said he would do it, I then contacted another ex. Octopus member Rick Williams who also said "yes".

Monday 18ᵗʰ December 1972

Nigel, Rick and me, now known as Kincade, met Terry Noone at Heathrow airport and flew to Amsterdam. We were taken to the TV studios at Hilversum to appear on Top Pop which was the Dutch equivalent to Top of the Pops. Also on the show was Hurricane Smith, the infamous Jonathan King and a group from Newcastle called Geordie. The lead singer of Geordie was an ex. paratrooper called Brian Johnson who would go on to be the lead singer with AC DC and is still with them today.

It was strange miming to someone else's voice but it seemed to go OK and afterwards we went out for a meal before flying home. Terry Noone explained to us that there had been a guy called John Knowles who had already performed a couple of TV spots as Kincade in Germany, but he'd had a disagreement with Larry Page and so we'd taken over. Terry also said there would probably be future work coming up. It didn't feel like being in a band, more like a part time job so I didn't have a problem with it.

Sunday 31ˢᵗ December 1972

1972 had been a strange and somewhat depressing year. I started wondering why I was so keen to break up Octopus when I had no idea what would follow. Continuing with the band, despite the problems at the time, would probably have been a better option.

1973
Wednesday 3rd January 1973

We had out first photo sessions as Kincade, one at the Penny Farthing office the other at the Railway Museum in Clapham where we were photographed aboard the world's fastest steam locomotive, Mallard, which was my idea. "Dreams are ten a Penny" had been a hit in several European countries and Larry Page was keen to establish us as the faces of Kincade even though we were in the bizarre situation of not having played or sung a single note on the record. There were several more European television appearances in the pipeline, the first being a three day trip to Holland in a few weeks time.

We discussed the situation of finance with Larry, because we felt that we should be put on some sort of retainer. I could not keep having time off work and would probably have to give up my job. I could see that Larry wasn't crazy about this suggestion but said he would give it some thought.

Wednesday 31st January 1973
We called in to Penny Farthing and collected tickets for our trip to Holland. While we were there Larry agreed to pay us a retainer of £15 per week each plus anything we made in television appearance fees.

We did an interview for an Australian pop magazine which due to the circumstances surrounding the formation of Kincade must have been full of bullshit.

Thursday 1st – Saturday 3rd February1973
We flew to Amsterdam and from there on to Groningen in the North of Holland to appear on a TV show called Zevensprongen which was a game show a bit like the Generation Game. It was a live show in front of a large studio audience. Clive Dunn, who was having a hit with "Grandad" at the time, was also appearing and we spent some time with him and his actress wife Priscilla Morgan, and managed to get him talking about his days

playing Corporal Jones in "Dads Army".

Tuesday 20th – Saturday 24th February1973

Kincade's first trip to Germany began when we arrived at Hamburg airport and were given rather a vigorous search by the customs. This was followed by a day of photo sessions and interviews.

On Wednesday we appeared on the top German pop show "Disco 73" where once again we mimed to "Dreams are Ten a Penny". Vinegar Joe were also appearing and in their line up was, Elkie Brooks and the late Robert Palmer. After the show we all went out to Hamburg's infamous red light district the Reeperbhan, with Elkie dressed as a guy since as it was deemed unwise for women to visit there. We visited the Top Ten Club where the Beatles had performed in the early days.

By Friday we had flown to Bremen for an important, but strange, radio show. It took place at an ice rink and we were interviewed before miming (on the radio?) to "Dreams are Ten a Penny", while walking round on the ice followed by a crowd of kids. We flew home on Saturday.

Friday 2nd March 1973

Although Radio One broadcast music non stop it wasn't all from records. The Musicians Union insisted that a certain amount of the musical output had to be specially recorded so as to give employment to musicians.

Kincade had been booked for one of these sessions so we contacted a drummer we knew called Alan Eden, spent an afternoon rehearsing the songs, and then it was off to the BBC for a three song recording session. This was the first time we had physically performed any of the Kincade material.

During the next few weeks these tracks were played several times on Radio One

Tuesday 27th – Saturday 31st March 1973

The Kincade Album which now featured our photos (back) Rick Willams (front) Nigel & Paul Griggs

It was off to Spain for a Kincade promotion trip and the first two days were spent in Madrid where we made one television appearance and numerous interviews on local radio stations which were becoming harder due to an added twist. John Knowles was the guy who had gone out as Kincade before we had taken over. John had made a bit of an impact and was now going out as John Kincade. The story was supposed to be that he had been the lead singer with the group but had left to go solo. The truth was that we had never even met and neither of us had sung a note on any of the songs, so the bullshit we had to give out was becoming much more involved, which we were none too happy about.

We flew to Barcelona for the second part of the trip and after more tedious interviews, and awkward questions about John Kincade, Rick lost his rag on air and had a real go at one guy who was interviewing us. I was really annoyed with Rick as we finished the trip under a bit of a cloud and never returned to Spain as Kincade.

Monday 2nd April 1973

Mungo Jerry with third from the left John Cook.

(Photo courtesy of Ray Dorset)

I had a phone call from ex. Octopus keyboard player John Cook who said that he had just joined Mungo Jerry.

Saturday 28th April 1973

Liverpool drew 0-0 at home to Leicester but secured the point that made them league champions for the first time since 1966. I celebrated this evening by getting rather inebriated and then painting Liverpool slogans all over my car.

Monday 21st May 1973

Kincade's record of "Dreams are Ten a Penny" had been released in the UK and today we were due to make an appearance on the children's TV show, "Lift off with Ayshea" at Granada studios in Manchester. Due to musician union rules we were not allowed to mime to the record and so had to record the song again and mime to the new track, and of course be paid a session fee. You may ask why we were not asked to play the song live. Well these shows were turned over very quickly and studios were not equipped to cope with balancing bands playing live, and there were two bands on "Lift Off" every week. It was far more practical for the bands to mime. As we needed a drummer for the recording we took Malcolm Green with us.

We recorded the track at a small independent studio, and I think I did a reasonable job imitating John Carter, (the original singer) and then drove to Granada. As we arrived we passed Barbara Knox (Rita in Coronation Street) hailing a cab. Chart group Vanity Fair were also on the show along with Ollie Beak, who was a glove puppet. Rehearsals took place in the afternoon, and the show was recorded in front of a live audience of kids. It all went well and the producer, a charming lady called Muriel Young, came round afterwards for a chat and to say thank you.

Wednesday 23rd May 1973

A couple of weeks ago Liverpool had beaten Borusia Munchengladbach 3-0 at home in the first leg of the UEFA Cup Final. Tonight Nigel and I watched them lose the second leg away 2-0 but won the cup 3-2 on aggregate. So two cups in one season and Bill Shankly voted manager of the year.

Friday 25th May 1973

Paul McCartney was touring with his new band, Wings, and tonight I went along to see him at the Hammersmith Odeon in London. The show was great and his new band, which was Paul and Linda, plus Denny Laine, Denny Siewell and ex. Joe Cocker guitarist, Henry McCullough, were excellent. It was the first time I had seen him on stage since the last British Beatles show on May 1st 1966, and the only disappointment was that he refused to perform any of the Beatles songs. I can appreciate that it was a new band with new material but it seemed that at that time he was in some sort of denial of ever having been a Beatle.

This attitude would change over the years and thirty years later, in 2003, I would see Paul McCartney's "Back in the World" show at London's Earls Court where out of a thirty six song set, twenty two would be Beatles classics. Possibly the best concert I have ever been to with Paul completely comfortable being an ex. Beatle.

Tuesday 10th July 1973

Armed with my acoustic guitar, a small PA system, and a lot of nerve, I began a solo residency at a pub called the Westminster in Bethnal Green, London. I had to perform a thirty minute spot once, sometimes twice, a week singing covers like "Imagine", "Annie's Song" and "American Pie" and was paid the princely sum of £8.00 per night. This residency would last well into 1974.

Wednesday 15th – Friday 17th August 1973

Another Kincade single had been a top ten hit in Germany. This one was called "Do You Remember Marilyn", so it was time to dust down the "bullshit" and hop on a plane. We flew to Hamburg and once again appeared on the TV show Disco 73. On the show with us were Suzi Quatro, singing her second hit, "48 Crash", and 10CC also with a second hit, "Rubber Bullets". The trip went well and Rick behaved himself.

Thursday 4th October 1973

Over the past couple of months there had been discussions at Penny Farthing about Kincade undertaking a three week tour of Germany. After it had been on, then off for the past week, it finally looked like going ahead, starting this coming Sunday. It would be a tour of discos and dance halls and we would be using backing tracks and singing live. We had argued with Larry page that we preferred to take a drummer and play live but he turned down this idea saying that backing tracks was the way it was done with these types of venues in Germany. We made a compromise saying that the three of us would take our instruments and perform a few songs live, without a drummer.

Today we were at the office to collect the backing tracks, plane tickets and the list of dates. The first problem arose when it was discovered that the tracks were just copies of the records which included all of the voices. We had no choice but to start the tour with these tracks while we waited for the correct ones to arrive. We were not happy as that meant performing in a live situation, miming to the singing and the playing.

Sunday 7th – Monday 29th October 1973

We flew to Bremen, with no-one from Penny Farthing accompanying us. At the airport we were met by a guy called Gerd-Michael Ebel who would be looking after us on the tour. He was a really nice guy and we agreed to call him Michael. We drove to Munster and found that for the first week we would be staying in an apartment above a club called the Batavia, which was one of our forthcoming gigs.

Some of the shows were great and some were disastrous, as some venues did not really accept us using backing tracks, especially when they had all the vocals on. Penny Farthing eventually sent us the correct tapes nearly two weeks into the tour.

On Sunday 21st October we had a particularly bad gig at a town called Bunde. Rick came off the stage in a rage and threw his Gibson Les Paul guitar on the floor and continued ranting and raving. I looked down at the guitar and noticed that the headstock was at a peculiar angle, I realized that he had broken the neck. I attracted Nigel's attention and pointed at Rick's guitar. Rick was still in a rage as we told him what had happened. There was an initial stunned silence and then he burst into tears. It was the real low point of the tour. The following day Michael, who had a music shop in Osnabruck, borrowed a guitar for Rick to use until the tour finished. We managed to persuade Rick that his guitar could be repaired, and later when it was it came back as good as new.

Sunday 28th October was the last gig and one of the worst, the audience would not accept us using backing tracks and were quite hostile. The promoter of the whole tour, a guy called Klaus Schulenberg, turned up and had a row with Michael and told him to go, so we never had a proper chance to say goodbye.

We flew home the following day reflecting on a badly organized tour with most of the finger of blame being pointed directly at Penny Farthing. Rick said that he wanted nothing more to do with Kincade and at that moment Nigel and I both felt the same.

Monday 3rd December 1973

John Cook phoned to say he had been sacked from Mungo Jerry. He had been in the band for eight months but in that time had managed to notch up a silver disc for playing on their number three hit "Alright Alright Alright".

We had received a call from Penny Farthing asking us to go back to Germany in a couple of weeks time for a television show which would feature a new Kincade single called "Big Hand for Annie". As Rick didn't want to go we said we would take John Cook on keyboards.

Wednesday 19th – Friday 21st December 1973

Final performance as Kincade

My wife said if I had looked like this when we met, I wouldn't have stood a chance.

We didn't know it at the time but this would be our final performance as Kincade. We flew to Hamburg for our third appearance on Disco 73 singing, what I thought was, the best single to date, "Big Hand for Annie". Unfortunately the German public did not agree and the record was not a hit. There would be a few discussions regarding future work but in fact it was all over and we were redundant.

1974

Tuesday 1st January 1974

1974 began with the country in the grip of "glam rock". At number one in the chart was Slade with "Merry Christmas Everybody" and at number four Wizzard with "I Wish it Could be Christmas Everyday" two songs that would haunt us for evermore, each December. Alvin Stardust was having his first hit with "My Coo-Ca-Choo" and my old mates Mud were a month away from their first number one, with "Tiger Feet".

I started the new year with my regular solo gig at the Westminster in Bethnal Green.

Tuesday 29th January 1974

There had been talk about another trip to Germany as Kincade, but this time taking a drummer and doing it properly. Today we heard from Penny Farthing that they were having difficulty arranging anything due to negative reports from the last tour.

Monday 11th February 1974

Penny Farthing phoned to confirm that Larry Page was no longer interested in being involved with Kincade, something we ourselves, had already realized.

Thursday 7th March 1974

My residency at the Westminster in Bethnal Green had come to an end and tonight I played at a disco called the Countdown, just off Oxford Street. This was the start of a residency that would last until May.

Saturday 4th May 1974

Shanks boards the Liverpool team bus then gives me a determined stare as he and the team leave for Wembley.

Liverpool were playing Newcastle in the FA cup final and I'd heard that the Liverpool team were staying nearby at the Sopwell House Hotel in St. Albans. Nigel and I drove there and took some photos of Bill Shankly and the team leaving on the coach for Wembley. We then drove back and watched the game on television. It was an easy 3-0 victory for Liverpool.

Sunday 12th May 1974

I had been writing songs on and off for a number of years. Today I wrote a song that was semi autobiographical called "Thomas J. Cricker". This would become the first of my songs ever to be released on record, when included on the first Guys n' Dolls album.

Wednesday 10th July 1974

I had become a jobbing musician. I'd registered with several agencies and was now gigging regularly, sometimes solo and sometimes I would drag Nigel out and perform as a duo calling ourselves Kincade. Some of the gigs were good others were terrible, but it was a living.

Saturday 10th August 1974

Bill Shankly had resigned as Liverpool's manager and today was his last game in charge, something Nigel and I couldn't miss. We drove to Wembley to see the Charity Shield which this year was between Liverpool and Leeds United. There was an emotional moment before the match when "Shanks" came out and walked the length of the pitch to say goodbye to the Kop, to a standing ovation. The game was drawn 1-1 with Liverpool eventually winning on penalties, but the occasion was marred by Liverpool's Kevin Keegan being involved in a fight with Leeds captain Billy Bremner resulting in them both being sent off and charged with bringing the game into disrepute.

Tuesday 1st October 1974

I popped in to see Mud who were rehearsing at the Lyceum ballroom in London. It was good to catch up as I hadn't seen them for a while. They were now big stars having had six top ten hits to date, including a number one with "Tiger Feet" and a number two with the follow up, "The Cat Crept In". I remember thinking, I should have joined them when I had the chance.

Thursday 24th October 1974

Vocalists Wanted

11p per word

A RECORD COMPANY IS FORM-ING A 6 PIECE POP VOCAL GROUP comprising 3 boys and 3 girls behind which there will be maximum promotion, publicity and finance, and will involve tours of Europe and North America. — For further details telephone 01-409 0146.

Today I bought the Melody Maker and found an advert from a record company, who were looking for three boys and three girls for a six piece vocal group. I phoned up and was told that I would receive a form to fill in and if they thought I was suitable I would then be contacted, and given an audition.

Tuesday 29th October 1974

A few days ago I had returned the form and as I was twenty nine years of age and far too old to be called a boy, I took four years off my age and wrote down twenty five. Today I was supposed to travel to London for an audition, but as it was pouring with rain and as it sounded like they were trying to form a group like the New Seekers, I decided to give it a miss.

I phoned the office of Ammo Productions and spoke to the secretary, who was called Jenny, and said that unfortunately I was unable to make the audition. Call it fate, or what you will but this next moment changed my life forever. Jenny could have just thanked me for phoning and left it at that but she didn't. She thanked me for letting her know and asked if I could come the following evening at 6.00pm. I was quite taken aback but said "yes".

Wednesday 30th October 1974

It was still pouring with rain and I had made up my mind that I couldn't be bothered going to the audition, after all it meant travelling in the middle of rush hour and to London's west end for a job that I probably didn't want. At about 4.00pm something changed my mind. I threw my acoustic guitar into the back of my beaten up Ford Cortina and drove the twenty odd miles up to Green Street near London's Marble Arch. It was an awful journey as my windscreen wipers were not working too well, and I breezed into Ammo's office with more a hint of annoyance than nerves. I met the three partners of Ammo Productions, Geoff Morrow, David Martin and Chris Arnold and sang John Denver's "Leaving on a Jet Plane". They seemed reasonably impressed and said they were interested in having me in the group and would let me know definitely in a few days time.

It was some time later I discovered that in 1963 Brian Epstein had rented a flat just along the street from the Ammo office at number 57, Green Street. This was the only address where all four Beatles had lived together, albeit only for a short while, in the early days of their success. The building is now visited by fans on Beatles tours of London.

Tuesday 5th November 1974

Geoff Morrow phoned to say that I had got the job and we would all be meeting, for the first time, at a restaurant in London on Friday evening. He also said they had decided the group would be called Guys n' Dolls. I put the phone down horrified, how was I going to tell all my "heavy" friends that I was in a group called Guys n' Dolls.

The bottom line was that in the space of six days I had auditioned, and been asked to join a new six piece vocal group. I had no idea who the other members were, no idea whether we were vocally or socially compatible, and no idea what sort of music we would be performing.

Friday 8th November 1974

I drove to London for what would be my first meeting with the other members of Guys n' Dolls. We were due to meet at Verreys restaurant in London's Regent Street at eight o'clock and I was the first to arrive, closely followed by a girl with long black hair wearing a duffel coat. This was Thereze Bazar. Next to arrive was a guy in a white jacket with blond hair, shirt unbuttoned, fake tan, and already looking every inch the pop star. This was Dominic Grant. The three guys from Ammo Productions walked in shortly after, and David Martin was with a very young looking girl with blond hair and her name was Julie Forsyth. David Van Day was next and everyone sat down but we were one girl short. About a half an hour later a dark haired girl called Martine Howard rushed in apologizing for being late. She was a member of the Young Generation dance troupe and had just finished working on the Les Dawson show. Being late was something we would have to get used to with Martine.

I got on well with Dominic straight away as we had a love of football in common and had both been in groups. The other four were all from stage schools and came across as very confident and outgoing which I had not experienced before having spent most of my time with laid back musicians. There was also quite an age difference, Dominic was twenty four and the others ranged between sixteen (Julie was the youngest) and eighteen. I was destined to be the old man of the group as in twelve days time I would be thirty, although having lied about my age when I applied for the job no one else knew.

During the meal the Ammo guys got us to sign a letter of intent, and then explained that we would be expected to sign a recording contract directly with Ammo Productions. They had a deal to release the Guys n' Dolls product through Magnet Records and our first record was going to be a song called "There's a Whole lot of Loving". They then handed us a demo disc with "There's a Whole lot of Loving" written on it. I assumed that this was a rough copy of the song for us to learn and asked when we were going to record it, and that is when they dropped the bomb shell. They said that this was the actual record that had been recorded by session musicians, Ammo's David martin had sung the boy's lead himself, and it was going to be released in a couple of months time. I thought "here we go again another Kincade situation" and I explained about the recent problems I had as a member of Kincade and didn't they think it would be better if our voices were on the record. Geoff Morrow said that they felt the track was perfect as it was, he called it a magic mix, and all the singers on the record were friends of theirs so there would be no problems, (famous last words). We continued with the meal generally getting to know each other, and at one point when Julie was out of ear shot, David Martin told us that she was Bruce Forsyth's daughter.

After the meal Geoff said that he would be in touch in the next few days and we all headed off. As I drove home I thought what the hell am I doing getting myself into another situation where I would be miming to a record I had not sung on. I arrived home and played "There's a Whole Lot of Loving" for the first time. A big orchestral opening, followed by a lead line sung by a girl and answered by a boy and then everybody in. It just wasn't the sort of record I would ever bother to listen to and I sat there deep in thought. I eventually decided, with many reservations, to give it a go and see what happened.

Guys n' Dolls would often be called a "manufactured group", but the way we were formed it was more like "quickly assembled".

Monday 11th November 1974

Geoff Morrow phoned to say that Guys n' Dolls would be having their first photo session the following week and he had arranged for me to have my hair styled before the session. As I was still in hippy mode, this was a wise move on his part.

Monday 18th November 1974

The first photo of Guys n' Dolls
(left to right)
(back)
Paul Griggs, Dominic Grant
(middle)
Martine Howard and Thereze Bazar
(front)
David Van Day and Julie Forsyth

Today I went to a rather "flash" salon in London and had my hair styled. For years I had worn my hair long, and because it was naturally curly tried many times in vain to straighten it. Today the stylist made no bones about it, I should have my hair in an afro style. I thought "why not" and he went to work.

I then met up with the rest of the group and we had our first photo session as Guys n' Dolls and as we had no stage costumes, just wore our own clothes.

Wednesday 20th November 1974

Today was my thirtieth birthday but the rest of the group thought I was twenty six and I hadn't decided exactly when I was going to tell them my real age, if ever.

David Martin was recording a solo record and had asked Dominic and myself to sing backing vocals. David was engaged to Julie's sister Debbie and had written a song based on a card that he had sent to her when they had been apart from each other. The song was called "Can't Smile Without You" and although David's version was not a hit it would achieve international success a few years later when covered by both the Carpenters and Barry Manilow.

Monday 25th November 1974

Guys n' Dolls met up at the Ammo office and from there we went to Magnet Records in York Street, just off Baker Street, and met the boss Michael Levy. From there we returned to the Ammo office and rehearsed "There's a Whole Lot of Loving" for the first time. It was clear from the first rehearsal that David Van Day was not a strong vocalist and in conversation with Geoff I was told that David was included in the group because he had an image that would appeal to younger girls, and this would turn out to be the case. We all went back to Julie's house in Whetstone, North London for a, getting to know each other, evening.

Magnet records boss Michael Levy eventually became Lord Levy when Tony Blair was elected prime minister. In 2007 he would be involved in the cash for honours case and subsequently be cleared of all involvement.

Friday 6th December 1974

The IRA were mounting a campaign of bombings in Great Britain and only two weeks ago there had been explosions in two pubs in Birmingham resulting in multiple deaths and injuries. I had become increasingly nervous about playing in pubs and today I was offered a part time job back in Hammonds music shop in Watford. I decided to accept and stop doing gigs until things started happening with Guys n' Dolls.

Monday 16th December 1974

I went with Dominic to Advision recording studios in London and met the Ammo boys who used us on one of their recording sessions. They had used us quite a bit in the past few weeks which was a great help financially because they paid us session fees.

On the way home I popped in to see John Cook the ex. Octopus keyboard player who was now living in north London. I had a bit of a shock when I arrived to find John straddled across a banister, stark naked, having his photograph taken for "Playgirl" magazine.

Tuesday 17th December 1974

I went along to the Magnet Records Christmas party with Dominic, and met fellow label artists Alvin Stardust and Pete Shelly. Lyndsey de Paul was also there.

Tuesday 31st December 1974

I spent New Years Eve with my family, wondering what Guys n' Dolls had in store for me in 1975.

1975

Thursday 2ⁿᵈ January 1975

Geoff Morrow phoned to say that although "There's a Whole Lot of Loving" was not being released until 10ᵗʰ January it would receive it's first Radio One play tomorrow on Tony Blackburn's breakfast show.

Friday 3ʳᵈ January 1975

Tony Blackburn played the record, raved about it, and said that he was going to play it again at the end of the programme which he did. In the afternoon it was reviewed on Radio One's "Round Table". It received good reviews from, among others, Les Gray from Mud, who had no idea that I was in the group.

What an amazing start, the record was seven days away from release and already had received three Radio One plays. I recalled all the futile waiting around the radio when the Cortinas and Octopus had records out, with "There's a Whole Lot of Loving" Ammo seemed to know exactly when it was going to be played.

Monday 6ᵗʰ January 1975

There was a piece in the Daily Express saying that Julie was Bruce Forsyth's daughter despite the fact that she had asked for it not to be used in the press. I guess either Ammo or Magnet Records couldn't resist such an obvious piece of publicity. Julie was not amused.

Friday 10ᵗʰ January 1975

"There's a Whole lot of Loving" was released today and I had a call to say that it was going to be Tony Blackburn's record of the week starting on Monday and we were booked to do one of the BBC's studio sessions next week, for the David Hamilton show. Despite a feeling inside that maybe I was about to become a bit of pop star, I spent the day working at Hammonds and was probably a little over excited at the prospect of what lay ahead.

Wednesday 15ᵗʰ January 1975

Dominic phoned to say the record had sold four and a half thousand copies since Friday which was a pretty good start.

149

Tuesday 21st January 1975

It had been decided that we would wear suits on stage, the boys in black and the girls white. We took delivery of the suits a few days ago and today we had our first photo session with them. I felt that the girls looked great and the boys were a little plain, but what did I know, I was just an old hippy.

Friday 7th February 1975

THE TEAM
(left to right)
(back) David Martin, Paul Griggs, Geoff Morrow, Thereze Bazar, Chris Arnold, David Van Day

(midddle) Martine Howard, Dominic Grant, Julie Forsyth, Steve Collier (Magnet Records)

(front) Brookie (Choreographer)

I had received a bit of a shock. We were starting to work on our stage act with a choreographer and it appeared that there were going to be dance routines involved. Julie, Martine, Thereze and David had all studied dance at stage school, while Dominic and I had two left feet. The choreographer Brookie was best known for being pursued by a statuesque Valerie Leon in the Hai Karate adverts of the early seventies. He was very patient with Dominic and I, where it would take the others about fifteen minutes to learn a routine Dominic and I would take hours.

We now had an agent called Alan Field from one of the top London agencies MAM, and he phoned to say that we had three weeks work at Bailey's night clubs starting in April, so we had a lot of work to do between now and then.

Tuesday 11ᵗʰ February 1975

Today we discovered that "There's a Whole lot of Loving" had reached number seventy three in the BBC charts and the sales figures were increasing.

Things were full on with Guys n' Dolls and we were needed almost everyday to do some sort of promotion so I handed in my notice to Hammonds saying I would be leaving at the end of the week. Ammo Productions said they would put us on a retainer of £50 a week which was good money in 1975.

Thursday 13ᵗʰ February 1975

The group met up at Magnet Records and from there we split up and, accompanied by a Magnet staff member, went off and toured record shops. In 1975 certain shops were designated to be chart return shops. At the end of the week they sent in details of records that had been sold and the charts would be compiled from this information. The list of chart return shops should have been kept secret but every record company knew which ones they were. Today I was teamed up with Thereze and our job was to visit some of these shops, chat nicely to the assistants, and dish out a few freebies in the hope that they would push our record a little harder.

Tuesday 18ᵗʰ February 1975

Dominic called early this morning with some amazing news. Our record was a breaker (i.e. just outside the top fifty) and we would be recording "Top of the Pops" tomorrow. Panic! Martine was abroad on holiday and, with some difficulty, was contacted and told to get the next plane home as we planned to all meet up at Ammo's office for frantic, last minute rehearsals later that day.

We found out that we would have to record the backing track first and mime to it on the show, so we had an intense couple of hours going over the harmonies, and movements with Brookie. This would be the first time that I had ever sung in public without a guitar, and it would have to be on national television.

Wednesday 19th February 1975

The BBC Camera script from Guys n' Dolls first appearance on "Top of the Pops"

A very early start and the group met up at the BBC's Lime Grove studios to record the backing track with the Top of the Pops orchestra. We all went into the booth which we realised was out of sight of the people in the control room. David Martin said that he would join us in the booth to supervise. In fact, because he couldn't be seen, he sang the boys lead and Dominic had to stand there and do nothing. I felt sorry for Dominic, he had a great voice, which sounded a bit like Scott Walker, and was so different to David's. It had got to the stage where him not singing on the record was a becoming a problem.

We finished the track and then travelled to the main BBC studios at White City, where "Top of The Pops" was recorded. I got quite a buzz as we walked into the Studio for the first time as I had always dreamed of being on Top of the Pops. I couldn't believe how small the studio seemed compared to the way it looked on television. The first people we saw were Slade who were rehearsing their latest record "How Does it Feel". We passed Babs from Pans People on the stairs, and like many others, I had a bit of a crush on her.

There was one rehearsal in the morning, the dress rehearsal was at four o'clock and the show was recorded around seven thirty. The song before us was Johnny Mathis "I'm Stone in Love with You" and the number one that week was Steve Harley and Cockney Rebel with "Make me Smile". It all seemed to go OK although Brookie said I didn't smile enough.

After the show Bruce Forsyth popped in to see Julie and we all ended up going out for a meal at Verrys, the restaurant where we first met.

Thursday 20th February 1975

This evening the group met up at Martine's house to watch our "Top of the Pops" debut. We were pleased with the way it looked but it did seem odd, Dominic miming to David Martin's voice.

Tuesday 25th February 1975

The BBC chart came out on a Tuesday and today "There's a Whole Lot of Loving" had moved up to 44. We were told that the sales figure for yesterday was 12,000 which was excellent.

Julie's mum had just moved into a card shop in Hampstead and today we performed the official opening ceremony.

Tuesday 4th March 1975

Ivor the Driver
With a van
named
"Smelly"

Everything was going well and I must admit I was thoroughly enjoying every minute. Everyday there was something to do, photo sessions, interviews, and of course rehearsals as there was barely a month to go before our first live show.

This morning we received more good news, as we now had a genuine hit record. "There's a Whole Lot of Loving" had moved up to 26 in the BBC chart and we were doing "Top of the Pops" again tomorrow. It had been decided that the whole group would look better in white suits so we went to our tailors, Barry of Chelsea, for a final fitting.

We now needed a road manager and two people had been interviewed. One was someone Julie knew called Ivor Parsley and the other a musician friend of mine, Bob Patmore. The outcome was that Ivor got the job and Bob ended up in the world of finance, something he turned out to be very good at. Today he is a multi millionaire, flies his own helicopter, and still lets me know how grateful he was not to get the job with Guys n' Dolls.

Even road managers have stage names and Ivor decided he was going to be called Ivor James. He started driving us around in a large Mercedes van fitted with aircraft seats, which Ammo had just bought. The previous owner had transported dogs and it never quite lost its canine aroma, so was nicknamed Smelly.

Wednesday 5th March 1975

Our second appearance on Top of the Pops and as we drove up to the gates of the BBC, we were recognized, for the first time, by a group of young girls waiting outside. We managed to draw a few screams from them which at the time I found a little odd but not unpleasant.

The show went well and it was Dominic's voice that was heard this time with no-one saying that it didn't sound like the record. It was the first outing for the boy's new white suits which had only been finished that morning. Also on the show were Neil Sedaka, the Goodies and once again Slade. The DJ was Jimmy Saville.

Sunday 9th March 1975

Today was our third television appearance in eighteen days. We recorded a guest appearance on the Lulu show at the Shepherds Bush Theatre, London, (now renamed The Shepherds Bush Empire) and I was able to get a couple of tickets for mum and dad to see the show. When we arrived at our dressing rooms we found that Lulu had sent a couple of bottles of champagne one for the guys and one for the dolls.

Tuesday 11th March 1975

Amazing news, we now had a top ten record as "There's a Whole Lot of Loving" had reached number nine in the BBC chart.

We spent most of the day at Advision studios in London trying to record our, all important, follow up single. Ammo had chosen a song called "Here I Go Again" and were keen for it to feature David and Thereze singing the lead parts. We had already been paired up for our performances, Dominic with Martine, David with Thereze and me with Julie and this would stay the same until the line up of the group changed.

I wasn't keen on this new song, but as I wasn't keen on our present number nine hit, kept my thoughts to myself. Ammo persevered with David singing the boy's part but it just wasn't working, and after recording until late into the night we called it a day.

Tuesday 18th March 1975

Today started off great and gradually went downhill. It began with the news that the record had moved up to number four in the BBC charts and we would be making our third appearance on Top of the Pops tomorrow.

The BBC had certain rules about Top of the Pops which went like this. To begin with you could not be on the show for two consecutive weeks unless your record was number one. The number one record was always featured. You could only be on if your record was going up or remaining in a stationary position in the top fifty. There were ten breakers, i.e. records outside the top fifty, and one of these was selected each week, and occasionally a new release would be featured.

 The musicians union insisted that each act had to record a new track of their song and could not use the original recording. The reality of this was bands would go to the studio, record a new track and then secretly swap the tapes and mime to their own records. The final rule was that one act a week had to use the Top of the Pops orchestra. This rule applied to groups like us who did not play instruments and starting from this week we would have to perform with the orchestra live in the studio.

We were back in the studio again and Geoff Morrow arrived looking rather grim faced. He had received a call from the Daily Mirror saying that they did not think Martine had sung on the record and that it was a session singer. A reporter was coming down to the studio to interview us and Ammo told Martine she would have to lie and say it was her on the record. When the reporter arrived we spent a very uncomfortable half hour with him. He said that he had been approached by a session singer called Kay Garner who claimed that she was singing the opening line of "There's a Whole Lot of Loving" and not Martine. Martine said it was her and Ammo told him there was an original demo version but, after the group had been formed, the song had been re-recorded with us singing. The reporter left, obviously unconvinced, while we were left to ponder the outcome.

We returned to recording and during this session, Martine's voice was hastily recorded on to the beginning of "There's a Whole Lot of Loving" which I felt was trying to shut the stable door after the horse had bolted. This version would be used on our forthcoming album and I have to say the voices are so similar that it's hard to tell which is which.

Wednesday 19th March 1975

This morning just Julie and I were needed at the studios to quickly record the B side of our next record, entitled, "Can't you Hear the Song". This only took about an hour, then we met the others at the BBC for Top of the Pops, and for the first time ever we performed "There's a Whole Lot of Loving" completely live with the orchestra. Also on the show this week were Cliff Richard, Lulu and the Bay City Rollers who at this time were at their peak and causing mayhem wherever they went.

Everyone was a bit subdued today as we wondered if or when some negative press would appear in the Daily Mirror.

Friday 21st March 1975

It's happened! Today there was an article in the Daily Mirror in which Kay Garner and another singer called Clare Torry, Ammo's "friends", claimed that along with Russell Stone and Tony Burrows they were the voices on "There's a Whole Lot of Loving". My immediate thoughts were that's it, we're finished, but in fact today was the start and end of it. It wasn't mentioned anywhere else in the press and this was the only time it was mentioned in the Daily Mirror.

Clare Torry sang the soulful wordless vocal at the end of Pink Floyd's "Great Gig in the Sky" on their album "Dark Side of the Moon" and in 2004 she successfully sued the group and EMI for unpaid royalties saying her contribution warranted her being named as a co-writer. There have been several similar cases over the years and there is a saying in the music business that, "Where there's a hit there's a writ".

Sunday 23rd to Monday 31st March 1975

It was time to record our first album so we travelled to Chipping Norton studios in the heart of Oxfordshire where, as the studio was residential, we were staying for the week. This would also be a good test of how well we all got on together in a confined space.

There was a lot of waiting around for the first two days as the musicians had arrived to put down the backing tracks and the group weren't needed. It was a completely different way of recording for me as, with Octopus I was heavily involved with the arranging and playing, in Guys n' Dolls I was just a singer. One of the songs we were recording was my composition "Thomas J. Cricker" and I had given a rough tape to the arranger Colin Frechter who went away and wrote out the music for the musicians.

We heard on Tuesday that "There's a Whole lot of Loving" had moved up to what would be it's highest position at number two in the charts, being held off the number one spot by the Bay City Rollers version of "Bye Bye Baby"

On the Wednesday we recorded the vocals on the two numbers written by members of the group, Thereze's "Give a little Love" and my "Thomas J. Cricker". I was a bit taken aback when I heard the backing track for my song as I had written it as a Rock song (a bit Status Quo) and the arrangement had a lot of brass on it. I got used to it and after the vocals were recorded I thought it sounded OK.

For the remainder of the week we recorded a couple of Ammo songs, a Beach Boys Medley, "River Deep and Mountain High" and finished off with an a cappella version of the Beatles, "She's Leaving Home" which as a Beatles fan I had strong reservations about. It turned out OK apart from some annoying backing vocals that went "chip chip chip". It was also finally decided that Dominic would sing lead on our next single "Here I Go Again".

It had turned into a busy week. Brookie had been with us for the past two days, and when we weren't recording we were frantically rehearsing our stage act as the first gig was barely a week away.

Tuesday 1st April 1975
"There's a Whole Lot of Loving" had remained at number two in the charts and tomorrow we would be making our fourth appearance on Top of the Pops.

Today the tracks we had recorded last week were played to Michael Levy at Magnet Records who gave the seal of approval, although, he said, for continuity, David Martin and not Dominic, should be the lead male voice on "Here I Go Again". Could this be an April fool joke, no, despite all the trouble caused by us not singing on the first single he was deadly serious. There were vociferous objections from nine voices and amazingly he backed down.

Wednesday 2nd April 1975
Today we arrived at BBC television centre to be greeted by a sea of Tartan. The "Rollers" were on the show and there was a crowd of very excited girls waiting to tear them limb from limb, although they did manage a few screams for us as we drove through the gates. We had to perform the song completely live once again but it turned out to be the best performance we had made so far.

Sunday 6th April 1975
Ivor arrived around lunchtime to collect me, my guitar and amp. We drove to the Ammo office, met up with the rest of the group, then off to Plymouth for our first week of live

dates. This was a real baptism of fire as we would be working every night for the next four weeks. We arrived at our hotel late in the evening, had a meal and an early night.

Monday 7th April 1975

Merlins nightclub in Plymouth was our first ever gig and we turned up in the afternoon for band call. The club had a resident band and Geoff had written out all of our arrangements so we could rehearse ready for our first performance this evening. The band call didn't go well and I was worried, we'd never performed the act with the band and they hadn't known which numbers we were going to perform until we arrived. Having been in bands I knew how long it took to rehearse one new number let alone a new act. This was the way it would be until we had our own musicians.

We returned to the club in the evening to ready ourselves for our debut and were all on edge, I don't think I had ever been so nervous before. The comedian Lennie Bennett was performing before us and we chatted to him before his spot. When he finished he came off stage, saw us all standing there, and shaking his head, said "They're a very tough audience". Bastard! He knew what he was doing and believe me we were nervous enough without his help. As Guys n' Dolls were with the same agency as Lennie Bennett we would often appear together, after tonight he was never our favourite person.

The music started up and we went on stage to our opening song, "Love Train" in a set that lasted sixty minutes. The show went pretty well, some of the singing was a bit off in places but no major cock ups and the audience, despite Lennie Bennett's misleading comment, were great. We came off stage feeling rather elated and relieved, and went back to the hotel where Brookie held a post mortem, picking up on points that could be improved on.

Saturday 12th April 1975

Tonight was our final day in Plymouth, it had been a good week with the act becoming tighter every night. The keyboard player of the club's resident band was a guy called Ray

Monk who been working with comedians Mike and Bernie Winters and had impressed us all. Ammo asked him to join us on a permanent basis as our musical director and he told us that he was committed to one more week at Merlins but would meet up with us after that.

After the last performance we packed up and set off through the night for Leicester.

Sunday 13th – Saturday 19th April 1975

We arrived at the Post House hotel in Leicester at around 9.30am and, as none of us had slept much on the journey went straight to bed for a few hours. This week we were at Baileys night club, which had been converted from a Ballroom and was quite large. The first show went well and the audience friendly and when we returned to the hotel we had our now customary post mortem from Brookie or his assistant Lamona. I liked Brookie but this was beginning to piss me off a little as he would sit us down and go through the whole act song by song, correcting small faults that we had made. He had gone mad the other night at Plymouth when we had decided to go back and perform an encore, I felt he wanted the show to be a bit too regimented, but that would soon change.

One of the songs in the act was my song "Thomas J. Cricker" and Brookie had written out a piece for me to say about the song which lasted about two minutes. This was so Julie could do a quick change and return from her solo number "My Guy". One night I was well into my carefully rehearsed chat and heard Julie return to the stage, trip, and promptly fall flat on her face. I didn't turn round to see if she was OK, I didn't make any comment, I think I had been so indoctrinated by Brookie that I just carried on word for word not wanting to make a mistake, as if nothing had happened. Julie never lets me forget that to this day.

On the Tuesday Ivor drove us to a small airfield just outside Leicester and we caught a small seven seater plane for our first trip abroad as Guys n' Dolls. We flew to Amsterdam to appear on the Dutch version of Top of the Pops, called Top Pop. I sat next to the pilot on the journey back and with the aid of a map, helped him find the small grass airfield so we could land. Very reassuring.

Mum and dad came to the last Leicester show along with several other of the group's mums and dads. They saw one of our best shows to date which ended with a standing ovation.

Sunday 20th – Saturday 27th April 1975

We met up with Ray Monk at Baileys club in Liverpool. It was fortunate for us that he had joined us today as the club's band were awful, and Ray spent the whole afternoon trying to teach them our programme.

After a shaky start with the band the week went well and on Saturday I went to see Liverpool beat QPR 3-0 at Anfield. This was my first ever visit and even though this was the last game of the season and Liverpool had just missed out on the league title the atmosphere was great. I went with Dominic and a couple of the others, we found ourselves sitting with Robin Askwith who starred in the "Confessions of " comedy sex films and was a QPR supporter.

Sunday 28th April – Saturday 3rd May 1975

We moved down to Birmingham and a smaller club called the Dolce Vita, where the house band was much better and there was a more intimate atmosphere.

Our second single "Here I Go Again" had been released last week and we were told we were needed for Top of the Pops. On Wednesday morning, having had very little sleep, we travelled down to the BBC and found that Mud were on the show with us. It was good to see them again and they were celebrating their third number one hit with an a cappella version of Buddy Holly's "Oh Boy".

I know my own musical tastes were far removed from that which I was performing with Guys n' Dolls, but I really didn't feel that "Here I Go Again" was a strong song and looking back at a tape of our performance on Top of the Pops find it embarrassing to watch. Dominic was singing with Thereze so there was immediately a height problem. Dominic was tall and Thereze wasn't and the routine was just too naff for words. The record would eventually struggle up to number thirty three in the charts, giving us our second top forty hit, mainly due to the impetus of following on from a number two hit. We didn't get clearance from Top of the Pops until 9.00pm and had a mad dash up the M1 to Birmingham where we were late on stage for our show.

We often had people drop in and see us at our shows and Thursday was a busy night. A guy called Danny O'Donovan who arranged Frank Sinatra's England shows was checking us out accompanied by television producer Stuart Morris, and Freddie Garrity from Freddie and the Dreamers popped in to say hello.

After the show on Saturday night we all went home for a few days. We had been away for four weeks and had performed for twenty seven consecutive nights. It had been hectic but enjoyable and had really made the act tight and together. Dominic and I, were starting to revolt against Brookie's strict, on stage, regimentation and inject some of our own personalities into the proceedings making it a lot more light hearted.

Wednesday 7th May 1975

My brother was on his travels again. Tim Reeves, the ex. Octopus drummer was over in France playing in a band called Ilbarritz, and had persuaded Nigel to join them. Today mum and dad took Nigel to the airport on his way to Biarritz, before coming on to the

BBC TV studios to see Guys n' Dolls appearing on the BBC 2 show Music Machine. This was introduced by singer Vince Hill and with us on the show was David Gates the lead singer from Bread. This pleased Thereze as she was a big fan.

Friday 9th May 1975

Tonight was our first performance in a theatre, when we supported Harry Secombe at the Winter Gardens in Bournemouth. It took a bit getting used to performing on a large stage after the confines of the smaller clubs but it went well. Julie's dad came along to see the show for the first time.

Saturday 11th May 1975

Saturday Scene was a children's television programme, introduced by Sally James, which we'd enjoy a happy relationship with over the coming months, and today we appeared at one of their road shows held at the Wimbledon Theatre. We performed along side fellow "Magnet" artist Alvin Stardust and were screamed at continuously throughout our short three song set. After the show the theatre was surrounded by screaming girls and we had a police escort of two motorcyclists with flashing lights driving down the wrong side of the road to get us away. Great fun.

Friday 16th May 1975

Ammo had decided to invite all of the main BBC Radio producers for a meal with Guys n' Dolls to say thank you for making "There's a Whole Lot of Loving" a big hit, (and make sure you play the next one) which we thought was a major error of judgement on their part. We spent a very awkward couple of hours each of us sitting next to a producer trying to make small talk, and to make matters worse, half way through the meal Ammo produced Parker Pens, each engraved "With love and thanks from Guys n' Dolls" and presented one to each producer. Brown nosing at its best----or 'worst'.

Sunday 18ᵗʰ May 1975

We had all been invited to a party at Geoff Morrow's house and when we arrived, found it was a wedding party as he had secretly married his girlfriend Marilyn that afternoon. Among others in attendance were David Essex, Kenny Jones (drummer with the Faces) Marianne Faithful and my old record boss Larry Page. We were subjected to our second, toe curling, embarrassing moment in two days when Geoff got us round the piano and made us sing "There's a Whole Lot of Loving" to the assembled gathering.

Sunday 8ᵗʰ June 1975

I suppose this could be termed as twenty four hours of misfortune. We had just completed a three day promotion trip to Spain and today were flying to Leeds and Bradford airport as we had shows in Sheffield. Last night I had my little finger slammed in a car door and it had turned black and was extremely painful. We flew from Madrid to Frankfurt to catch a connecting flight and somewhere in Frankfurt airport I managed to lose my passport. On arrival at Leeds and Bradford I had no problem with immigration but when it came to collect our luggage, the large case containing our costumes came through, but our entire personal luggage was missing. Great!

The outcome was the luggage arrived the following day, my passport turned up two weeks later, the girls camouflaged my black finger nail with nail varnish and we had a great week at the Fiesta in Sheffield. On the Friday we even managed to fly to Edinburgh and Glasgow for a day time promotion trip and make it back for the evening show.

Thursday 3ʳᵈ July 1975

Where ever we were working Magnet nearly always arranged for us to do promotion. Today we travelled from Stockton where we were appearing, up to Newcastle for a personal appearance at the record section of a department store. We were taken to the managers office who warned us that not many people had turned up, we walked down to the record department and to say there wasn't many was an understatement, there was nobody there at all. We stayed there for about ten minutes with Ivor embarrassingly walking up to people saying, "would you like to come and meet Guys n' Dolls", before we called it a day.

Monday 7th July 1975

Guys n' Dolls with their silver discs. Michael Levy (now Lord Levy) is second from the right. Standing next to Dominic at the back is DJ Ed Stewart.

Our next record was to be a song called "Lets all get Together" and guess what? I hated it. It was supposed to be an anti war song about everyone coming together and living in harmony. One of the early mixes had American and Russian voices at the beginning saying "may all the world live together in peace". The lyrics were so crass, and a few years ago there was a TV programme which had a spot called "Criminal Records"; one of the records featured was "Let's all get Together".

> *Let's all get together, let's all get along,*
> *We'll be friends forever, friendship can't be wrong,*
> *Love is round the corner, Let's give it a try,*
> *Let's all get together, let's all do it especially you and I.*

Today we were at CBS studios in London recording this epic, before going on to Magnet records where Michael Levy presented us with silver discs for selling more than 250,000 copies of "There's a Whole Lot of Loving". I'd always wanted a silver disc, but couldn't help feeling that I had got this, a little under false pretences, so it now hangs in the downstairs toilet.

Monday 14th July 1975

Hello your highness, I'll be meeting your Dad next year and your Mum in 2007

Today was our first show in front of royalty. We appeared at a marathon show at London's Cambridge Theatre, in front of HRH Princess Anne and her new husband Captain Mark Phillips. There seemed to be hundreds of acts and everybody was sharing dressing rooms, and I remember sharing ours with a young, brash, Lenny Henry. He was 16 years of age and just won a talent show called New Faces and was beginning to make his mark in the business. The girls were sharing with comedienne Marti Caine, and our paths would cross several times over the coming years. She was one of the nicest people in the business.

The show seemed to go on forever and I felt rather sorry for the royal couple. All we had to do was perform "There's a Whole lot of Loving" and afterwards be presented to Princess Anne and her husband. When they were introduced to Dominic, Princess Anne asked him where we were playing next and Dominic replied Batley Variety Club in Yorkshire. Mark Phillips said "We're up that way next week" and Dominic came out with "Oh you must come and see us". Mark Phillips gave a nervous smile and the couple moved on.

Wednesday 16th July 1975

On stage at the Royal Albert Hall, but where's the audience?

Two days on, and another show in front of royalty. This afternoon we performed at The Royal Albert Hall along side Lulu and Alvin Stardust for a show called "Help the Police", this time in front of the Duchess of Kent. It was an odd show that had pop music and displays, including gymnastics in the arena of the hall. This meant that the audience were a long way from the stage and it was a little hard for the singers to make contact with them. Half way through our four song set, Michael Levy came on stage to re-present our gold discs for "There's a Whole Lot of Loving". Michael was never one to miss a photo opportunity.

We met the Duchess of Kent informally in the interval, she was very down to earth and told us that her daughter Lady Helen Windsor was a huge fan of the Bay City Rollers and had pictures all over her bedroom.

Friday 1st August 1975

Tonight we appeared at the Black Kat Club in Sunderland which was part of Sunderland F.C. it was the first gig for our new permanent drummer Dave Morris. Dominic had known Dave in the sixties when he was in a group called Doctor Marigolds Prescription. The situation where we had been playing with a different drummer every week had been driving me crazy so to have Dave, who was excellent, meant we finally had consistency.

Wednesday 20th August 1975

Our record "Let's all Get Together" had been released three weeks ago and had so far struggled to reach number 150 in the charts. Miraculously Magnet had managed to secure us an appearance on Top of the Pops as a new release, which it wasn't really. We wore the white suits emblazoned with emblems from different countries of the world and the audience were given flags to wave, and it all seemed a bit naff.

The record would peak at number 54 the following week and so was a miss. We would have to think very carefully about our next release.

Monday 2nd September 1975

Princess
Alexandra meets
Julie
In the background
is Frankie
Vaughan

Guys n' Dolls appeared at the opening of the Greenwood theatre in South London and this was our third appearance in front of royalty. The special guests were Princess Alexandra and her husband Angus Ogilvy. Also on the bill were Lyn Paul (formerly from the New Seekers), Frankie Vaughan and a member of the "Carry On" team Bernard Bresslaw. For me it was great to meet Bernard Bresslaw as I remembered him playing a character called Private Popeye Popplewell in a TV show called the Army Game that I watched in the fifties. I even managed to get him to sing a few bars of his hit record "Mad Passionate Love".

Tuesday 9th September 1975

Today I ran head first into the bureaucracy of the musicians union, of which I was a member. Guys n' Dolls had travelled down from Manchester for an appearance on the Saturday morning pop music show, Supersonic. Ray Monk had gone down earlier to record our backing tracks, which were "Let's all get Together" and my song "Thomas J. Cricker". There was a guy from the musicians union, who we had seen before as he was always hanging around the music shows. When it came to our rehearsal, as usual with "Thomas J. Cricker", I would play guitar. The union guy came up to me in the studio and said that because someone else had played guitar on the backing track it was against union rules for me to mime to it. I explained that it was my own song, I had composed the guitar part and I was a member of the union. He would have none of it and stood firm, I wasn't best pleased and felt he was being petty and unhelpful. The musicians union should be looking after the interests of all musicians, but he certainly wasn't looking after mine. After that I petulantly resigned from the musicians union and joined Equity, the actors union, which I felt would be handy if I ever had the call to play James Bond.

Saturday 27ᵗʰ September 1975

It was back to London's Wimbledon theatre for another Saturday Scene road show with Sally James and today we appeared with the Wombles and Marc Bolan. I was standing back stage holding my Gibson SG guitar; Marc Bolan had a Gibson Les Paul. Marc said "Nice SG, what year is it", I replied "it's a 68 what about yours", we then proceeded to have a typical guitarist's conversation about the merits of various guitars. He was great, but a bit "cosmic". Another person who featured on these road shows was a character called Eric the Frog. This was someone dressed in a frog outfit, and that someone was Eric Hall, whose nickname was "I'll get a limo", and now well known as a "monster" football agent.

Marc Bolan was killed in a car crash less than two years later on 16ᵗʰ September 1977, when a car driven by his girlfriend, singer Gloria Jones, crashed in Barnes, South West London.

Sunday 28ᵗʰ September – Thursday 9ᵗʰ October 1975

We were given ten days off for a much needed holiday, and I went to Majorca to stay with my friends from the Octopus days, the Haywoods. For the last two days I flew to Marbella and met up with Julie, David and Thereze in Porto Banus. From there we all flew back to Amsterdam, joined the others and went straight back to work doing three days of Dutch TV and promotion.

Tuesday 14ᵗʰ October 1975

The Other Guys n' Dolls (left to right) Phil Kershaw, Wendell Sowerby, Janet Wright, Sue Parkinson, Lenny Calvert.

Another problem for the group had arisen when it had been discovered that there was another group already called Guys n' Dolls who came from County Durham. Over the past few months there had been threats of legal action, but the situation was sorted when Ammo productions and John Wray, the manager of the other group, came up with a compromise. The other group would change their name to "Kissin' Cousins" and Ammo would write and produce a record for them.

Today, as part of the deal, Guys n' Dolls had a photo session with "Kissin Cousins". I was in hospital following complications after a tooth extraction, so the other five went along without me.

Saturday 18th October 1975

Ammo productions had been managing the group up to this point but realised they were more record producers than managers. They had appointed a guy called Brian Longley to take over the day to day running of the group.

Thursday 6th November 1975

We were back at Baileys nightclub in Leicester this week and a couple of nights ago footballer Frank Worthington had dropped in to say, "hello". Today he took the boys down to the Leicester City training ground and kitted us out for a training session. Frank told me that a few years ago Bill Shankly nearly signed him for Liverpool but as he was a bit of a drinker and hell raiser he failed the medical due to high blood pressure. He was great company and got us tickets in the director's box for Saturday's match.

Friday 7th November 1975

Guys n' Dolls at the races with future champion jockey Joe Mercer

Today we were off to the races at Doncaster as there was a race on the card called the "Guys n' Dolls Maiden Plate". We presented the prize to the winner and did a short TV interview. It was an enjoyable day marred only by one of the horses being injured and having to be destroyed right in front of the stand.

Saturday 8th November 1975

It was one year ago today that we all met, and what a year it had been. We celebrated with champagne at our last show of the week at Leicester. My Mum and Dad were there along with Frank Worthington, Malcolm Allured, one of the drummers from Showaddywaddy, and a friend of Frank's called Phil. Now Phil was a lovable but shady character and when my dad asked him what he did for a living, Phil said he was a burglar. We never discovered if he was serious or not but from that day on his name was Phil Tealeaf.

One tradition we keep to this day. Every year on the 8th November I ring Dominic and Julie or they ring me, at 8.00pm, to say "happy anniversary".

Sunday 16th November 1975

I had been looking forward to today, as we were to appear at the Empire Pool Wembley (now Wembley Arena) for the Saturday Scene awards show in front of around 8,000 people. Magnet records had organised a limousine so we could arrive in style.

One of our regular fans was a girl called Liz who was totally in love with Dominic, and a little bit crazy. We drove down the side of the Empire Pool to the stage door, and in front of us we can see an apparition of flailing arms and legs running towards us screaming Dominic! Dominic! It was Liz and with a total disregard for any sort of reasoning she hurled herself onto the bonnet of our, still moving limousine. Her head hit the windscreen with a thud and her nose was instantly broken. The outcome was she went to hospital, stayed there for two days, and of course missed the show.

It was a great day, and there I was standing on the same stage that the Beatles stood for their last British show just over nine years ago. The majority of the crowd were Rollers fans but gave us a great reception waving their tartan scarves in time with the music. Also on the bill were the Bay City Rollers, Gary Glitter, Alvin Stardust, Smokie and Linda Lewis. It's always great to meet a legend and one of the people who came on stage to present the awards, was the forces sweetheart from world war two, Dame Vera Lynn.

Tuesday 18th November 1975

Our manager Brian Longley was never one to miss out on a bit of publicity. Today we all went to see Liz in hospital accompanied by a photographer from the Daily Mirror. It was a much more subdued and embarrassed Liz lying in bed with a large bandage covering her nose. We took her some gifts and stayed for about thirty minutes, and of course got the photograph which duly appeared in the Mirror the following day.

Thursday 20th November 1975

I spent my 31st birthday performing at Hendon Hall Hotel. This was followed bit a bit of a party at Geoff Morrow's house where I drank far too much Champagne, and heard the latest Queen record Bohemian Rhapsody for the first time and thought it was sensational.

I had finally come clean about my real age a few months ago when I had to use my passport for a foreign trip and realised that my date of birth was inside. I needn't have worried neither Ammo, nor the rest of the group were the slightest bit bothered.

Friday 28th November 1975

Brian Longley had come up with the idea for recording a cover of "You Don't Have To Say You Love Me" as our next single. Dusty Springfield had a number one hit with it in 1966 and I liked the song. The only worry was that a version of the song by Elvis Presley had reached number nine in the charts in 1970 and it might be too soon for another.

We spent the day in Lansdowne Studios recording what we hoped would be our next single and the group were much more involved with the arrangement than before. At the end of the day we thought it sounded great, all we had to do now was convince Michael Levy.

Monday 1st December 1975

We took "You Don't Have To Say You Love Me" to play to Michael Levy. There was always a little ritual that took place with a new record. We would go to his office he would pour us drinks and we would all sit down. Michael would then play the track, sitting at his desk listening intently sometime with his head in his hands. At the end he would pause, then jump up, thump the desk and shout "It's a fucking smash". Today was different, he said he wasn't sure and would take it home and let us know tomorrow.

Tuesday 2nd December 1975

Michael Levy phoned Ammo and said that he had played our record to his wife and she didn't like the drum sound so it should be re-mixed.------ HIS WIFE! Ammo were understandably annoyed and did nothing for a few days, they then confidently breezed in to see Michael with exactly the same version, saying "we've remixed it and it sounds great". Michael played it thumped the desk and said "It's a fucking smash".

Sunday 14th – Saturday 20th December 1975

Our last weeks work before Christmas turned out to be our best week so far. We flew to Edinburgh to perform at a club called La Fabrique in Bo'ness, under the shadow of the Forth Bridge. The first night ended in chaos when girls rushed the stage and during the confusion of getting us off stage Thereze was mistaken for a fan and for a few moments was refused entry to our dressing room. She wasn't amused.

On the Thursday we had to fly back to London during the day to record the Chrstmas Top of the Pops and once again met up with Mud. The final show at Bo'ness ended with a small party backstage, with all the staff that had been great. Scottish audiences were among the best we would ever play to.

Thursday 25th- Friday 26th December 1975

After the hectic year I had just experience I spent a quiet enjoyable Christmas with Mum, Dad and Nigel, who had come home from France unexpectedly. I reflected on the past twelve months, which, despite the fact I was having a problem with the music we were playing, I had enjoyed immensely. I can't deny that I'd always wanted my fifteen minutes of fame and was now hoping that this might be extended to at least thirty. Who knows what 1976 would bring.

1976

Friday 9th January 1976

On the day Guys n' Dolls fourth single "You Don't Have To Say You Love Me" was released we were coming to the end of a week, appearing at Talk of the West in Newquay, Cornwall.

Sunday 18th – Saturday 24th January 1976

This week we appeared at a north London club called Neros, situated opposite Mornington Crescent underground station in Camden. This was an old converted theatre originally called Camden Palace and at one time used by the BBC. The anarchic fifties radio programme The Goon Show, that launched the careers of Peter Sellers, Harry Secombe and Spike Milligan, (which I listened to and loved), had been recorded there.

I had seen a very attractive girl in the audience on the Monday night; she had blonde hair and a lovely smile and was there again on the Wednesday and Thursday. Guys n' Dolls always wore red carnations in their buttons holes and at the end of the show gave them out to members of the audience. On the Friday, she was there again and I managed to give her mine. I wanted to meet her but it was difficult to go out into the audience after the show, and we would always leave the club soon after we had changed. On the Saturday I decided to write a note and try and get it to her. If she wasn't there, well that would be that, but we took to the stage and she was once again in the crowd. We finished the show, took our bow, and I went to where she was standing, grabbed her hand and gave her my carnation along with the note, which had my phone number, asking her to phone me the following day.

Sunday 25th January 1976

Being a bit of a "pop star", I arrogantly thought that she would phone me, which she did. It was only after I had got to know her that I realised she wasn't the kind of girl who normally rings up strange men in tight lycra trousers (which the boys wore at the time) and if it hadn't been for her mates persuading her she wouldn't have phoned at all. We met that evening and I wasn't disappointed, her name was Lynne Seeley and I thought she was great. I had assumed that, as she had seen five of our shows, she must have been a huge Guys n' Dolls fan. The truth was that she was a nurse from the nearby University College Hospital and she and her fellow nurses were given free tickets and went to Nero's most nights. She was down to earth, totally unimpressed with my, so called, pop status and I was quite smitten. It was unfortunate that we were about to go away the following morning, working solidly for the next three weeks, but I said I would phone her and hopefully meet up on my return.

That was the start, and thirty one years and two kids later we are still together.

Tuesday 3rd February 1976

This week we were in Birmingham but today we travelled back to London for a "heavy" meeting with Ammo. There had been a gradual downturn in relations with them and there was possibly a conflict of interests, being signed both recording and management to the same company, so today we told them that we'd like Brian Longley to manage us on his own. They were not too happy but they agreed.

We then went along to see Colin Wild at a place called Carnaby Cavern, off Carnaby Street. Colin specialised in stage costumes and had supplied many of the outfits worn by the top groups during the "Glam Rock" period. He was making a new set of costumes for us, which were identical cat suits for the boys and the girls.

Wednesday 4th February 1976

We made the first of many appearances on a lunchtime TV show called Pebble Mill at One. This was a live show broadcast daily at 1.00pm in the foyer of the Pebble Mill Studios in Birmingham. Guests were interviewed and a musical act opened and closed the show. We always performed live and Ray Monk was able to book his own musicians, usually people who worked with us regularly, along with our own drummer Dave Morris. It was an enjoyable relaxed show and the live sound was always far superior to Top of the Pops. Today we performed our new single "You Don't Have To say You Love Me" and a song from the act, "The Locomotion".

Wednesday 11th February 1976

Our single was a breaker this week and today we travelled to London from Stoke on Trent for Top of the Pops. We wore our cat suits for the first time, and from their design (see photo above) it's obvious that, "Jaws" was the popular film of the moment. We sang the song live and I was allowed to play the lead guitar figure featured on the record. As we always wore black and white I had recently bought a White Fender Stratocaster from my old friend Alan Shacklock to match the costume. Guys n' Dolls now had a second roadie called Dave (Tank) Chambers, who came more from the rock fraternity so he looked after my guitar and amplifier with the utmost care and pride.

After we had clearance from Top of the Pops it was back up the motorway for the show at Stoke on Trent. There was always so much promotion to do when a single was released and this was the first of three trips from Stoke to London and back in four days.

Thursday 19th – Friday 20th February 1976

On the way to Hamburg (left to right) Dominic Grant, Brian Longley, David Van Day, Thereze Bazar. Brian is sitting on the seat that converts into a toilet.

Our first promotion trip to Germany was in a small nine seater plane, and we flew to Hamburg for a TV show. Appearing with us were David Essex and one of Dominic's heroes Scott Walker. Scott was a bit strange and uncommunicative and spent most of the time trying to hide his face.

It was on to Glasgow for another TV show and during the flight I had an upset tummy and badly needed the loo. The toilet on our small plane was the back seat which turned into a sort of commode and there was very little room. Brian Longley had the job of trying to retain what dignity I had left, covering me with a coat while I did what I had to. Fortunately this happened very close to our landing in Glasgow as the atmosphere in the plane had changed somewhat.

Saturday 21st February 1976

This TV show we were appearing on was called the Alexander Brothers hour and I found out that one of the other artists was the guy who first inspired me to be involved with music, Lonnie Donegan. We had a short rehearsal and I met one of my all time heroes.

Sunday 22nd February 1976

I shared a cab with Lonnie back to the studio, and when we arrived two girls ran up to me, completely ignoring Lonnie, and asked for my autograph. I felt rather uncomfortable with this as here was one of my greatest heroes and the girls had no idea who he was. Lonnie wasn't at all bothered and we went inside. Between rehearsals I spent a lot of time talking to him about music and reminiscing. It can be a great experience or a disappointment to meet one of your heroes but Lonnie didn't disappoint. He gave me a copy of his latest album and allowed me to have a go on his custom built Stan Francis twelve string guitar which I had only seen in pictures years ago. There was so much Lonnie Donegan still ingrained in me that it seemed I knew more about him than he did.

Wednesday 25th February 1976

"You Don't Have To Say You Love Me" had moved up to No. 29 in the charts so we had our second top thirty hit and today another appearance on Top of the Pops. Dominic's hair must have been looking even camper than usual, and during rehearsals Robin Nash, the producer, came down and had a real go at him about his hair in front of everyone, saying that he was coming across a bit too gay. I thought Dominic was going to hit him, which would not have been the best career move, but he kept his cool and went to the dressing room and got to work with the brush and hair dryer.

Thursday 4ᵗʰ March 1976

**Alvin Stardust
with Julie and
Dominic inside
Westminster
Cathedral**

*(Photo by Robin
Jones)*

Westminster cathedral was launching a one million pound restoration appeal with a special concert featuring Alvin Stardust and Guys n' Dolls. The concert was held in the cathedral in front of the Duke of Edinburgh, with appearances from the likes of Eamon Andrews and actress Susan Hampshire.

Just as we are about to perform Dominic had to perform his usual ritual of a last minute pee. Since we had started Dominic had peed in many sinks, pint glasses and even behind the scenery at the Basil Brush Show, tonight he had a dilemma as we were standing in the cathedral with no obvious choice of a place to relieve himself. He found a small stone staircase leading up to who knows where, and disappeared. About a minute later he walked down the stairs followed by a river of urine and at the bottom of the stairs encountered a group of nuns waiting to go up.

It was an odd show; we walked on to the stage? to be confronted by a sea of clergymen in strange hats and right in front of us was HRH the Duke of Edinburgh. I had told the group a joke, and they dared me to say it during the show so half way through I said, "It's very nice to be here in this wonderful cathedral, especially for me as my father was in the church. He was a cannon, but they fired him". There was a deafening silence, which for some reason I found incredibly funny, and I heard someone go "tut tut". The only person who was smiling was the Duke of Edinburgh.

Afterwards we were all introduced to the Duke and he told me that after we had performed, a clergyman walked on stage and said "I'm a cannon perhaps I should be fired" and the place erupted. Perhaps it's the way you tell em'.

Wednesday 10th March 1976

Our second top ten hit as "You Don't Have To Say You Love Me" reached No.9 in the charts and today we made another appearance on Top Of The Pops. Afterwards Dominic, myself and a few friends went out for Dominic's stag night as he was getting married the following day.

Dominic had been living with a girl called Karen for a few years but he and Julie had begun a relationship a few months after the group started. He had now decided, more out of guilt than anything else, that he and Julie had to end their relationship and he would, "do the right thing" and marry Karen. I and many others could plainly see that this was the wrong move, but Dominic was adamant and try as we might nobody could talk him out of it.

Thursday 11th March 1976

Dominic married Karen at 2.30pm this afternoon. It was obvious that Julie couldn't attend so none of the group went which must have seemed odd. There were only eight people at the wedding, close family, and our manager Brian Longley.

While this was going on Julie, Thereze and I were doing an interview and a photo session. At the session we met Leslie and Debbie Ash (Debs from "Men Behaving Badly"), who were school friends of Julie's and were really pleased to see her, but it made things more difficult as she was really upset and struggled to put on a brave face. Brian Longley phoned Julie at the session and said that it looked bad that none of us were at the wedding and we should come down later, but there was no way that was going to happen

Saturday 13th March 1976

Two days after Dominic's wedding Guys n' Dolls were booked to play in Carlisle, so we all met up at Euston station and travelled up by train. We checked in to our hotel, and because Julie was still feeling very down after Dominic's wedding, the girls ordered a couple of bottles of champagne and got very pissed. David and Thereze ended up having a fight, and when Dominic tried to intervene, Thereze screamed at him "and you can fuck off". We went on stage, the girls were still pissed, the boys were annoyed, the audience didn't seem to notice, and we went down really well.

Tuesday 16th March 1976

On the day that "You Don't Have Say You Love Me" peaked at No.5 in the charts, we were in Holland recording a TV show with Gilbert O'Sullivan and Gloria Gaynor.

Friday 26th March 1976

Our relationship with Ammo had deteriorated further over the past weeks; we had received a royalty statement from them which said the group had earned around three hundred pounds in royalties but were still in debt to Ammo for several thousand pounds which we couldn't understand. We had sold a considerable amount of records and had been working solidly for the past twelve months and were still only drawing £50 per week. Coupled to this Michael Levy and Magnet records were not that impressed with the material Ammo were coming up with and were anxious for us to have a different producer.

Today Ammo received a letter from our solicitor stating that we wished to sever connections with them.

Saturday 27th March 1976

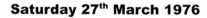

The BBC had started broadcasting a programme called "Saturday Night at the Mill" which was a slightly more upmarket version of "Pebble Mill at One". It was broadcast live at 11.00pm and tonight we were appearing with Bruce Forsyth, and had been rehearsing a special item with him for the past couple of days. First of all Bruce did a father and daughter interview with Julie. He then asked to sing with the group and Julie said no. We then sang "Love Train" and when I walked to the front to sing a solo verse, Bruce, who by this time was dressed up in a white suit like us, took my place in the line. When I tried to get back he passed me a note and told me that I was wanted on the phone and spent the rest of the song making fun of Dominic. It's one of my favourites out of all the television shows we did, and a privilege to work with Bruce.

Monday 19th April 1976

Mick Mills the Ipswich Town footballer was having his testimonial year and we had been invited to perform a special show for him and the rest of the team. It was a small audience just the team, their wives, some of the staff and the club manager, who at that time was Bobby Robson.

After the show Mick Mills came round for a chat and brought with him one of his team mates, the striker David Johnson. Little did I know that the next time I met Dave he would be wearing the red of Liverpool FC.

Thursday 29th April 1976

Today we had a photo session where we recreated characters from the original "Guys n' Dolls" musical

Tuesday 4th May 1976

Liverpool won at Wolves 1-3 which meant they were league champions again. All they had to do now was win the UEFA cup and they were 3-2 up after winning the first leg against Bruges at home. The second leg was in two weeks time when Guys n' Dolls would be working in Liverpool.

Tuesday 18th May 1976

ANFIELD In the players tunnel and the dugout where Bob Paisley sat

It never ceased to amaze me that a little bit of fame can get you into places.

We had been in Liverpool since Sunday working at a club called Allinsons, and staying at the Holiday Inn. The manager there was a guy called Stuart who, when he found out I was a Liverpool fan, arranged for me to have a tour of Anfield. Stuart (also a red) took me to the ground and we met Peter Robinson the club secretary who gave me a club badge and a tie. I then went on a tour, first to the trophy room and then out on to the pitch passing through the tunnel that the players use, with the sign that Bill Shankly had put up to put fear into opponents which said, "THIS IS ANFIELD". I wanted to see the famous boot room where tactics are sorted out and when we knocked on the door and went in, there was Bob Paisley, Joe Fagin and Ronnie Moran sitting, probably plotting the downfall of Bruges.

The team had returned from training and I was introduced to Kevin Keegan and Emlyn Hughes, I was a bit like a kid in a toy shop. They were about to leave for Belgium for the second leg of the UEFA Cup final and I wished them luck.

Wednesday 19th May 1976
This evening before our show, I had been invited to Radio City, the local radio station, to listen to the commentary of the UEFA cup final. At half time I was interviewed and they played a couple of Guys n' Dolls records. Liverpool drew the match at Bruges 1-1 but won the cup 4-3 on aggregate. So two cups again, not a bad season.

Thursday 20th May 1976

That's Emlyn Hughes holding up the UEFA Cup. Honest.

Stuart took me to Liverpool's Speke airport (now John Lennon Airport) to see the victorious Liverpool team come home with the UEFA cup. There were about two thousand people and the atmosphere was great.

Sunday 23rd to Saturday 29th May 1976
From Liverpool we drove to Glasgow for the start of a week of shows in Scotland. Monday was a night off so we managed to blag some tickets to see Elton John performing at the Glasgow Apollo and he was on top form.

We performed in Aberdeen, Dundee then back to the Pavillion Theatre in Glasgow for two nights and the audiences were wild. I had never thought of us as being the type of group that provoked hysteria but Glasgow was something else. We were screamed at during our shows with girls trying to rush onto the stage. When it came to getting out of the theatre each of us were taken individually, surrounded by Brian and the two roadies for protection, and virtually thrown into the car, and one night Martine had a handful of hair pulled out. On the last night around twenty girls stayed outside our hotel, all night singing.

Thursday 3rd June 1976

Tony Macaulay was a writer and producer of some standing, having written or produced songs for Elvis Presley, the Foundations, the Drifters and many more. Michael Levy wanted him to produce our next album and today we went to his house to listen to some material. He played us some songs and we decided to record a number called "If Only for the Good Times" as a potential next single. It was more up tempo than our previous records and was a much better song than anything we had heard up until then, and even I didn't mind it too much.

Saturday 12th June 1976

It was the last day of our week's run at the Lakeside Club in Frimley Green, Surrey, now home of the world darts championship. It was run by a guy called Bob Potter who was rather annoyed one night when Martine brought her dog into the dressing room saying, "I don't want dogs in here; I've got Shirley Bassey coming next week".

Two girls came into the dressing room for autographs and the stage manager / bouncer took exception to this and started dragging them out by their hair, which was totally out of order. Dominic saw red and waded into the guy, who was much bigger than him, and threw him out of the room giving him a black eye in the process. It's the only time I've ever seen Dominic involved in a fight.

Tuesday 15th June 1976

Guys n' Dolls had been given their own one hour TV special by London Weekend Television and had started intensive rehearsals and having fittings for costumes. It was being produced by Mike Mansfield who we had built up a good relationship with following several appearances on his "Supersonic" shows. There was a bit of a panic as it was to be recorded in two weeks time.

Tuesday 29th June 1976

A busy day. First it was a visit to our solicitors regarding the new contract we were about to sign with Magnet records. Then it was last minute costume fittings and on to a meeting with Michael Levy where the contract was duly signed. London Weekend television was next for a band call and to see the set for our special which looked fantastic. There was a large stage with steps each side leading to another narrow stage at the back. This created a square and the orchestra were in the middle of the square.

Wednesday 30th June 1976

Today was the recording of our TV special at London Weekend television. We spent all day rehearsing the format of the show with our guests, Tina Charles and Biddu. There were a couple of numbers which we had been rehearsing specially for the occasion. One of these was "The Continental", a song and dance from the 1934 Fred Astaire and Ginger Rogers film "The Gay Divorcee" (when gay meant happy). Julie sang this and had been teamed up with me for the dance routine, probably because my dancing had been compared to Fred Astaire's. This had been giving me nightmares for the past two weeks and I was praying I wouldn't mess up on the night as we had a very tight schedule time wise.

The show was recorded at 7.30pm in front of a live audience including friends and family. Mum and Dad had broken their holiday to be at the show and my wife to be, Lynne, was also there. The show went really well and I got through "The Continental" with no problems, and was rather pleased with myself thinking, "not bad for an old hippy". We were a bit rushed at the end when the final section had to be re-recorded due to a technical problem but all in all it felt good, and we all went for drinks afterwards with our nearest and dearest.

Friday 23rd July 1976

The new single "If Only for the Good Times" was released today and we had begun recording tracks for our second album with Tony Macaulay. It had been agreed that one of my songs "Lovely Lady" would be included. It can be a bit of a fight to have your songs considered when the producer is also a writer, and wants to get his own songs recorded.

Today I was in Advision studios to record the backing track. I had worked out the format with Ray Monk who had written a string quartet backing, Tony Macaulay didn't even turn up so we were able to get on with it ourselves and it was great to be able to have more input than before. I played guitar, Ray Monk was on Keyboards, and on drums was our own Dave Morris.

Saturday 31st July 1976

(left to right)
Sally James,
Yours truly,
Thereze Bazar

The group had recently bought a Daimler eight seater limousine to replace "Smelly" the van that belonged to Ammo. Today Ivor drove us in the limo to Lewisham Town Hall for an appearance on "The Sally James Road Show". When we arrived, we discovered that the guys from Ammo were there with their new all girl group called Glamourpuss. There had been no contact with Ammo since the split and we had heard that they were thinking of suing us for breach of contract. It was a difficult situation for Julie as her sister Debbie was about to marry David Martin so there was a bit of a family divide. It turned into a bit of an awkward afternoon as Debbie was there with David, but we all managed to keep things civilised.

Friday 6th August 1976

Thereze and David went into the studio as Tony Macaulay was recording the backing track for a song of Thereze's that she wanted to be included on the next album. They upset Tony by trying to tell him how to do his job which culminated in a huge row and Tony phoning Michael Levy, telling him that he didn't want Thereze or David in the studio again.

Julie had been unwell for the past couple of weeks and her Mum phoned Brian and said that she would have to go into hospital next week for tests. We had been through a period of almost non stop working from morning until night and I think everyone was tired. Our new single had reached No.71 in the charts and for the first time had not made it onto the Radio One play list (which means it would not be played) and needed strong promotion, but Brian decided that we should have a few days off next week to recharge our batteries.

Tuesday 10th August 1976

So much for our few days off. Brian phoned to say that our record was a breaker at No. 64 and we had Top of the Pops tomorrow. Julie was in hospital having tests as she was still unwell, and her mother, Penny said that she would not be able to do the show. Brian used all his powers of diplomacy and persuasion and Penny said she would see what she could do. Brian was not really flavour of the month with Penny, who at the time had sided with David Martin and Ammo over the split and Julie herself was having a bit of a hard time at home.

Wednesday 11th August 1976

We had our first Top of the Pops rehearsal without Julie but she arrived in time for the dress rehearsal. We sang live in the studio with the orchestra and it went well. Now we hoped the record might get onto the Radio One playlist.

Wednesday 18th August 1976

The record was still a breaker but had dropped to No. 66 and was still not on the Radio One playlist so it looked as if it wasn't going to be a hit.

We spent eight hours in the studio with Tony Macaulay recording three more songs for the album. There was an uneasy truce between Tony Macaulay, and David and Thereze, who were present but keeping a low profile.

Saturday 21st August 1976

One of our young fans, a girl called Clare Lambourne, had written in to the Jimmy Saville TV show "Jim'll Fix It" asking to meet Guys n' Dolls. Today we appeared on the show performing our latest single and then met Clare who sang a bit of "There's a Whole Lot of Loving" with us. I found Jimmy Saville a bit remote and rather odd.

The actor Peter Cushing was on the show with us and was such a nice person a real gentleman. Dominic asked him for an autograph something I'd never seen him do before or since.

.

Tuesday 24th August 1976

Today we had a meeting with Michael Levy to hear the new album. Michael didn't like much of what he heard but did say he thought my track "Lovely Lady" was one of the best, so I left the office feeling rather smug.

We didn't know what was going to happen next as Michael was talking about scrapping some of the tracks and getting a new producer. He was unhappy with Tony Macaulay and there were the problems between him, David and Thereze. It's a shame it didn't work out with Tony as there was no doubting his track record and what might have been. In a few months he would go on to produce David Soul and have four top ten hits in a year including two number ones.

Saturday 4th September 1976

The Guys n' Dolls one hour TV special was shown today and it came out well, and today I think it's one of our best pieces of work.

Saturday 15th September 1976

Tony Macaulay was now history and Keith Rossiter and Steve Elson were to be our new producers. We had a long session with them at Morgan Studios in Willesden North London recording two new songs.

Sunday 19th September 1976

GUYS N' DOLLS FC
(back) Dominic Grant, Dave (Tank) Chambers, Paul Griggs.

(middle) David Van Day, Ray Monk, Ivor the Driver.

(front) Julie Forsyth, Martine Howard, Thereze Bazar.

Dominic and I were invited to play in a charity football match at Barnet FC for a show biz team. Dominic was a pretty good player and I was hopeless but we were told it was just a fun game nothing serious. I can't remember many of the other players apart from Peter Duncan (actor and Blue Peter presenter) and ex. Spurs player Alan Gilzean who was the captain. Sally James and Debbie Ash were there to give some moral support.

There were twelve players on the Show Biz team so Dominic started and I was supposed to substitute him when he got tired. This happened after about five minutes when Dominic came over and said "OK Griggsy I'm knackered, your turn". On I went, they said it was just a fun game but Alan Gilzean was taking it very seriously, shouting at everyone, and I just stood as far away from the action as possible hoping the ball wouldn't come to me although I almost scored with one of my only kicks of the game. Almost but not quite.

At the end we were all presented with medals by Jeanette Charles the woman who impersonates Her Majesty the Queen.

Monday 27th September 1976

Our second album was complete and we went to Magnet to hear the final running order. It ended up having three producers as four of Tony Macauley's songs remained, there was one from Ammo and the rest from Steve Elson and Keith Rossiter, but it sounded OK. It had been decided that the next single was to be "Stoney Ground" which meant I would be singing lead for the first time, and it was a much more up tempo song than previous singles.

One of the songs on the album was called "I've Been Loving You" and we were told that it had been specially written for us by Elton John and Bernie Taupin. I thought the song was very ordinary and the lyrics naïve, nothing like his present material. It turned out that it was Elton's first ever solo record released by "Phillips" in 1968 which sunk without trace, and we had been the victims of record company bullshit.

Friday 8th October 1976

We appeared on The Basil Brush show, Basil took the piss out of my hair, and I nearly changed my views on fox hunting.

Thursday 21st October 1976

Eric (I'll get a limo) Hall, phoned to ask if I wanted to see Paul McCartney and Wings in concert this evening. I thought for about half a second and said "yes". Eric got a limo and I went with him, David Van Day and the TV producer Mike Mansfield to Wembley's Empire Pool and saw a great show. Afterwards Eric, who could talk his way into anywhere, managed to get us all into the after show party backstage. There were a lot of well known faces, including some of the guys from 10CC and Peter Frampton, who was appearing the following evening. I stood talking to Jake Hooper from the band Arrows with his wife Lorna Luft, who happened to be Judy Garland's daughter. Paul and Linda

McCartney arrived and Lorna made a swift beeline for him saying, "I must say hello to Paul, I met him with my Mom in 1964". I would like to have met Paul but that night the opportunity did not arise.

Monday 25th – Saturday 30th October 1976

I had always wanted to appear on the stage of the London Palladium ever since I had seen Bruce Forsyth introduce almost every top name imaginable, including the Beatles, on Sunday Night at the London Palladium in the fifties and sixties. Tonight we were to begin a week of shows at this illustrious venue supporting the funny but always unpredictable Freddie Starr.

Having never set foot in the Palladium before, I was a bit awestruck. We sat in the stalls watching Freddie rehearsing before being introduced to him and getting on with our own band call. The first show went well even though we were all a bit nervous, and I kept thinking this is where the Beatles stood in 1963.

On the second night Michael Levy presented us with silver discs for the just released "Good Times" album. I guess he just couldn't resist coming on to the stage of the Palladium, as I was convinced that we could not have possibly achieved gold status of £100,000 worth of albums in just over a week. There had been a huge campaign for the album with major displays in shops but the resulting royalties we eventually received did not add up to a silver disc. I heard that a lot of records went into the shops on a sale or return basis and although it sold well, I suspect that £100,000 worth went in but a lot were returned unsold.

It was a busy week; we had to promote our new single "Stoney Ground" during the day with two shows at the Palladium most nights. On the Wednesday we even performed a late show at the Hilton Hotel, appearing with Bob Monkhouse. We all got on well with Freddie Starr; he was quite outrageous but great company. One night the song writer Tony Hatch called to see Freddie when Dominic was in the dressing room. Now Tony Hatch has a large indentation on his forehead and on this night Dominic may have had a little too much firewater. Freddie introduced Tony to Dominic who blurted out "where did you get that bloody great scar". Even Freddie was shocked.

We finished an enjoyable week with Freddie dragging us all on stage at the end of the last performance; I looked along the line and noticed the actress Dora Bryan was there as well. I don't know where she came from as she wasn't part of the show. We were now ready for a further four weeks with him, touring Great Britain.

Saturday 6th November 1976

With Adolf Starr

(Photo by Paul Smith)

We had been on the road with Freddie Starr for almost a week and last night we played the first of two days in Manchester. The musical intro had started for us to go on stage and as always last thing, I checked my flies. Horror of horrors the zip had broken and to make matters worse I was wearing blue underpants. I had no spare white trousers with me so I just buttoned my jacket and the rest of the group said no one would notice. Throughout the act I couldn't help noticing people nudging each other followed by smiles.

Today we bought the local papers to see if there was a write up about the show. There was, dominated by my blue underpants.

Wednesday 10th November 1976

Our record "Stoney Ground" had reached 38 in the charts which would be its highest position. Today we had another appearance on Top of the Pops and as we had a show to go to in Peterborough the BBC let us record our spot early without the audience. There was dense fog on the journey, we were in two cars and the one with Thereze and Julie got lost and it was fast approaching the time for our spot, closing the first half of the show. It was Freddie's show and Brian had to explain to him that we were sorry but we weren't ready to go on. Some top of the bill acts would have gone mad, Freddie just said that it wasn't a problem that he would go on and do a short spot, followed by the interval, by which time we hoped the other car would arrive which it did. After a mad scramble and a slightly longer interval we all made it on stage to open the second half. This was 1976 and the mobile phone was a dream of the future.

Friday 12th November 1976

Freddie was always unpredictable, he would often walk on stage in the middle of our act, and one night he came on dressed as Tarzan, lifted Dominic on to his shoulders, and staggered around while Dominic was still trying to sing. On another occasion he went up to Thereze and rubbed her face affectionately, the only problem was his hands were covered in black ink.

Tonight we were at the Theatre Royal in Nottingham, Dominic had a bit of a sore throat and mentioned this to Freddie who said "I've just the thing" and gave Dominic a couple of tablets and said "these will do the trick". About half an hour later Dominic complained of feeling rather strange as if he was drunk. Freddie had given him a large dose of valium and we were about to go on stage. We gave Dominic some strong coffee and Brian took him for a walk outside dressed in his white suit and a passer by was heard to say "isn't that the bloke from Guys n' Dolls, he looks pissed to me". None of this really worked and Dominic struggled through the act about a beat behind the rest of us. Half way through Freddie, who thought the whole thing was hilarious, came on stage with a stool and said, "I think you might need this".

We returned to our hotel with Freddie and all had a meal together. We were eating our dessert when one of us, I can't remember who, flicked a bit of trifle at someone who flicked a bit back. This turned into a full scale food fight during which Freddie emptied half a bottle of ketchup into my hair which by now was in a ridiculously large afro style and had taken on a life of its own. It took two days of washing to get the ketchup completely out.

This sort of behaviour was completely out of order for a nice clean cut group like Guys n' Dolls but a helluva lot of fun.

Many years later DJ Steve Wright was discussing Guys n' Dolls on his radio show and referred to me as "the plonker with the perm". As my hair was naturally curly I'm afraid the statement was only half correct.

Sunday 14th November 1976

Tonight's venue was the Liverpool Empire, and between shows Freddie's roadie, Stan, asked if I could I come to Freddie's dressing room as he wanted to see me. Due to past events I was immediately suspicious, and as I was wearing my white suit, hurriedly changed into my jeans. I crept upstairs to the dressing room, half expecting Freddie to jump out with a fire extinguisher or suchlike. I knocked on the door, went in and there standing in front of me was the legendary Liverpool manager Bill Shankly, who said in that familiar Scottish voice "Hello young man". It was great to meet him and we talked for a while, and at one point Freddie, who is an Everton FC fan said, "Now that you've finished with Liverpool you should manage Everton, they need you". Shanks turned and said, "Ah Freddie I canna do that".

I will always be grateful to Freddie for that meeting with one of my all time heroes.

Saturday 20th November 1976

We had played at the Newcastle City Hall last night and I had gone to bed early. I was woken just after midnight with the rest of the group standing round my bed singing "happy birthday to you" and pouring champagne and gateau all over me. They then left me covered in gunge lying in a bed that was totally uninhabitable. I was sharing a room with David, so I got up, showered, locked and bolted the door and went to sleep in David's bed. Sometime after I thought I heard knocking at the door and David's plaintive voice saying "Paul, let me in, it wasn't my idea". I just turned over and went back to sleep.

The following night we were back in Liverpool and Brian had arranged for a private room at the St. Georges Hotel with some food to celebrate my birthday. The group, the band and the roadies all came along but I'm afraid none of the food was eaten. Thereze and David began another food fight and everyone waded in, except Julie who was out of there so fast. One fan had managed to gate crash and all he wanted was to get our autographs which he managed to do, completely avoiding any of the flying food, and left the room totally unscathed. The outcome of the evening was that Guys n' Dolls were charged around £250 for the damage to the room and Freddie Starr wasn't even present.

About a week later a well known rock band tried to check into the St. Georges Hotel only to be told "No more bands as we had Guys n' Dolls here last week and they were trouble".

Wednesday 24th November 1976

After a day off we were back on tour travelling up to Halifax. Our "flash" Daimler Limousine was somewhere near Leicester when it suddenly began making a loud knocking noise and ground to a halt, and it was obvious it wasn't going any further. We were taken to Leicester services and after about an hour Ivor managed to hire a transit van with no seats, so we all bundled in the back, sat on the floor and travelled the remaining one hundred miles in discomfort. Some fans were waiting at the stage door and our image took a bit of a knock as we climbed out of the transit to sign autographs.

After Freddie's spot we had to go back at the end and take a bow, Brian said as we'd had such a bad day we wouldn't hang around and as soon as we'd come off stage we'd go straight out of the theatre, in our costumes, and into a waiting car before the audience came out.

We took our bows and ran like mad to the front of the theatre and climbed into the waiting car, David and Thereze were squashed in the front and the rest of us in the back. We shut the doors and said to the driver "Go! Go! Go!". He turned, looked at us with a bemused look on his face and said "What are you doing, I'm waiting for my wife". The audience, were by now coming out of the theatre, and standing beside the car was our manager Brian pointing to the car behind saying "It's that one".

Monday 29th November 1976

Freddie with the sausages up his shirt

(Photo by Paul Smith)

It was the last day with Freddie Starr, and we had reached Wolverhampton. As he had been full of surprises for us during the tour it was time to turn the tables. Every night he would sing a rather rude song about sausages, and one line said "I got 12 pounds of sausages and stuffed them up my shirt". We found a local butchers shop and bought 12 pounds of sausages, as he finished the song we went on stage each carry two pounds of sausages and presented them to him and he stuffed them up his shirt. This was followed by the last food fight of the tour, as Freddie began throwing sausages at the audience who then threw them back, resulting in the Wolverhampton Civic Centre being covered in sausage meat and once again Guys n' Dolls receiving the cleaning bill.

We gave Freddie a world war one German helmet, complete with spike, as a goodbye present. It had been a great few weeks working with him, we'd had a lot of laughs, probably far too much food had been used in an inappropriate manner, and Guys n' Dolls had got about as "Rock n' Roll" as they ever would.

Wednesday 8ᵗʰ December 1976

It was back down to earth today as we had a meeting with our solicitors regarding Ammo. They had decided to sue us for breach of contract and it looked as if it would go to Crown Court which would involve barristers and probably a lot of money.

Sunday 12ᵗʰ December 1976

I went to Victoria station and met my brother Nigel who had returned from France. The band he was in had broken up and he had run out of money. It was good to see him again.

Tuesday 14ᵗʰ December 1976

Today we recorded a session for the Alyn Ainsworth BBC Radio show. David was not in the best of moods and had a tantrum at the studios. It was the first time I wrote in my diary that David's days in the group could be numbered. He and Thereze, who by now thought they knew everything about show business, were often having rows with Brian our manager about group policy, and the strong relationship within the group at the beginning, was starting to crack. Dominic, Julie and I were pretty tight together and Martine was now in a relationship with a guy called Michael Richardson who was Freddie Starr's drummer, and who she would eventually marry.

Sunday 19ᵗʰ December 1976

Today was another royal show at the Drury Lane theatre in front of HRH Princess

Margaret. We appeared with, among others, Gary Glitter, Mark Bolan and Twiggy who was trying to carve out a singing career at that time.

Sunday 26th – Friday 31st December 1976

I spent Christmas Day with Lynne and my family; it was the only day off over Christmas. On Boxing Day I took Lynne back to her flat in London, called for Dominic and then collected Julie, who was by now sharing a flat with David and Thereze but had been staying with her dad for Christmas. We then drove down to Bournemouth where Guys n' Dolls were appearing in a Christmas show for two weeks with Norman Wisdom. Bournemouth in wintertime was a bit bleak as were the shows. The audiences were quite elderly and the houses were far from full.

On New Years Eve we did the show and then had a few drinks to celebrate and reflect. It had been a pretty good year; we'd had our second top ten record and made thirty two appearances on British television. Recently the atmosphere within the group had changed and I wondered whether we'd all be together at the end of 1977.

1977

Saturday 1st January – Saturday 8th January 1977

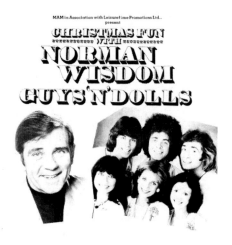

MAM in Association with Leisuretime Promotions Ltd.,
present
CHRISTMAS FUN
with
NORMAN WISDOM
GUYS'N'DOLLS

The first week of 1977 was spent finishing off our Christmas shows with Norman Wisdom. We didn't enjoy the same sort of relationship with Norman Wisdom as we had with Freddie Starr. He was a bit uncommunicative and his act seemed to be a little dated although he went down well with the rather elderly Bournemouth audiences.

Monday 10th January 1977

Today we were back in the studio with Steve Elson and Keith Rossiter trying to find a song that would be our next single. As we had a hit with a cover of "You Don't Have to Say You Love Me" this was the route we were pursuing so we recorded cover versions of "You're My World" a hit for Cilla Black and "Angel of the Morning" originally by P.P. Arnold. We sang them with our usual formula of Dominic and Martine singing the lead parts, they sounded OK I suppose, but as usual I wasn't convinced either of them were hits.

Friday 4th February 1977

The decision was that "You're My World" was to be our next single and it was released today. On the B-side was a song written by David and Thereze called "Just Loving You". We had decided that, as we now had our own music publishing company called Guys n' Dolls Music, the group would always write the B. sides of our singles and share the profit between us all. This was because the writers share was the same for the A side and the B side and it would generate income for the group.

At that time the writer/publisher share of royalties was approximately 6% of the wholesale price of a record.

Tuesday 8th February - Friday 11th February 1977

A busy few days, on Tuesday we rehearsed and recorded the Larry Grayson show for London Weekend Television. With us was American actor Dennis Weaver who at the time played McCloud a cowboy detective in the American series of the same name. He was a bit of a red neck and I'm not sure what he made of the overly camp Larry Grayson.

As we had to be in Germany the following morning, as soon as we received studio clearance we drove straight to Heathrow Airport and boarded a small ten seater plane for the flight to Dusseldorf. I was still very nervous about flying, but for some strange reason felt happier in the smaller planes, I probably thought they would glide more easily should the engines fail.

We sang two songs on a TV show called "Starparade" which featured the James Last Orchestra and Roger Whittaker and went out live in front of an audience of 7000.

On Friday we stopped off in Luxemburg to visit the famous Radio Luxemburg studios and were interviewed by Tony Prince, before flying home.

Tuesday 15th February 1977

Another hectic day as we travelled down from Manchester for yet another appearance on Mike Mansfield's "Supersonic" and this time we appeared with Cliff Richard and the Damned.

The era of "Punk" was upon us; it was only a few months ago that the Sex Pistols had made their infamous appearance on the Today programme with Bill Grundy, and the Damned were one of the groups that had come to prominence. It was reported in the press that Cliff Richard had objected to appearing with the Damned due to his Christian beliefs but there was absolutely no evidence of this and Cliff could be seen chatting to them with no problems at all. Another story created by a publicist?

Wednesday 16th February 1977

We were appearing for the week at Talk of the North in Eccles near Manchester, and the owner a guy called Joe Pullen arranged for me Dominic and David to sit in the director's box at Old Trafford for the match between Liverpool and Manchester United. First we had drinks in the director's bar and bumped into Bill Shankly again. We had a chat before taking our seats and I noticed that Shanks was sitting a couple of rows in front of us with the Manchester United directors and not Liverpool's.

After he had resigned as Liverpool's manager Bill Shankly had found it hard to let go. At first he would turn up to train with the Liverpool team until it became difficult for his successor Bob Paisley who had to remind Shanks that he was manager now. Liverpool never gave him a directorship or his own seat at the ground, which Manchester United gave Sir Matt Busby on his retirement, and Shanks became rather alienated from the club that he loved which was a great shame.

It was a good game even though it ended in a 0-0 draw, and we rushed back for the evening show.

Wednesday 23rd February 1977

Yet another TV show, this time we were at Yorkshire Television in Leeds to record the Les Dawson Show. We appeared in a sketch, Les and the Guys playing Greek waiters, and the Dolls and Lulu were guests at a restaurant. Zorbas dance was playing and we served food in time with the music, which got faster and the food went everywhere but we were quite experienced at throwing food around.

Tuesday 8th March 1977

Our latest single "You're My World" had only reached 80 in the charts and today dropped to 91 so this was our worst performing single to date. We met at Brian's office for a discussion about recording but these days it was getting difficult to debate anything without the whole thing turning into a pointless argument.

Wednesday 16th March 1977

Liverpool had lost 1-0 against St Etienne in the first leg of the quarter final of the European Cup. Tonight was the second leg at Anfield and on a whim I phoned Stuart the manager of the Holiday Inn at Liverpool to see if there was any chance of a ticket for the match if I came up. He said no problem, so I caught the train to Liverpool and checked in at the Holiday Inn.

The game would go down as one of the best games in Liverpool's history. Kevin Keegan scored in the first minute but St. Etienne equalized before half time which meant they had scored an away goal and Liverpool needed two. With twenty minutes to go Ray Kennedy scored but we needed one more. On came super-sub David Fairclough and with five minutes to go scored the winner. I have never experienced an atmosphere like it with the crowd going absolutely crazy.

My ticket enabled me to go to the director's lounge and I met up again with David Johnson who had recently signed for Liverpool from Ipswich. The UEFA Cup and the Division One (now premiership) trophy were on display and all in all it was a great night.

Friday18th March – Wednesday 23rd March 1977

Despite the fact that "You're My World" had bombed in the UK it had been released in

Holland by our Dutch label, Negram, and early signs indicated that it was going to be a hit. We undertook a very intense five days Dutch promotional trip which included four television appearances with numerous radio shows and photo sessions. Our final TV appearance was a "Parkinson" type of show with the legendary Tommy Cooper and a guy who impersonated American President, Jimmy Carter. We convinced Martine that it really was Jimmy Carter so she had a photo taken with him.

We flew back on the same flight as Tommy Cooper and walked behind him through Heathrow Airport, I just couldn't believe the size of his feet.

Friday 25th March 1977

Lynne had a few days off and had come to Cardiff, where we were appearing, to stay for a few days and as I really know how to treat a lady, we went out for the day.

I have an unashamed love of steam trains that goes back to train spotting as a boy and endures to this day. I took Lynne to Woodham's scrap yard on Barry Island where there were still over one hundred British steam locomotives waiting to be scrapped. At the time Lynne couldn't understand why I would want to wander around these rotting metal hulks getting quite emotional.

Dai Woodham, who owned the yard, never scrapped any of these locomotives and by the late eighties every one of them had been saved for preservation.

Monday 4th April 1977

My brother called round for a chat on his way to an audition, I said that when he got back we should meet at Mum and Dad's as Lynne and I were going to tell them that we were getting engaged. That evening we cracked open a bottle of champagne to celebrate and Nigel had barely got the glass to his lips when the phone rang with a call that would change his life. It was former Octopus drummer Malcolm Green who had recently joined New Zealand band Split Enz, led by Tim Finn. Guitarist Phil Judd and bassist Mike Chunn had both left the group and Malcolm had recommended Nigel for the bass player's job, and so he headed straight off for an audition in north London. They spent the night jamming together, Tim Finn asked him to come back the following day and he was in.

They had been auditioning lead guitarists and getting nowhere so Tim contacted his brother Neil Finn in New Zealand. Three days later (7/4/1977) Neil arrived in the UK and the new line up for Split Enz was complete. They were scheduled to make their debut in just over three weeks time on 29th April at one of the old Octopus gigs, St.Albans City Hall.

Tuesday 5th April 1977

I have already mentioned my preference for travelling on smaller planes. Today Guys n'

Dolls had to travel to Dublin for a TV show and fly back the same day in an eight seater plane. Arriving at Stanstead Airport we were confronted by a plane which looked as if it been borrowed from a museum, and a rather scruffy looking pilot. We boarded the plane which began to taxi ready for take off, when someone noticed the back door wasn't shut. The pilot stopped the plane and with some difficulty closed the door. We reached the end of the runway when the pilot had a message to say that the case containing our stage clothes hadn't been put on the plane and was still on the ground where the plane had been parked. The pilot cursed under his breath and we went back for the case. The plane eventually took off and seemed to be travelling quite low and very slowly, when we crossed the Welsh mountains seemed to struggle to climb over them. I felt sure there was something wrong and for some bizarre reason started to sing Buddy Holly songs in my head. The journey home was just as bad and at one point I saw sparks coming out of one of the engines, but thank god we got back, safe, but scared stiff.

Wednesday 6th April 1977

Brian asked Dominic and I to come to the office for a meeting. There had been a bad vibe in the group for some time with ridiculous rows over the direction the group should be taking, and most of the negative feeling was coming from David and Thereze. We seriously discussed that in the best interests of the group, on and off the stage, they should be sacked. They were vocally the weakest members and David still had problems singing harmony parts. Although nothing else happened at this time it was the beginning of the end of Guys n' Dolls as a six piece.

Saturday 9th April 1977

Liverpool striker Dave Johnson with his wife Carol

A few weeks ago Guys n' Dolls had visited a fan who was seriously ill in Alder Hay children's hospital in Liverpool. I met a guy called Ken Head who did the commentary for Hospital Radio at the Liverpool games and he invited me to join him in the commentary box for a match.

I arrived in Liverpool and went to Ken's house which was only two hundred yards from the ground. We walked to the ground and first he took me into Anfield's press room and showed me where all the newspaper reporters sit watching the game with phones in front of them ready to send in their match reports. Who should we find in there, but Bill Shankly holding court to a group of press guys and talking about, what else, football. I stopped to listen and it was obvious that Shanks had lost none of his passion for the game, although he looked a bit of a solitary figure.

We made our way to the commentary box which was quite an ordeal. First we climbed some stairs which were like a fire escape at the side of the main stand. These lead to the roof, we then crossed inside the roof to a ladder which dropped down to the gantry that hung under the main stand and where the TV cameras and commentators were situated. The view of the pitch was incredible, we were in a little booth and beside us was Brian Moore getting ready to give the commentary for ITV Sport.

It was an easy 2-1 win for Liverpool against Manchester City and I was asked to comment throughout the game and thoroughly enjoyed myself. It was looking as if Liverpool were in a strong position to win the title again, and they were still in the FA and European cups. I found David Johnson after the match and arranged for him and his wife Carol to come to our show that evening in nearby New Brighton. Dave promised me a ticket if Liverpool reached the FA Cup final.

Wednesday 13th April - Thursday 21st April 1977

Electrola, our German record label had arranged an intense eight day promotion trip which included three television appearances. There was a bit of a tug of war between Germany and Holland and on the Monday our Dutch record company sent over a private jet, (I thought that was pretty cool) and whisked us off to Holland for the day to appear on a TV show called Disco Circus. "You're my world" had by now reached number sixteen in Holland.

Despite the best efforts of Electrola Guys n' Dolls never had a hit in Germany.

Friday 22nd April 1977

Lynne and I had been together nearly eighteen months and in that time, due to the constant demands of Guys n' Dolls, I hadn't seen that much of her. The group had decided to have a week off starting this Sunday. We all planned to go away and I was to have my first holiday with Lynne in Majorca. Today Brian told me that he had arranged a very lucrative booking next Friday at the Inter Continental Hotel in London and I would have to come home two days early.

I don't think in general I caused Brian too many problems, but when he told me about cutting short the holiday I went ballistic and basically said I wasn't prepared to do it. We had a rather heated discussion and did not part on the best of terms.

Looking back with the benefit of hindsight I can see Brian's dilemma in wanting us to do the gig. Guys n' Dolls was a business and fees we earned from gigs were a major part of our income. Every week there was a wage bill of fourteen people to pay, there were the six members of Guys n' Dolls, our own four piece band, two roadies, a manager and an agent. Our record sales had been fair but we hadn't cracked the main overseas markets of Germany, America and Japan where the big money was. Each year we received an advance from Magnet records that had to be recouped before we could be in profit. The income from TV appearances was small, an appearance on Top of the Pops earned the group £150 before management and agent's commissions were deducted, and when we went abroad for promotional trips any fees would be eaten up by the expenses.

There is a misconception with the public that anybody seen on television must be earning a fortune, the reality is somewhat different. Today there is more money to be made, merchandising and sponsorship plays a much bigger part than it did in the seventies.

Sunday 24th April – Sunday 1st May 1977

Lynne and I spent a relaxing week in Majorca staying with the Haywoods, my friends from the Octopus days. By coincidence David and Thereze were also on the island staying nearby, and we decided to have a day out together. We hired a sailing boat and loaded it up with food and drink and sailed along the coast stopping at a remote beach. Despite the fact that there was an obvious divide in the group with David and Thereze on one side, we spent a very enjoyable day together.

David and Thereze went home early to do the disputed gig in London on the Friday. I stubbornly remained in Majorca and the group performed as a five piece without me.

Monday 2nd May 1977

We had been booked for two weeks at London's supposedly prestigious Talk of the Town nightclub, and it wasn't a pleasant experience. There was a complete cabaret show with Guys n' Dolls performing their normal act at the end. The show was produced by a guy called Robert Nesbit who drove us and our band crazy by subjecting us to hours of rehearsal, going through each song line by line to set the lighting, it was purgatory. The whole place seemed to be living in the past.

Tuesday 3rd May 1977

When we arrived at the Talk of the Town this evening Robert Nesbit wanted to see me. I was now doing most of the talking between numbers during the act, including a couple of jokes. Robert Nesbit thought one of my jokes was too rude for Talk of the Town and wanted me to change it. The joke in question, if you can call it a joke, was when I introduced David by saying, "David comes from Brighton. Actually he's from Hove which is the posh part of Brighton where the seagulls fly upside down". That was it, quite disgusting really.

Wednesday 4th May 1977

Last night we'd had problems with The Talk of the Town's so called "state of the art" sound system, so this afternoon we went in to try and sort things out. While were there, despite the fact I had dropped the 'filthy' pigeon joke, Robert Nesbit said he still wasn't happy with some of my on stage chat, and now he was seriously pissing me off.

Thursday 5th May 1977

Not much sleep as we had an early flight from Heathrow to Cologne for a daytime television show. Our record company were still trying hard to make "You're my World" a hit in Germany.

This evening's show at the Talk of the Town went OK. The sound was better and there was no sign of Robert Nesbit waiting to pounce on me after the show.

Magnet records boss Michael Levy came to see us tonight accompanied by a dozen Israeli war widows, whose holiday he had personally sponsored. We were in our dressing room after the show when Michael knocked on the door. He said "David, Thereze and Martine could you come outside for a minute". Julie, Dominic and I remained in the dressing room, intrigued. A short while later we could hear the strains of Hava Nagila being sung outside our dressing room by Michael Levy, twelve Israeli war widows and the Jewish half of Guys n' Dolls. The three gentiles of the group burst out laughing. Michael had got it slightly wrong as Martine was not strictly Jewish.

Saturday 7th May 1977

Today I celebrated my engagement to Lynne in the most romantic way possible. I took her to see Liverpool play Queens Park Rangers at Loftus Road. Liverpool only needed a win to become First Division champions, but could only manage a 0-0 draw so they still needed a point. We bumped into Elton Welsby, a TV commentator that I knew slightly, and he took us to the after match press conference. It was great to be there but a bit of a dull affair as Bob Paisley and the QPR manager Dave Sexton were not the most eloquent talkers.

Julie's Dad and his wife Anthea Redfearn came to this evenings show, and Brian bought some champagne for a bit of a celebration.

Monday 9th May 1977

After the abject failure, in the UK, of our last single "You're My World" Michael Levy resorted to some desperate measures for our next release. The now infamous Jonathan King had suggested that Guys n' Dolls record a song called "Mamacita", which was totally different from anything we had recorded before and quite frankly, crap. This wasn't just my opinion it was unanimous. It was in the style of Una Paloma Blanca and Levy was totally sold on the song which we all thought sounded like "Rupert the Bear".

We went along to meet Jonathan King who appeared quite arrogant, he began by telling us that he thought that most artists were c--ts, and the conversation went downhill from there. He told us to learn the song as we would be recording it on Thursday.

We were into the second week at Talk of the Town and none of us were enjoying it much. The audiences consisted of large parties of foreign visitors the majority of whom didn't know who we were, or care very much. There was a lot of petty officialdom back stage mostly by my new best friend Robert Nesbit, who by now had been christened the Prince of Darkness, and we couldn't wait for this week to be over.

Thursday 12th May 1977

The big day had come, our recording session with Jonathan King. Dominic had learned the lead vocal to Mamacita, but when we got there King wanted all the boys to try it, and I had barely listened to it. The three of us had a go and our illustrious producer in his infinite wisdom decided that I was the best one to sing it, which considering it was such an awful song was a back handed compliment.

The backing track was played and I sang the song thinking that I would be allowed a couple of run throughs before we recorded it properly. When the track finished Jonathan King said that's fine now we'll double track it. I couldn't believe it, we ran through the song again I double tracked my voice, and that was that, it had taken ten minutes. The whole group then went into the studio to record the harmony parts and in the end the whole session had lasted less than an hour. We left the studio with Jonathan King saying "Who's had more hits, Rupert the Bear or me".

Saturday 14th May 1977

It was our last day at Talk of the Town and a busy one. We boarded another small plane at Leavesden airfield near Watford, flew to Holland for a children's television show and on arrival were informed that our single "You're My World" had just reached number one in the Dutch charts, which was great news. We returned to the UK and the day got even better, Liverpool had drawn 0-0 at home to West Ham and were league champions once again, and next Saturday was the FA Cup Final followed four days later by the European Cup Final.

The day finished on a bit of a low note as our last show at Talk of the Town was not good and we couldn't get out of the place fast enough.

Sunday 15th May 1977

An early photo of
Split Enz with
Nigel doing the
monkey
impersonation at
the front.

*(Picture courtesy of Split
Enz archive)*

Nigel had been a member of Split Enz for just over a month and today they were playing quite a prestigious gig at London's Victoria Palace theatre so I took Mum and Dad along to see them. I really enjoyed the gig and was quite surprised that my brother was now on stage dressed in a strange costume with bizarre make up, some would say a bit like Guys n' Dolls.

Thursday 19th May 1977

This week we were in Dublin and someone suggested we go fishing, so Dominic, Ivor and I bought some basic gear and went to a place called Blessington Lakes. We managed to catch a few roach and perch and if you'll pardon the pun, we were hooked. Fishing would become almost an obsession with Dominic and me when we were on the road with the group.

Saturday 21st May 1977

It was cup final day, Dave Johnson had sent me a ticket and the plan was to get me to the match and back to Dublin for the evening show. I caught a plane from Dublin to London and a friend of our manager, a guy called Steve, met me at Heathrow and dropped me off at the ground. It was my first ever Cup Final and the atmosphere was great, I was sitting with wives and friends of the team, but as always at the old Wembley Stadium you seemed to be a long way from the action because of the running track which went round the outside of the pitch. It was a good game but the wrong result as Manchester United beat Liverpool 2-1.

After the match I walked about a mile to a predetermined spot, to avoid the crowds, and met Steve who rushed me back to Heathrow for the Dublin flight. Everything went to plan and I made it to the show feeling rather deflated as we had lost.

Wednesday 25th May 1977

We were in the middle of a week performing at one of our favourite clubs, the Fiesta in Stockton on Tees. Before this evening's show I saw Liverpool beat Borussia Munchengladbach 3-1 in Rome to lift the European Cup for the first time in their history. A great night and when it came to our encore at the show, I went back on stage wearing a Liverpool strip.

Saturday 4th June 1977

Last night we had performed at a restaurant in Braintree in Essex. After the gig there was a huge row, with David and Thereze having a real go at Brian saying we shouldn't be playing places like this and it all got rather nasty. I left them to it and drove home.

Brian phoned me this morning to say that David and Thereze wanted him sacked. I wrote in my diary that unless something drastic happens the group might as well break up. It had been over a year since we had our last hit record added to the fact that the cabaret scene where most of our work came from was in decline. We had begun to notice that in some clubs, where previously we had performed for a whole week, they were now cutting back and only opening for a few days. We had to work to survive and maybe we would have to play places that we wouldn't have considered a year ago.

Wednesday 8th June 1977

Our turbulent recording situation had taken another turn, the Jonathan King episode was fortunately a one off and Magnet records had decided that our next album would be produced by Ben Findon and Mike Myers. Today we went to Ben's house to meet them for the first time and to hear some of their material. Julie Dominic and I went for a drink afterwards and the three of us agreed that David and Thereze were causing far too many problems and for the sake of the group should be sacked.

Thursday 9th June 1977

Away from all the trials and tribulations of Guys n' Dolls, I spent a rare and enjoyable day with Lynne. We went for a meal and then on to the Thames embankment where we watched the Queens Silver Jubilee river procession and firework display. We could see the Queen watching on the other side of the river, and I found it hard to believe it was twenty five years since I watched her coronation on Dad's home made television.

Tuesday 21st June 1977

"You're My World" had become a huge hit in Holland, it had remained at number one in the charts for three weeks and would remain in the top forty for a total of fourteen weeks making it the biggest selling Dutch single of the year. Because of this success our first two albums had been re-released and were selling well.

We should have flown to Holland last night but I was at Lynne's parents in Abingdon and Brian couldn't contact me, so this morning we boarded another small plane at Luton and made a mad dash to Holland for another appearance on Top Pop. It was then on to the north of Holland for a strange TV show where we sang on a raft in the middle of a lake. Over the next few years we would perform in many odd circumstances for Dutch television.

Tuesday 28th June 1977

Every year the BBC entered a programme for the Knockke (Belgium) television festival and this year Guys n' Dolls had been invited to take part in the BBC entry along side Rolf Harris and Bonnie Tyler. The boys were to be dressed as Musketeers and the girls as wenches, so today we had been to Burmans and Nathans, the film and television costumiers, to be fitted out.

It was then on to the BBC rehearsal studios at Acton. We rehearsed the show and had to do a couple of dance routines with the Nigel Lythgoe dancers which caused Dominic and me a few problems but Nigel was quite understanding and didn't make it too complicated.

Nigel Lythgoe is now the executive producer of "American Idol".

Sunday 3rd July – Tuesday 5th July 1977

We arrived in Knockke from Preston, where we had been performing, and went straight into more rehearsals, and found Rolf Harris in the studio painting one of his large murals for part of the scenery. It was only a half an hour show but there was a lot crammed into it. Rolf Harris was playing D'Artagnane with the Guys as his musketeers, Bonnie Tyler had been "Lost in France" (cue for her song) and had to be rescued by a stunt act with live horses in the studio, which was a bit dangerous but worked well. We sang the dreadful "Mamacita" in full costume and everyone lived happily ever after. It was an enjoyable few days and it was great to be working with Rolf Harris although he wouldn't stop making his strange mouth noises.

After the show I went for a walk on the beach with Dominic and Julie, we bumped into his holiness Cliff Richard with my old mate Tony Rivers. I hadn't seen Tony for years and now he was one of Cliff's backing vocalists and is credited with the vocal arrangement on the record "Miss You Nights". Cliff was appearing in concert the following evening.

Wednesday 6ᵗʰ July 1977

In four days time Guys n' Dolls would be a four piece group. David and Thereze have already been cut from this picture of the Hilversum presentation.

We drove from Knockke to Hilversum in Holland for a press conference and a presentation at Negram our record company. "You're My World" and our first two albums had achieved gold status and we were each presented with triple gold records.

In Holland a gold single is for sales of over 100,000 and a gold album 25,000.

Saturday 9ᵗʰ July 1977

The BBC were putting on a series of music shows called Pop at the Mill which were recorded on a special stage set up in the grounds of the Pebble Mill television studios in Birmingham. Tonight we appeared alongside Billy J. Kramer in front of an audience that included a lot of our fans.

We had a very loyal group of fans who would regularly turn up at our shows, dressed in the black and white that we always wore, sometimes travelling hundreds of miles to be there. One particular couple called Will and Phyl Taylor, were quite elderly but would think nothing of travelling all over the country from their home in Brigg, Lincolnshire to see our shows. Will was an undertaker who would regularly change from his sombre black work suit into a white suit and carnation when he came to see us, and was a bit of a character.

 Most of our fans were great and caused us no problems but we had a few whose sanity I would question.

Sunday 10ᵗʰ July 1977
Today's show at the Princess Theatre, Torquay was to be our last as a six piece group, but at the time we didn't know it. We were scheduled to perform two shows and after the first there was a huge row between Dominic and Martine, over what, I can't remember. We struggled through the second show with a horrible atmosphere, after which Martine stormed out saying that she was leaving the group. I can remember Thereze shrugging her shoulders and suggesting it wouldn't be a problem and the five of us could carry on. I had the feeling she thought she would be taking over Martine's role as the lead girl singer.

Monday 11ᵗʰ July 1977
I had returned home last night and this morning, phoned Brian and flippantly asked if he could find out what the future line up of Guys n' Dolls would be, and then went fishing. Brian phoned back later and asked me to come to the office for a meeting. After a long discussion it was concluded that the main problem in the group was the disruptive influence of David and Thereze and the only course of action was for them to be sacked immediately and the group, remain as a four piece.

Tuesday 12ᵗʰ July 1977
While Dominic, Julie, Martine and I were discussing our next album with Ben Findon and Mike Myers, Brian had called David and Thereze to the office. He bluntly told them that they were sacked and would take no further part in Guys n' Dolls activities. Obviously it came as a shock and they took it very badly, there was the added problem that Julie was sharing a flat with them. David and Thereze went back to the flat and threw all of Julie's belongings out on to the street. Fortunately Brian's assistant had followed them home and managed to gather up everything as it was hurtling out of the door. Brian phoned Julie and warned her not to return to the flat so she stayed with a friend for a while until she sorted out her own flat in Kilburn.

Tonight Guys n' Dolls were due to perform at Wembley Conference centre for the agent Michael Black, who was understandably nervous about the situation. We were a little concerned ourselves as we had never performed as a four piece, but we talked through the act and vocally there wasn't much to change. The show was fine and afterwards a smiling Michael Black came backstage and said he hadn't noticed any difference.

Friday 15th July 1977

Brian had agreed with David and Thereze that they could say they left the group of their own choice and today the following piece appeared in the press.

Singers David Van Day and Thereze Bazar have danced their way out of the top pop group Guys n'Dolls. Thereze 21 and 20 year old David are teaming up to write and produce records. "But there's no romance" they insisted.

The rest of the £5000-a-week song-and-dance group, are sticking together but will remain as a quartet.

David and Thereze have been with the chart-busting sextet since it was formed three years ago. They shot to fame with songs like "Theres a Whole Lot of Loving".

Said David, "We might even write them a hit record".

Saturday 23rd July 1977

Our first week's work as a four piece was at a venue called Bunny's Club in Cleethorpes. The week went well and there were no apparent repercussions on us being four instead of six, that was until Brian went to collect our fee. The management said they were withholding a percentage of our money and a heated discussion ensued culminating with Brian physically taking the cash that we were owed from a drawer in the manager's desk and leaving.

I suppose there may have been an argument for a possible reduction of the fee, but this should have been negotiated before the commencement of the engagement, not at the end. We never heard any more about this incident.

Sunday 31st July – Tuesday 2nd August

We were hoping the departure of David and Thereze would not affect the popularity we had built up in Holland which by now was exceeding the success we had achieved in the UK. Today we recorded our own Dutch TV special in the seaside town of Schreveningen. We were filmed at various locations in the town including the beach and the fairground and introduced the other acts on the show speaking in very bad Dutch. Our new single in Holland was "Mamacita", God help us.

Despite Michael Levy's faith in "Mamacita" it had completely bombed in the UK receiving hardly any radio plays and not charting at all. The lack of success was so richly deserved.

Sunday 14th August 1977

We were in the middle of recording what would be our third album and as usual I found the process boring to the extreme with the majority of the time hanging around for hours on end waiting to sing my part. One of my songs, "I Must Go Home Alone" was to be included and our producers Ben Findon and Mike Myers had allowed me artistic control of the session. We recorded the backing track and found that the session drummer that had been brought in was the jazz drummer Chris Karan featured regularly with Harry Stoneham's band on the Parkinson show, and who played with the Dudley Moore Trio. This worked well as the song had a bit of a "nightclub" feel to it.

We then recorded the vocals before working on the instrumental solo. One of the recent innovations in the music world was the voice box, this first came to prominence with Peter Frampton's song "Show me the Way", although many years ago a song called "Sparky's Magic Piano" used a similar principal. The sound from a guitar or keyboard is fed up a small plastic tube and into the players mouth. By opening and closing the mouth the sound changes and is picked up by a microphone, and if you mouth words you can distinguish what they are. There was a bit of a scare when they were first introduced, it was said that if the volume was too high it could make your teeth fall out.

I had built myself a voice box and after a bit of experimenting recorded the solo and urged on by the rest of the group mouthed out a tirade of abuse directed at Magnet records. Very childish, but satisfying and for anyone who would like to work out what I said, our records are still available today, in all good charity shops.

Tuesday 16th August 1977

Guys n' Dolls were in the middle of a two week mini summer season in Cleethorpes, playing in a small theatre at the end of the rather rickety looking pier. It seemed so precarious, arriving each night we were amazed it was still standing.

Tonight we returned to our rented house, to discover that Elvis Presley had died which, although I wasn't a big fan, still came as a shock. I phoned Lynne and broke the news to her as she was a fan. Ever since we met I had promised to take her to one of Elvis' shows in Las Vegas, now it was too late.

Despite our misgivings Cleethorpes pier is still standing and the theatre is now a modern nightclub.

Wednesday 14th September 1977

There were still a few years to go before the promotional video became common place, but Guys n' Dolls did make the occasional film clip for use abroad. Our new single was to be a ballad called "Let's Make Love" and ITN news studios had been hired by producer Mike Mansfield for this purpose. The idea was that there would be two couples Dominic with Martine, me with Julie, sitting at tables drinking champagne and being rather romantic. The unfortunate thing, or should that be fortunate, was that the champagne was real and I like champagne. After running through the song numerous times I was pissed and the final take shows me with glazed eyes virtually falling on Julie. I cringe when I see this today, we all have embarrassing moments and that is definitely one of mine.

Monday 19th September 1977

Brian had decided we needed our own publicist and today we went to meet him. He was actually a guy who shared an office with Brian but was destined for greater things. His name was Max Clifford.

Friday 23rd September 1977

This week we were appearing in Birmingham at the Night Out club but at lunchtime today we made one of our regular appearances on Pebble Mill at One, and now I was relaxing in my hotel room watching crappy afternoon television. Suddenly there was a knock on my door and a panicking Julie calling out "Paul! Karen's here".

The situation was that eighteen months ago Dominic had stopped his relationship with Julie and against advice from friends and family had married his long time girlfriend Karen. It was so obviously a wrong move and it wasn't long after the wedding that Dominic and Julie had resumed their relationship and because of the schedule with Guys n' Dolls he was hardly ever at home.

On hearing Julie at the door I panicked (Julie always says much more than her) and we began taking Julie's belongings out of the room they shared and into mine, expecting any moment to be confronted by Karen. We sat in my room and waited, eventually I went to see what was happening and could see Dominic and Karen deep in conversation at the bar. Eventually Dominic came upstairs, white faced, this morning Karen had phoned the hotel to speak to Dominic and the receptionist told her that he was with his wife so Karen came to sort things out. Now the marriage was over and she had gone home.

Something had to happen sooner or later and in the long run it was for the best. Thirty years on, one divorce, a marriage and two kids later, not necessarily in that order, Dominic and Julie are still together and remain my closest friends.

Wednesday 12th October – Thursday 20th October 1977

Arriving at Rotterdam at the beginning of our first tour of Holland and Belgium

We toured Holland and Belgium for the very first time playing six shows in large concert halls in the major cities and received a great reception from the audiences. One of the customs in Holland is for the audience to give flowers and each night our dressing room resembled a florist.

The Sunday Mirror sent over a reporter who followed us around for a couple of days and the following week there was a two page spread about Dominic and Julie's relationship.

Tuesday 1st November 1977

Guys n' Dolls were in the middle of a short UK tour and tonight played in my hometown of Hatfield, not only that but the Forum theatre was literally two hundred yards from my flat so I could walk there. It was great to see familiar faces in the audience including of course, Mum, Dad, Lynne and Nigel.

We appeared with a band called Flintlock that featured a guy called Mike Holloway. Mike was currently appearing in a long running children's television programme called The Tomorrow People and was a bit of a heart throb with young girls. This meant the audiences on the tour were a bit disparate, with very young girls screaming at Flintlock and an older audience who had come to see us.

Love Affair were also on the bill, but there wasn't one original member left from the line-up that had four top ten hits in the late sixties, including the number one, "Everlasting Love". They were, however, managed by Mo Bacon, the original drummer, who now owned the name. Today there are many sixties and seventies chart groups doing the rounds with very few, if any, original members and mostly the audiences don't seem to notice or care.

Friday 25th November 1977
We were back in Holland for a charity telethon in The Hague which lasted a marathon five and a half hours. Included in the line-up were, jazz pianist Oscar Peterson, Manhatten Transfer, fifties crooner Johnnie Ray and Don Maclean who performed an amazing live version of "Vincent". Queen Juliana and Prince Bernhardt were in the audience for part of the show but quite understandably, didn't stay for the whole evening.

All the artists were staying at the same hotel and after the show we were treated to an impromptu performance by Oscar Peterson in the bar.

Tuesday 6th – Tuesday 13th December 1977

A few months ago a group of Thai businessmen had come to see us with a view to us undertaking a tour of Thailand. I had never travelled outside of Europe but today we were off to the Far East. We flew Thai Air and at that time they had no wide bodied jets, so we travelled, for the sixteen hour journey, in a rather small and uncomfortable DC8 aircraft.

In the last few months the promoters had done a great job promoting the group and we arrived at Bangkok airport to be mobbed by a crowd of around three hundred people, mainly girls, and given many garlands of flowers.

The first two days were quite relaxing, sight seeing, spending a lot of time around the hotel pool and doing some promotional work for the sponsors of the tour. We performed a total of six shows in large ballrooms at three different hotels, they were all sold out and the audiences were amazing, knowing the words and singing along to most of our songs.

The music business in Thailand was almost entirely a bootleg industry; any top album could be bought for less than one pound on unauthorized cassettes. There was no vinyl and CDs were still a thing of the future. Although a lot of our product was sold in Thailand we never received one penny in royalties.

One of the habits I had developed since joining Guys n' Dolls was collecting hotel keys. This probably started out with me genuinely forgetting to hand in my key but developed into a hobby. We had checked into the Indra Regent Hotel and when I saw the key thought it would be the centrepiece of my collection. The key ring was in the shape of a temple, embossed with elephants, and made of brass. On checking out I put the key in my bag, but as our car was about to draw away from the hotel, a receptionist came running out calling "Mr. Gliggs, Mr Gliggs you haven't handed in your key." I pretended to look in my bag and said "no I don't seem to have it". She persisted and I thought I would have to back down when she suggested I should unload my case and check. Dominic was getting a little edgy saying "Griggsy, I don't think you'll get away with this one", but I managed it and we all drove off to the airport along with my illegal contraband.

It had been a great trip and this was the first of four visits we would make to Thailand.

Thursday 15ᵗʰ December 1977
I took Lynne back to the place where I first met her, it's name had changed from Nero's to the Music Machine and had more of a disco feel than a nightclub. We saw Mud for the first time in quite a while and thought their act was excellent and it was the best I'd seen them play. They were having a crisis with their recording career as it had been over a year since their last hit "Lean on Me" and this in fact was their last ever hit.

Monday 19ᵗʰ December – Saturday 24ᵗʰ December 1977
After the trip to Thailand it was down to earth with a crash as we played a depressing week of shows at a place called the Roxy in Harlesden north London. The Roxy was a converted cinema and we were appearing with Eurovision Song Contest winner Dana, and DJ (diddy) David Hamilton.

There were only about fifty to a hundred people in each night in a venue that held around a thousand. There was a balcony which most nights was completely empty but one night I noticed two people looking rather lost up there so I announced "tonight in the balcony we are pleased to welcome the entire Tony Blackburn fan club." This was mostly for the benefit of David Hamilton who enjoyed a friendly rivalry with Tony.

Saturday 31st December 1977

This year we were able to have Christmas and New Year completely off and reflect on a year with a major change, the group now two thirds of its original size but with a much improved atmosphere. We didn't have a hit record during 1977 and Magnet seemed to have no idea which direction to take having put us with three different sets of producers, giving us no real continuity in the studio.

1978

Thursday 5th January 1978

Number one in the charts this first week of 1978 was Paul McCartney and Wings with "Mull of Kintyre" which was in the middle of an eight week spell at the top. Number two was "The Floral Dance" by the Brighouse and Rastrick Brass Band" and at number three "How Deep is Your Love" by the Bee Gees. At number twenty, on the way down from being a number three hit was "Rocking All Over The World" by Status Quo. I loved "Quo" and it wouldn't be long before I would persuade Guys n' Dolls that this would be a great song to close the act, and it would remain our closing song for the rest of the group's existence.

Today we had a meeting with Michael Levy at Magnet records who told us that despite the success we'd enjoyed in Holland, we were still quite heavily in debt to them due to disappointing UK record sales last year. We then had a meeting with our accountant who said that we were spending more than we were earning and would have to find ways of cutting our expenses. It was decided that we would have to stay in more economical places when we were on the road and unfortunately would have to get rid of Ivor, our first roadie. We had two roadies and because Ivor wasn't familiar with our PA system and sound balancing he had to be the one to go. It was very sad as he had been with us from the beginning and was a good guy.

Thursday 12th January 1978

Tony Hiller had produced and co-written "Save Your Kisses For Me" for Brotherhood of Man which had won the Eurovision Song Contest in 1976, the group were about to topple "Mull of Kintyre" from the number one spot with their latest release "Figaro". Michael Levy had decided that Tony should produce Guys n' Dolls and today we had a meeting with him when he played us a very dreary song called "People Over the World". This was another, 'lets all live together peacefully', sort of lyric, and had been chosen as our next potential single.

Tuesday 17th January – Friday 20th 1978

We flew to Zurich where we appeared as guests on a TV programme that was choosing the Swiss entry for the next Eurovision Song Contest. It was then on to Paris where we appeared in a strange French variety show, which lasted for two hours. The acts sat around tables in a night club setting and then got up and sang. We were on early and then had to sit through the rest of the show which seemed endless; it finally finished with the camera panning around focussing on all of the acts that had appeared. There was a marvellous close up of Julie ---- fast asleep.

Saturday 4th February 1978

It was a quick return to Paris as our French record company were keen to promote our single "Let's Make Love" and had booked us to record two important television shows in one day.

We had arrived in Paris last night but this morning when we reached the television station, found that there had been a sudden industrial strike by technicians and both shows were called off. There was nothing we could do except catch the next flight home. The shows were never re-scheduled, and as France was a difficult market to penetrate, with timing being essential when promoting a record, we lost the momentum that we were trying to achieve.

Monday 27th February 1978

Fortunately the Tony Hiller track "People over the World", suggested as our next single, had been tried, tested and dismissed as unsuitable. We had a meeting with Michael Levy, and Brian our manager suggested that we had a go at producing ourselves. Brian had found a couple of songs and as we had an excellent arranger in Ray Monk, plus a great band, we felt able to handle this. Michael wasn't convinced, and had a look on his face that suggested the lunatics wanted to take over the asylum. He came up with a compromise; we could go in the studio and co-produce with a new producer called Pete Smith, and to this we agreed, after all there were four of us and only one of him.

There was currently an advertising campaign for OXO cubes featuring a song called "Only Oxo Does It" and obviously we couldn't sing these lyrics as the blatant advertising meant it would never be played. Brian suggested changing it to "Only Loving Does It" and as the advert was heard every night the tune would be in everyone's head. That was the theory anyway. Brian had also found a great song called "You and I" written by a composer I admired, Albert Hammond.

This evening we were in Roundhouse studio in Chalk Farm to record the backing tracks for both songs. We all worked well together; I enjoyed being part of the creative process again and even got to play the lead guitar solo on "Only Loving Does It".

Wednesday 1st March 1978

Today we went back to the studios to lay down vocals for the two new tracks and also to record the B side. This was a song of mine called "Starlight Starbright" and as it only needed acoustic guitar and bass, I dragged Nigel along, on a rare day off from Split Enz, and the two of us recorded the backing track. It was the first time we had played together for four years.

Saturday 11th March 1978

Millwall were playing at home in the FA Cup to first division Ipswich Town, Dominic being a huge Millwall fan had agreed to sponsor the match ball and had been invited to sit in the directors box at the Den, he went along with Julie and our manager Brian Longley. It turned into a nightmare as Millwall lost the match 1-6, fighting broke out amongst rival fans, and Brian was hit in the back with a meat pie which ruined his leather coat. Dominic was supposed to receive the match ball as a souvenir but after the match it couldn't be found.

Wednesday 12th April 1978

This week Guys n' Dolls should have been appearing at a club called Fagins in Manchester, unfortunately Dominic and Martine were both ill and so the whole week had to be cancelled.

Liverpool were again in the semi final of the European Cup and had lost the first leg away to Borussia Munchengladbach 2-1. Tonight was the second leg at Anfield and Dave Johnson had invited Lynne and I to stay at his house for a couple of days and to go and see the match. Dave wasn't playing as he had a serious leg injury that would require surgery after scoring the away goal in the first leg. We went to the match and it was an easy win for Liverpool 3-0 so they were in the European Cup Final again. This year it was to be held at Wembley and Dave had promised me a ticket.

Friday 14th April 1978

Dominic and Martine had recovered sufficiently for us to make another promotional trip to Holland for a television show. We were walking down a corridor in the Hilversum TV studios when someone leapt on my back; it was Paul Green the guy I worked with in Hammonds Music shop in 1972. He was now a member of Suzi Quatro's band who were also on the show, along with Mud, so it was a bit of a meeting of old friends.

Thursday 20th April 1978

It was now two years since Guys n' Dolls had split with Ammo productions but the prospect of a court case with them was still rumbling away in the background. Our solicitor had suggested that we should have an informal chat with them to see if it could be settled out of court and I had been the one elected to have a meeting alone with Geoff Morrow.

I met Geoff at the Dorchester hotel in London and at first it was a bit awkward but we settled down and talked for around half an hour. We didn't really achieve much but I came away with the distinct impression that he was reluctant for the whole thing to end up in court.

Tuesday 2nd May 1978

My unused ticket for the European Cup Final. The cost, £10 and that included a meal.

Our record "Only Loving Does It" had been released a couple of weeks ago and today climbed to 53 in the charts. We thought we might get an appearance on Top of the Pops, but unfortunately the answer was, possibly next week, which I prayed wouldn't happen as I had a ticket for the European Cup Final at Wembley on that day.

Tuesday 9th May 1978

The unthinkable has happened, despite the record dropping to 60 in the chart, we are booked to appear on this week's Top of the Pops which is recorded tomorrow night starting at 7.30pm. The European Cup final at Wembley, which is only a couple of miles from the BBC studio, kicks off at 7.15pm, my ticket was for seat in a private box that entitled me to a pre match meal.

I naturally had a wobbly and told Brian that the rest of the group could do the programme without me. This was impossible, common sense prevailed, and I knew I would have to miss the match.

Wednesday 10th May 1978

Trying to play the solo. Good job you can't see my face; and so say all of us.

I gave the twin towers of Wembley a mournful look as we passed close by before arriving at the BBC television studios. It was a live performance of "Only Loving Does It" with the Top of the Pops orchestra with the added problem of me playing the guitar solo. The orchestra was about twenty five yards away from us on the other side of the studio. We had to hear them through a small, ancient speaker in a grey box that was wheeled around the studio acting as a monitor so that artists could hear either the playback of the track or as in our case the orchestra. Another difficulty was that the guitarist in the band was playing a harmony line on top of what I was playing.

I wanted to see as much of the European cup final as possible. This was being shown on ITV and I was at the BBC, but eventually found a TV in reception showing the game. I watched about thirty minutes before we had our call to perform. We now had a noisy studio audience and it was even harder to hear the orchestra, but we managed to get through and there was a close up of me with my face contorted in concentration, trying to synchronise my guitar playing with the distant guitarist.

When we had finished I went back to the television and found that Kenny Dalglish had already scored what would be the only goal of the match and Liverpool went on to beat Bruges and win the European cup for the second year in a row.

After Top of the Pops finished I collected Lynne and went to the Holiday Inn at Swiss Cottage where the Liverpool team were staying. I met Dave Johnson who hobbled in on crutches and shortly after, the team arrived carrying the European cup. They had a celebration banquet which was attended by all the team, their wives and officials and some of the Liverpool players from the past, but my abiding memory was of Bill Shankly looking immaculate in his suit, red shirt, tie, and a pair of slippers.

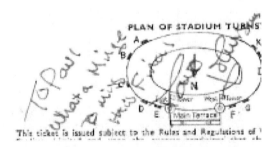

Dave Johnson signed my unused ticket and wrote "What a Minge to miss this final".

Tuesday 23rd May 1978

Our record "Only Loving Does It" today reached 42 in the charts, which would be its highest position and our last chart entry in the UK.

Friday 9th June 1978

We were performing more one nighters than a couple of years ago and this was due to the decline of the cabaret club scene in the UK. Today Guys n' Dolls and their band were flown in two small planes by the RAF from their bass in Northwood to Wildenwrath in West Germany for a show. They had removed all of their fighter planes from one of the hangers and erected a large stage, we performed in front of 3,000 people and it was a great night.

Sunday 16th July 1978

In the middle of our performance at a theatre in Paignton we noticed the audience had started to laugh, and natural instinct, I immediately checked my flies, all OK so what was it? I turned round and discovered that Freddie Starr had come on stage dressed as Elvis, picked up my guitar and was standing there, straight faced, as if he was a member of our band. He was in the middle of a summer season nearby and we hadn't seen him since the tour of 1976. It was good to catch up; we planned to see his show the following night.

Monday 24th July 1978

Dominic had come up with the idea for recording "Something's Got a Hold of my Heart", originally recorded by Gene Pitney. A few days a go we had recorded the backing track with our band and tonight it was time for the b side which was a song of mine called "Son Caliu". This was the name of the house in Majorca belonging to my friends the Haywoods. I recorded the track with the Split Enz rhythm section, Nigel and Malcolm Green with me on guitar which was also three quarters of the Octopus line up. Both tracks came out well and this was the first time we had been in the studio producing completely on our own.

Tuesday 22nd August 1978

Ever since 1975 there had been talk of Guys n' Dolls appearing with Frank Sinatra, and a few weeks ago it had been confirmed that this would finally happen in September when he was due to perform for six nights at the Royal Festival Hall in London. We would be a support act along with our dear 'friend' Lennie Bennett who had now teamed up with comedian Jerry Stevens as a double act. Today there were final fittings for the new costumes we planned to wear for the shows.

Tuesday 5th September 1978

The Eurovision Song Contest was often considered as a possible vehicle for resurrecting a flagging recording career and this year, much to our dismay, Michael Levy had this in mind for Guys n' Dolls. Today we were back in the studio with Ben Findon and Mike Myers recording their overly dramatic ballad "How Do You Mend a Broken Heart". The idea was that this would be entered into "A Song for Europe", and hopefully reach the final twelve from which the British entry would be chosen. We had also heard that a song we had recorded a few months ago called "The Same Old Way" had been selected for the final of the Yamaha International Song Festival and we would be off to Japan for the finals in November.

Friday 8th September 1978

Our shows with Frank Sinatra were to begin this coming Monday and today we had to attend a rehearsal at the Royal Festival Hall. Appearing with Sinatra was something I had been looking forward to, although I wasn't particularly a fan he was probably the biggest star in the world at that time. Frank Sinatra stories were legendary, he was allegedly a difficult man to work with, he hated the press and there were all sorts of allegations of Mafia connections so it was with a mixture of anticipation and trepidation that we approached the shows.

Sinatra had come and gone when we arrived and already there had been some sort of back stage disagreement. We rehearsed with our band augmented with most of Sinatra's orchestra and it seemed to go OK but the Festival Hall itself was a rather stark soulless sort of building, lacking in atmosphere. Passes were issued to everyone in our party and we were told that without them we would not be allowed in.

Saturday 9th September 1978

We all went to see Martine marry Freddie Starr's drummer Michael Richardson at Beaconsfield registry office, followed by a party held in a marquee at her parent's house in Bushey near Watford.

Monday 11th September 1978

I was allowed to take this picture of Sinatra. This is the view we had of his shows from the side of the stage.

This afternoon we had a final rehearsal at the Royal Festival Hall in preparation for the opening night with Sinatra of whom there was no sign.

I wasn't one for being nervous but tonight was different; we opened the show and performed for about thirty minutes followed by Lennie Bennett and Jerry Stevens before an intermission. There were no wings at the Royal Festival Hall just a room at the side of the stage, and although there were quite strong security measures in force we were allowed to stay in this room to watch the show. Suddenly he was there, Frank Sinatra walked in accompanied by two personal bodyguards and as he walked passed us, turned and said, "Hi kids I'm Frank". I resisted the urge to say "Frank who?" and we sat there mesmerised. There was no announcement he just walked on stage to a tumultuous reception and went straight into his opening song "Night and Day". He performed nineteen songs before coming off stage, getting straight into his limousine and disappearing into the night.

One of Sinatra's body guards who stayed in the room with us during the performances was a guy called Jilly Rizzo who had originally owned a restaurant in New York called Rizzo's, which Frank Sinatra and the rat pack used to frequent. He was a man of few words, looked mean and was almost as wide as he was tall and had reportedly roughed up a few press photographers over the years. Jilly was a lifelong friend of Sinatra's and was killed in a road accident in 1995.

Tuesday 12th September 1978

After our spot this evening Dominic needed the toilet and unfortunately emerged from the men's room the same time as Frank Sinatra was walking past on his way to the stage with his bodyguards. Obviously they needed a clear path for Frank, and Dominic must have posed a major security threat so the two bodyguards picked him up and threw him back into the men's room. There was a lot of testosterone flowing that week.

Wednesday 13th September 1978

Today we had two shows; Julie's Dad attended the second one and had asked to meet Frank Sinatra. Despite Bruce Forsyth being one of our best loved performers this was not easy, but Julie managed to arrange for her Dad to meet Sinatra just before he went on stage. They met but the meeting was brief, Sinatra shook hands with Bruce and said "Hello sir, pleased to meet you I've heard a lot about you", he seemed to live in his own remote world, reluctant to talk much to anyone outside his close circle. We sat watching the show every night and apart from the brief greeting on the opening night he would walk past us without saying a word.

Thursday 14th September 1978

The whole week of Sinatra concerts had been sold out for months and tickets were going for silly money on the black market. Tonight when we took to the stage I had to smile when I noticed that sitting in an aisle seat in the middle of the front row, probably the best seat in the house, was Stan Flashman the well known ticket tout. Almost every night there would be familiar faces in the audience, and also sitting in the front row this evening, was world cup winning captain, Bobby Moore.

Tonight Julie narrowly escaped a potentially unpleasant situation. One of the security guys, not Sinatra's, told Julie that she was wanted on the phone and led her to a room. She went in followed by the guy and as she picked up the phone heard the door being locked. There was nobody on the phone and it was obvious by now that this guy's intentions were less than honourable. Just as Julie realised what was going on there was a knock on the door. It was Dominic who had followed suspecting all was not as it seemed. Julie just said "they must have hung up" and hurriedly left the room. As there was no harm done Julie decided not to take the matter any further.

Friday 15th September 1978

Every night in the middle of his act, Sinatra would light up a cigarette and chat to the audience for about five minutes. He would talk about his life, his films, every night it was different. Tonight he had a go at the press about not mentioning Guys n' Dolls (he called us the kids) in the reviews of the show.

When he had finished his chat he would walk over to the side of the stage where we were sitting and throw his unfinished cigarette away, and every night one of us would pick it up. I think Martine and Julie still have a few of these, and I wonder what price they would fetch on e.bay.

Saturday 16th September 1978

Our last day with Frank Sinatra and we performed two shows. His final song, which he admitted wasn't one of his favourites, was "My Way" and as he left the stage he agreed to have photos taken with us and although it looks as if we were all good friends there was once again very little communication.

On the whole it had been an enjoyable and eventful week and naturally one of the highlights of my career. Twelve years ago I was in a band supporting Cream with Eric Clapton and now I had supported Frank Sinatra, how diverse the business that is 'show' can be.

Wednesday 11th October 1978

Today we parted company with our manager Brian Longley after being together for over three years. The relationship had deteriorated somewhat over the last few months and in the end we parted by mutual consent. Our agent Alan Field took over managerial duties.

Wednesday 1st November 1978

It had been fifteen months since David Van Day and Thereze Bazar's departure from Guys n' Dolls, and we'd seen nothing of them during that time. We recently heard that they had signed to Carrerre Records under the name Dollar and were about to release their first record, "Shooting Star". This morning we were checking in at Heathrow airport on our way to a TV show in Dublin and spotted David and Thereze walking past a few yards from us. We saw them and they saw us but both parties pretended they hadn't.

Sunday 5th November - Monday 6th 1978

We were off to Tokyo for the Yamaha International Song Festival which featured artists from all over the world in a song contest a bit like Eurovision. There was a special Japan Airways flight with a section specifically for the contestants and their entourage. Alan Field came with us as our manager, along with our musical director Ray Monk, plus our song's co-writer Pete Smith, and Barry Johnson from Magnet records. Among others on the flight were Tina Charles, ex. Monkee, Micky Dolenz, who turned out to be a bit of a pain, and a vocal group called Original Cast which included our ex. manager and Julie's brother in law, David Martin. David as part of Ammo productions was still in the process of suing us for breach of contract.

We flew the polar route to Japan stopping for two hours in Anchorage, Alaska, the first time I had ever set foot in the USA. It was winter and the airport was surrounded by snow covered mountains and the scenery was amazing. We flew on to Tokyo arriving at 7.00pm their time and after checking in to the Grand Palace Hotel, went straight to bed.

Thursday 9th November 1978

Out and about in Tokyo

After a quiet first few days relaxing and sight seeing, today was the first rehearsal at the world famous Nippon Budokan Hall. The Beatles caused some controversy when they appeared at the Budokan in 1966 as it was then deemed to be too spiritual a building for pop music and was mainly used for sumo wrestling.

There were thirty six songs in total and the contest was to take place over three days, the first two days being semi finals followed by the Grand Final. Guys n' Dolls were in the first semi final, and this morning we were taken to the Budokan and before we could rehearse had to sit through orientation. The building was huge and held ten thousand people but there was a small area roped off and we were shepherded in with some of the organisers standing guard in case we tried to escape. The Japanese are a very precise race, everything had to be organised and timed to the second, the orientation consisted mostly of stating the obvious especially when they held up diagrams of how to hold and how not to hold a microphone; this raised a few smiles from the contestants, most of whom had been in the business for many years and had a pretty good idea how a microphone should be held.

This evening Yamaha held a reception for everyone involved in the contest, and most of the acts I had never heard of although many were big stars in their own countries. Apart from the aforementioned Tina Charles and Micky Dolenz, there was Astrud Gilberto best known for her 1964 hit "Girl From Ipanema" representing Brazil, Scott English who wrote "Mandy" for Barry Manilow was singing for the USA. Albert Hammond who had written the song "You and I" which we had recently recorded and Dick James the Beatles ex. music publisher who I had first met in the Octopus days were also in attendance.

Before becoming a music publisher Dick James had been a singer and was famous for singing the Robin Hood theme for the fifties television series. I had consumed a few drinks (as you do) and thought it would be a good idea to go up to him and ask him to sing a chorus of "Robin Hood". Embarrassingly I did this and amazingly he obliged.

Friday 10ᵗʰ - Saturday 11ᵗʰ November 1978

The semi finals were spread over two days and after all thirty six songs had been performed the judges had to reduce this number to sixteen for the grand final. Due to different styles, cultures and languages the songs were fairly disparate and I could not see how the songs could be judged one against the other. Our song was called "The Same Old Way" and had been co-written by Pete Smith and Peter Waterman, who at the time was working at Magnet Records and was still a few years away from the phenomenal success he would achieve as a producer.

Sunday 12ᵗʰ November 1978

On stage at the Budokan

Guys n' Dolls had reached the last sixteen and tonight was the grand final. It was quite nerve racking back stage; the Japanese efficiency meant that there always had to be four acts queuing at the side of the stage ready to perform. We entered the queue at number four and gradually moved up until it was our turn to take to the stage. This created tension and we were all nervous but the performance went well.

The prize giving was a rather strange affair as out of eighteen acts, eleven received prizes. Tina Charles won the grand prize with her song "Love Rocks", and there were various awards for outstanding songs and performances. Guys n' Dolls received an outstanding song award but as usual I didn't think the song was outstanding.

World Popular Song Festival in Tokyo '78

CERTIFICATE OF MERIT
having become friends through music

Idle Prize chosen by the girls

Guys'n'Dolls "Paul"

Dominic and I with Tina Charles	My Certificate for the "Idle Prize"

At the after show party there was another strange prize giving presentation where, for no apparent reason, some of the artists were presented with expensive cameras, and cassette players and Micky Dolenz was given a motor bike. These may have been enticements to get certain acts to attend the contest, we never did find out. Guys n' Dolls received four cardboard Japanese lanterns and we were not amused. Individually I was awarded the "Idol Prize", voted for by the girls, and was quite chuffed until I received the certificate which read "Idle Prize", and couldn't figure out if it was a misspelling or an astute piece of observation.

The master of ceremonies for the Yamaha Song Festival had been Kyu Sakamoto who in 1963 had reached number six in the UK charts with "Sukiyaki". He would be tragically killed in 1985 when the plane he was travelling on, a Japan Airlines Boeing 747, suffered a major structural failure and flew, out of control for thirty minutes before crashing into a mountain killing 505 of the 509 passengers, the worst single aircraft crash in aviation history.

Monday 13th – Thursday 23rd November1978

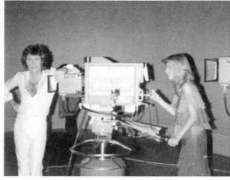

The contestants were packing up to go home and we said goodbye to some new found friends, and Micky Dolenz. Three days after the contest only Guys n' Dolls remained along with Barry Johnson from Magnet records. We had been asked to stay a further ten days by our record company Toshiba, to promote "The Same Old Way" which was being released as a single. Interviews for magazines were an integral part of Japanese promotion and everyday we had to endure numerous interviews, each of which seemed to last forever due to the need for an interpreter. Every interview began with the same two questions, "do you think you are like Abba?" (The biggest group in the world at that time.) and "can you explain the meaning of the lyrics to your song". The Japanese were always looking for deep, meaningful lyrics to songs, but I defy anyone to find anything deep or meaningful in:

> *Baby now I've found you gonna put my arms around you,*
> *In the same old way, in the same old way, hey hey hey.*

Apart from the interviews we made several appearances on local and national television. The guys from the record company looked after us well and on the 20th November took us all out to celebrate my thirty fourth birthday at a traditional Japanese restaurant. After ten days of constant promotion, answering the same questions every day, with hardly any time to ourselves, we were getting a little "stir crazy" and were ready for home.

**Pissed off in Tokyo.
(a severe case of
over-acting)**

On the day of our departure I managed to get away with the hotel key for my collection but we had a bit of a shock at the airport when it was found that we had an excess baggage bill of £400. Fortunately the record company, in a final gesture of kindness, sorted this out for us and we boarded the plane armed with souvenirs from the land of the rising sun, the cost of which far exceed the prize money from the contest, $500 US between the four of us.

Friday 24th November 1978
We arrived at Heathrow, glad to be back, very tired, and quite relieved that it was all over,

but it wasn't. There was a work to rule by the customs officers at the airport and everyone had to go through the red channel and have their luggage searched, it took us another three hours before we met up with friends and family. Lynne was there to meet me with Mum and Dad and when we got home Nigel came over, it was the first time I had seen him in ages.

Nigel had now been with Split Enz for eighteen months and was at present sharing a house in Radlett with drummer Malcolm Green and keyboard player Eddie Rayner, Neil Finn and percussionist Noel Crombie were in Chorley Wood and Tim Finn lived in North London. During his time with the band they had released two albums, "Dizrythmia" in 1977 and "Frenzy" in 1978. The first songs that made an impression on me were from "Dizrythmia" and I particularly liked "Charlie" and "My Mistake" both songs which Nigel first began learning at his Split Enz audition. I was quite envious of Nigel being part of a band in which he obviously enjoyed the music he was performing, it made me once again question why I was in a Guys n' Dolls.

Thursday 30th November 1978

Dollar's first single "Shooting Star" entered the charts at number twenty seven which gave us food for thought. It was more a production than performance record and David and Thereze's voices were double tracked and heavily processed with effects but I had to admit I thought it was OK.

Tonight we were playing a gig in Cardiff, but during our trip to Japan our roadie John had done a runner and completely vanished so there was nobody to take our gear to the gig. In the end our band managed to borrow some instruments and we struggled through.

Saturday 9th December 1978

I had just seen Liverpool beat Nottingham Forest 2-0 at Anfield and this evening Guys n' Dolls played their last night at the Hamilton club in Birkenhead with four of the Liverpool team in the audience. There was Dave Johnson, Phil Thompson, Steve Heighway and Ray Clemence along with future Liverpool manager Roy Evans, who at that time was managing the reserve team. It was a great night, we dragged Dave Johnson up on stage to sing with us and all went back to his house afterwards for a bit of a party before travelling home.

Tuesday 19th December 1978

I had a call from Michael Levy to say that we were in the final twelve for "A Song For Europe" to be held at the Royal Albert Hall in February, when the song to represent Great Britain in the Eurovision Song Contest would be selected. I think he expected me to be jumping around with joy but I wasn't.

Sunday 31st December 1978

We spent Christmas and New Year with our families having had another eventful year, sharing a stage with Frank Sinatra, visiting Japan and making over twenty appearances on British television. Although we had enjoyed several hits in Holland, chart success in this country had eluded us and to rub salt into the wound, Dollar had finished 1978 with "Shooting Star" at number eighteen in the charts and still rising.

1979

Monday 1st January 1979

1979 began with the Village People topping the chart singing "YMCA" followed by Boney M's version of "Mary's Boy Child". Peaking at number fourteen was Dollar with "Shooting Star".

We should have been starting a week at the Golden Garter club in Manchester but the country had been experiencing freezing temperatures, snow and a petrol strike making any sort of travel a nightmare. We now had a new roadie, a German guy called Dieter and his van for the equipment was snowed in. We decided to get us and the band and as much gear as we could manage, on a train and up to Manchester. The train journey was a nightmare with serious delays due to the weather causing points to freeze and we eventually arrived at Manchester far too late for the show. We couldn't even get taxis and ended up bribing a guy driving a newspaper van to take us, our band and equipment to the hotel arriving after midnight. A great start to the New Year.

Friday 5th January 1979

I had arranged to meet Dave Johnson at Anfield and then go to see his wife Carol and their new baby Katy. On arrival at Anfield I walked in to the players lounge to be greeted by almost the entire Liverpool team singing "There's a Whole Lot Of Loving" (quite an ego trip for a Liverpool fan). Before we left I asked Dave if there was any chance of having a photo taken with the European Cup and he said "no problem". There was a problem because we couldn't find the cup and nobody else seemed to know where it was. Eventually we were told it was in the director's lounge and discovered it stuffed under a counter with an old pair of socks inside, such irreverence.

Liverpool had already been knocked out of this year's European Cup competition by Nottingham Forest who would go on to win the trophy.

Sunday 14th January 1979

Went to Mum and Dad's for Sunday dinner and to say goodbye to Nigel, who was off on his travels again. Split Enz were flying to New Zealand primarily to appear in the huge Nambassa Festival in Waihi in front of 60,000 people on 28th January and then to spend February and March touring Australia. A track called "I See Red", which Split Enz had recorded at Ringo Starr's Startling Studios back in 1977, looked like becoming an Australian hit and would be the beginning of major success for the band. Although he didn't know it at the time, tomorrow Nigel would effectively be emigrating as he'd eventually settle down in Melbourne, Australia remaining his home to this day. The family wouldn't see him again for another twenty months by which time Split Enz would be superstars in the Antipodes.

Tuesday 23rd January 1979

The weather this month had been horrendous with freezing temperatures and a large amount of snow and ice. Today we should have been leaving for our second trip to Thailand but during the night there had been heavy snow and when we arrived at Heathrow, after our taxi was involved in a minor accident skidding in the ice, we were told that the airport was closed and all flights were cancelled.

Wednesday 24th January – Saturday 3rd February 1979

We had armed guards to take us to and from the stage, probably because of all the gold in our costumes

Who's the little guy on the right?

Guys n' Dolls finally left the freezing shores of Britain for the tropical temperatures of Bangkok, the trip was made more enjoyable as I was able to take Lynne, and Martine her husband Michael. Even though our arrival was a day later than scheduled, there was still a large crowd of girls waiting to greet us at the airport.

We performed seven concerts the last being a really wild affair in a university with no air conditioning and probably the hottest conditions in which we had ever performed. Once again the hospitality shown to us was second to none and we had a few days relaxing in Pattya before returning home.

Monday 5th March 1979

The 'Song For Europe' competition was looming and none of us were very enthusiastic, but today we visited the BBC rehearsal studios in Acton for the first get together of contestants. The big television show at that time was Fawlty Towers and who should be coming out of the lift as we were about to enter but John Cleese. I was hooked on the programme and just seeing him made me smile. On entering the rehearsal room, still set up for Fawlty Towers, we found Andrew Sachs who played Manuel, the Spanish waiter. We had a chat and told him how much we enjoyed the show. Andrew went a bit "luvvie" on us and said "yes it seems to have the right amount of comedy and pathos". No Andrew, it's just bloody funny!

There were twelve acts in the competition and with the exception of Guys n' Dolls and the Nolans all the others were unknown.

Thursday 8th March 1979

It was our second day at the Royal Albert Hall rehearsing for tonight's Song For Europe contest which was due to be broadcast live. Around five o'clock everything seemed to stop and there were small groups of technicians and staff having discussions. At six o'clock only two hours before the live transmission, it was announced that an unofficial strike had been called by technicians and the contest was cancelled.

There was mayhem, as some of the four thousand people who were going to make up the studio audience started to gather outside. All of the contestants had friends and family turning up and were frantically trying to find them to break the news that the show was off. I managed to find Mum, Dad and Lynne and got them inside the Albert Hall while we pondered our next move. It was eventually decided that the contest would go ahead with recordings of the songs played to the various panels around the country and then voted on. Nothing would be broadcast but the result would be announced on television later in the evening. Michael Levy suggested that we all go back to the Magnet office and await the result. He laid on food and drink and it turned into a bit of a party. At 9.20pm the party came to an abrupt halt when we received a phone call to say that, the then unknown, Black Lace had won with a song called "Mary Ann" and Guys n' Dolls placed a lowly tenth out of twelve. The atmosphere became subdued and everybody drifted off home. Despite not really wanting to be in the contest I felt deflated, but felt very sorry for the unknown acts that had missed out on a chance of performing on stage at the Royal Albert Hall and appearing on television, an opportunity that might not come their way again.

Michael Levy said that he would still release our record, but the reality was that failed "Song for Europe" entries have no chance of chart success and even Black lace would only make it to number 42 in the charts and be placed seventh in the actual Eurovision Song Contest.

Thursday 15th March 1979

Billy Connolly Dominic and Yours truly.   **Nutbush City Limits.**

We were back in Manchester for the week staying at one of our favourite places a nightclub cum hotel called the Sandpiper. Last night Billy Connolly checked in with his road crew, in the middle of their U.K. tour. They were a crazy bunch and one of the highlights of the evening was a dance routine that Billy and the crew had worked out for Tina Turner's "Nutbush City Limits".

We spent this afternoon with Billy who was great company with many stories to tell; he was as funny off stage as on. In a few weeks time we were due to appear in Glasgow and he invited us to visit his home in Drymen near Loch Lomond, and promised to take Dominic and I fishing.

Thursday 22nd March 1979

I went with Dominic to meet up with our ex. manager Brian Longley and sort out his compensation due to the termination of his management agreement. I liked Brian and it was a shame the relationship ended but we all remained friendly and managed to finalise things without the need for legal intervention.

Saturday 14th April 1979

Ray Clemence heeds my advice to watch out for the high balls.

My name's Phil Thompson and I'm going to score on Monday. Not sure who for.

Once again we were spending a week in Manchester staying at the Sandpiper. This afternoon I went to see Liverpool beat Manchester United 2-0 at Anfield, later in the evening Dave Johnson, Phil Thompson, Ray Clemence and their wives, came along to our show at the Golden Garter. As it was Martine's birthday we decided to all go back to the Sandpiper for a drink, but the one drink turned into several bottles of champagne and a very drunken game of charades. I realised that Liverpool had a game on Monday against Aston Villa and through my champagne haze tried to become sensible and remind three of the first team that it might be wise to take it a bit easy. Waste of time, and the party carried on into the night and finally broke up around three o'clock. We travelled back home as the sun was rising.

Monday 16th April 1979

Liverpool were on their way to another league title in a season where goalkeeper Ray Clemence would concede only sixteen goals but tonight was a disaster. Liverpool were beaten at Aston Villa 3-1 and the participants of the party two nights ago were all involved. Aston Villa's first goal was a gift from Ray Clemence who made a complete hash of an easy save, their second was an own goal courtesy of Phil Thompson, the only redeeming feature was Dave Johnson scoring for Liverpool. I wondered how much our little soiree was a factor in the defeat.

Dave Johnson was a regular player for Liverpool who were the top side in the country at that time; his wages were £500 per week plus £100 per point for every game he participated in. At this time it was still two points for a win so if Liverpool played and won two games in a week his wages would be boosted to £900. This was excellent money at the time but in no way compares with the over inflated wages that premiership players receive today. Dave's medal tally while at Liverpool is impressive; four League Championships (now the Premiership), three European Cups (now the Champions League), three League Cups (now the Carling Cup) and eight caps playing for England scoring six goals in the process. He is still involved with Liverpool to this day, looking after hospitality on match days.

Saturday 21st April 1979

Guys n' Dolls were on their way to Bridlington, Dominic was driving and I was map reading. I thought it would be a good idea to go over the Humber Bridge. Unfortunately they had not finished building it, and as we couldn't wait we had to make a twenty mile detour.

Saturday 28th April 1979

It was the last day of a short run of dates at a club called McTavishes in Bo'ness near Edinburgh and today we drove to Drymen to visit Billy Connolly and his wife Iris at their home. He had a small holding in the country with lots of animals including a couple of donkeys but admitted he was more of a town person. We had an enjoyable day, Billy took us down to Loch Lomond but unfortunately there was no time for fishing as we had to get back to Edinburgh for a radio interview. In a couple of year's time Billy and Iris would separate and he would go on to marry Pamela Stephenson.

Tuesday 1st May 1979

Since Guys n' Dolls parted company with Brian Longley we had been looked after by our agent Alan Field but had been searching for someone to take on the roll as full time manager. Martine suggested an old school friend, Robert Earl who had become a very successful businessman and today we went along for a meeting. The meeting went well but in the end we decided against him which in retrospect was probably a mistake. Robert would take a major roll in the running of the Hard Rock Café chain of restaurants and in a few years time would create Planet Hollywood partnered by, Bruce Willis, Arnold Schwarzenegger, Sylvester Stallone and Demi Moore.

Friday 4th May 1979

Lynne and I had planned to get married in September and had been looking at houses for the past few months. We must have seen around thirty properties and found nothing we liked. This evening we went to see a cottage in Tewin, a small village about six miles from my home in Hatfield. It was a private sale and the owners said they would not be home but we were welcome to take a look from the outside. It was a small forester's cottage that backed on to open fields as far as the eye could see. There was a plaque on the wall that dated it as 1903, and as we walked up the path, knew immediately that it was going to be our home.

I had first visited Tewin while still at school, in history lessons we had learned about a highwayman called Walter Clibbon who had been shot dead during a failed robbery in 1782, his body then hung on display in a local pub called The Horns. He was buried where he fell in an unconsecrated roadside grave near the village, with a large post marking the spot, allegedly having been driven through his body. I was quite fascinated by the story and had cycled to Tewin to find Clibbon's Post and returned several times over the years.

Thursday 24th May 1979
We made one of our regular appearances on the lunchtime "Pebble Mill at One" TV show and just for a change performed the old Lonnie Donegan song "Have a Drink on Me", a bit out of character for Guys n' Dolls as a group, but not for me.

When we returned to the hotel we had a call from Michael Levy who confirmed, as expected, that our recording contract with Magnet records was not being renewed. Our three year contract was ending and Michael Levy had the option of re-signing us which would involve paying us an advance, we were considerably in debt to the company and as our UK record sales had been poor it made good business sense on his part not to take up the option and write off the debt. We were not unhappy with this situation as our relationship with Magnet was not what it once was and there had been some interest shown from EMI Holland.

Monday 11th June 1979
I had a recording set up at my flat so that I could work on songs that I had written. It had consisted of a two track semi professional Revox tape machine with dubbing facility meaning I could bounce between tracks and record multiple voices and instruments by myself. The musical instrument industry had realised that there was a market for home recording and today I bought one of the latest Teac four track tape machines which would give me much more flexibility.

Up to their White Album of 1968 the Beatles had recorded all of their material on two and four track machines.

Monday 18th June 1979
We were off to Billy Smart's Circus at Windsor for a television show where we performed in the middle of the circus ring with Charles Aznavour and Lionel Blair. We played "Rocking All Over The World" live with a band that was provided and it was not the best choice of song in these circumstances as the band could not rock.

Thursday 21st June 1979

Our failed 'Song for Europe" entry "How do you mend a broken Heart" had, as expected, completely bombed in the UK, but in Holland it was becoming a hit. Today we flew to Holland to appear on the Tros Top 50 TV show, and then stayed over to have business discussions with EMI Holland.

We had a meeting with Roek Williams, one of the bosses, who said that now our contract with Magnet records had finished, EMI Holland would like us to sign directly with them. It was something we had to think carefully about. We still had a high profile in the UK as we were doing a lot of television and live shows but our records weren't selling and at present we had no record company. In Holland we had enjoyed a run of hits since 1975 and our relationship with EMI had always been excellent with a lot of the staff becoming friends. We said we would go away and seriously discuss it.

Saturday 7th July 1979

Our German roadie Dieter had to suddenly return to Germany as his mother was ill, when I received the news I was with the ex. Octopus/Kincade guitarist Rick Williams who immediately offered to help out. I was a bit dubious about the idea but as we had a gig that evening, I said "yes".

Tonight Guys n' Dolls were in Minehead, and we had one of our nightmare journeys as our car broke down and we had to be towed to a garage and then rent another, reaching the gig very late. When we arrived we found Rick having a stand up row with comedienne Faith Brown who was appearing on the show with us. Julie managed to smooth things over, and I regretted asking Rick to roadie.

Thursday 12th July 1979

Liverpool goalkeeper Ray Clemence was having his testimonial year and had asked us to perform a show for him in his home town of Skegness. The show culminated in us dragging him on stage to sing the Liverpool anthem "You'll Never Walk Alone". The key he started in was a little too high and as the song gradually gets even higher, by the end I thought he was going to burst a blood vessel.

Tuesday 24th July - Friday 27th July 1979

Having a great
time in the
Shetland Islands.
Wish you were
here,
and we weren't.
(more over-acting)

The Shetlands was our next unlikely port of call as we had been booked to perform three shows entertaining the oil workers. We flew to Glasgow and while we were waiting for the connection to Lerwick I went to make a phone call and had to wait while a rather inebriated Scotsman finished his call. I eventually made my call and as I was putting the phone down, the guy came back and said "I've losht my wallet I musht have left it by the phone", he couldn't find it and immediately accused me of taking it. I said I hadn't and walked away. Five minutes later I could see him walking towards me with a police officer saying "he'sh the one, he took it". I explained I hadn't and said I was quite prepared to have my bag searched and empty my pockets. The police officer took a cursory look in my bag and apologized for the inconvenience, walking away the man was by now getting rather belligerent almost screaming "why don't you arresht him".

We arrived in Lerwick and found the Shetland Islands to be rather cold and bleak. We travelled to the oil depot and discovered that there was a strict rule of no fraternization between men and women even if they were married. Dominic, myself and the band were taken to a large ship that had been converted into living quarters. The girls were taken to the women's quarters which were about two miles away, we felt a bit like prisoners. We were really annoyed that we had not been told about the conditions. The men's quarters had inside cabins like cupboards with bunk beds and no windows, but we probably had the better deal as there was six of us along with sixties chart group the Fortunes who were also on the show and we ended up playing a marathon pool tournament for the whole time we were there.

The shows were a bit scary as each night we performed to five hundred drunken, noisy, lecherous oil riggers and you can imagine the comments aimed at the girls. At one point in the act Dominic and I sing the Dr. Hook song "A Little Bit More" and take a verse each and sing it to a woman in the audience. My verse was first and on the first night there was only one woman in the audience, I sang to her and wondered what Dominic was going to do. I saw him making his way towards the biggest, hairiest, guy in the room, all chains and tattoos, and start singing to him. I thought "Dominic you're dead" but the guy suddenly smiled, put his arm around Dominic and they both camped it up a treat. This really broke the ice and kept the audience on our side.

We were all glad when it was time to fly home, especially Julie and Martine who had endured a miserable few days stuck in the women's quarters. I can't say they were the most enjoyable shows we'd ever done but I did manage to come third out of eleven in the pool tournament.

Sunday 16th September 1979
As I was to be married next Saturday, today was my last gig as a single man and by coincidence it was a return to the Forum in Hatfield, close to my flat.

Wednesday 19th July 1979
I was supposed to have my stag night tonight, Dave Johnson had invited Dominic and I to see Liverpool play and then to go out with some of the team for drinks afterwards. I was so busy moving things from my old flat to the new house that I phoned Dave and said I wouldn't be coming, but arranged to go out with Dominic the following night.

Thursday 20th July 1979
Spent all day moving things into the house, plumbing in the washing machine, moving furniture around and by evening time was knackered. I phoned Dominic and said the stag night was off. He had different ideas and said he was still going out, and he went out on my stag night, with a few friends, and without me.

Saturday 22nd September 1979

Today I married Lynne with Dominic as my best man, (the best I could find). We had taken over ownership of the cottage in Tewin several weeks ago which meant we could be married in the village church, St. Peters, only two hundred yards away. Everything went well, Lynne looked beautiful, and after the ceremony we moved on to our reception with family and friends in Hatfield.

Nigel was unable to attend our wedding due to his commitments with Split Enz on the other side of the world. They had spent the year gigging in Australia and New Zealand and were about to go into the studios to record the bands fourth album "True Colours" which was destined to achieve unprecedented success. The likelihood of them returning to live in the UK seeming increasingly remote. In a few days time Lynne and I would be setting off for our honeymoon in Crete.

Thursday 11th October 1979

Guys n' Dolls flew to Holland for a meeting with EMI to discuss future recording. We had considered everything carefully and decided we would sign directly to EMI Holland and concentrate on making records for the Dutch market where we continued to have success. There was a song we put forward called "You Can" which was written by our band, and EMI said that we could go in and record it ourselves.

Thursday 8th - Friday 9th November 1979

John Kurlander

(Photo courtesy of John Kurlander)

EMI Holland had booked studio time for us at the world famous Abbey Road studios in St. Johns Wood, where the Beatles recorded. Studio one was where the Beatles made their live worldwide television broadcast recording "All You Need is Love" back in 1967, and today we recorded "You Can" along with one of my songs "The Affair That Never Was". Our engineer was John Kurlander who I later found out had worked on a lot of the

Beatles final album "Abbey Road".

Friday 16th November 1979

Today we were back at Abbey Road to mix the two, already recorded tracks. For me it was a great experience as we were working in Studio 2, the main room used by the Beatles. It looked so familiar having seen it so many times in photographs and even though we were only using the control room I just had to walk down the very familiar staircase and stand in the eerily empty studio where the Beatles would have been producing their masterpieces.

I managed to get John Kurlander talking about his time working with the Beatles on the Abbey Road album. He said that at times the atmosphere was a bit strained and there would often be two studios on the go with individual Beatles working on their own songs. John also said that it was he who was responsible for the gap before the very last track on Abbey Road, "Her Majesty". Paul McCartney said he didn't like "Her Majesty" and that it should be thrown away. It was EMI policy never to throw anything away so John spliced it onto the end of a mix of the album with a long piece of leader tape and added a note that it should be discarded. As every Beatles fan knows, it never was.

Friday 30th November 1979

EMI Holland were keen for Guys n' Dolls to work with a producer called Gerrard Stellard, and today we flew to Holland for our first session with him at Wisselord Studios in Hilversum. We recorded a song called "Love Lost in a Day" which Gerrard (we would call him Gerry from now on) had written, his approach seemed much more up to date than previous producers we had worked with, and amazingly I quite liked the song.

Wednesday 5th December 1979

It looked as if our long awaited court case with Ammo Productions was to start next month. Today our solicitors had arranged a meeting for both parties in a last ditch attempt to resolve the issue without going to court. Unfortunately the meeting was unsuccessful.

Sunday 9th December 1979

Paul McCartney and Wings were in the middle of a UK tour and tonight I took Lynne to see them at the Empire Pool Wembley and was somewhat disappointed with the show, the sound wasn't good and I found the set list to be a bit obscure in places. Although they included four Beatles songs, "Got to get you into my Life", "Fool on the Hill", "Let it Be" and "Yesterday" it all seemed a little lacklustre and short on crowd pleasers.

Tuesday 18th December 1979

Today we were appearing at Chesford Grange in Kenilworth and with a half an hour to go before the show there was no sign of Martine. We received a phone call to say that Martine had been involved in a road traffic accident and was in hospital. She wasn't seriously hurt but one of two new estate cars that we had purchased only ten days ago was a write-off. Julie, Dominic and I decided to do the show as a three piece and my wife Lynne went off to collect Martine.

Monday 31st December 1979

Lynne and I had spent an enjoyable first Christmas as a married couple, at our new home with both sets of parents. For Guys n' Dolls it had been a changeable year, with the ending of our recording contract with Magnet records and the signing of a new deal in Holland. We had no chart success but our ex members David Van Day and Thereze Bazar now working as Dollar had hit the charts three times during the year including a number four hit with "Love's Gotta Hold On Me". This played havoc with my ego.

1980

Tuesday 1st January 1980

The beginning of the new decade saw Pink Floyd topping the charts with "Another Brick in the Wall", Abba followed at number two with "I Have a Dream". A new entry at forty two was Dollar with their latest release, a hi tech cover of the Beatles "I Wanna Hold Your Hand" which I can't say I was fond of but it would give them their second top ten hit peaking at number 9.

Wednesday 16th January 1980

On his arrival at Tokyo's Narita Airport with Wings, Paul McCartney was arrested by customs officials when marijuana was found in his luggage. He was questioned, handcuffed and locked up and would remain in prison for the next ten days, his eleven date tour cancelled.

Monday 21st January 1980

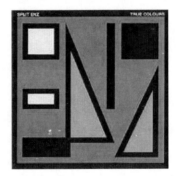

> **Split Enz Album**
> **True Colours**

While Guys n' Dolls were meeting with their solicitors in London to discuss next week's court case with Ammo productions, twelve thousand miles away in Australia the Split Enz album "True Colours" and the single "I Got You" were being simultaneously released.

Friday 25th January 1980

It had been decided that Guys n' Dolls first release in Holland, under our new deal with EMI, was to be a Gerrard Stellard composition called "Our Song" and we were back in Wisselord studios in Hilversum to record it.

Paul McCartney had been released from prison in Japan and deported; he was flying back to Amsterdam's Schipol aiport. We were staying at Schipol's Hilton Hotel and the rumour was that Paul would be checking in later tonight. The reality was he arrived at Schipol and immediately chartered a private plane to fly him home to England.

Monday 28th January 1980

It was the first day of our court case with Ammo productions held at the high court in the Strand. Unfortunately Julie was ill and couldn't attend, I took Lynne along and met up with Dominic and Martine and for the first time in almost three years we met David and Thereze. At first it was a little awkward but it soon settled down and we started chatting, past differences were temporarily put aside as we united in a common cause. There were a few press photographers taking pictures as we entered the High Court and took our seats on the right side of the room. On the left was David, Geoff and Chris from Ammo productions, their legal team and Julie's sister Debbie with their mother Penny. I thought it was going to be quite interesting but was in fact quite tedious and the first day was taken up with Ammo's council outlining their case which was littered with long legal statements and seemed to go on forever.

We left the court and were met by the press, and as my wife Lynne has similar hair and bears a passing resemblance to Julie, reporters came up and asked her what her Dad thought of the situation. I don't think Lynne's Dad would have had too much to say on the subject and I tried to explain that Lynne wasn't Julie but one woman from the Daily Express wasn't convinced and persisted. We eventually got away and I said we should get Lynne a T shirt with "I am not Julie Forsyth" printed on it.

Tuesday 29th January 1980

Our second day in court and Ammo's council finished their case and now it was our turn. One of the things I found odd was that Ammo claimed we owed them £12,906 and Guys n' Dolls entering a counter claim that Ammo owed us £928. Both parties had access to the same information yet each came up with two different sets of results in favour of their own side.

Our council raised some points including, in the event of us winning the case, Ammo should put £5000 into the court to cover our costs. The judge adjourned for the day to consider this.

Wednesday 30th January 1980

A very short day in court as the judge agreed with our council and said that Ammo productions should put £5000 into court for the case to continue. Ammo's council immediately said they would appeal, and court was adjourned. We said goodbye to David and Thereze and since that day our paths have never crossed.

Dave Johnson was picked to play for England for the first time.

Friday 1st February 1980

It was the day of Ammo's appeal and we couldn't attend as we were working in Edinburgh. The appeal was held in front of Lord Denning, who as Master of the Rolls was the most senior judge in the court of appeals and well known for his common sense approach to cases. He dismissed the appeal and said that Ammo had two months to put the money into court for the case to continue. In the event they were unable to do this and we never returned to court. The only people to win were the barristers; it cost us and Ammo a considerable amount in court costs which, as there was no judgement, we each had to pay.

Tuesday 19th February 1980

This evening I met our village policeman for the first time. The long arm of the law had finally caught up with me concerning a couple of parking tickets that I thought I had got away with. He was quite relieved when I paid up because if I hadn't he would have had to arrest me which would have been difficult as he only had his bike outside.

Saturday 23rd February 1980

We all went to Linda Nolan's surprise twenty first birthday party in Ilford. She was now married to Brian Hudson the former drummer with Tony Rivers and the Castaways. I couldn't believe how many Nolan brothers and sisters there were, seemed to be hundreds.

Tuesday 4th March – Friday 7th March 1980

We spent four nights working at the Heathrow Hotel for a large corporate event with magician Paul Daniels. Love him or loathe him he is a brilliant magician and performed card tricks right under our noses in the dressing room that were amazing. Also on the bill was a comedian called Dave Ismay who we had worked with previously. Dominic is really good at remembering people, the only problem being he can't remember where he's met them. Dave Ismay came into our dressing room to say hello, he was wearing a suit and bow tie. Dominic remembered his face but got the circumstances wrong and said "Hi, how are you? Julie will have an orange juice, Paul a brandy and I'll have" -------- oops.

It was during these dates that I met a guy called Bev Walker who managed sports personalities and was there with Judo champion Brian Jacks. I would end up working with Bev in a few years time.

Monday 10th March 1980

We heard from Nigel that Split Enz were about to embark on a lengthy tour of Australia with the news that their album "True Colours" and single "I Got You" were both top of their respective charts. The album would stay at number one for ten weeks, the single eight weeks and in numbers of sales both would turn multi platinum. It was a similar story in New Zealand.

Saturday 19th April 1980

Our first release in Holland under our new deal with EMI was called "Our Song". It had been released a couple of weeks ago and had just entered the charts. We had been recording a new album for the past few weeks and the sessions had taken place both in Holland and England. Tonight we were in Lansdowne studios in London finishing the final track.

Julie and Dominic were expecting their first child in August, Julie had decided she would be able to carry on working until June.

Saturday 3rd May 1980

Today Liverpool became League Champions yet again after beating Aston Villa 3-1 with Dave Johnson getting a couple.

Tuesday 6th May 1980

We met a guy called Chris Youle who at one time worked for Carrerre records, Dollar's label, and discussed the possibility of him becoming our manager. He was slightly unorthodox and was petrified of flying, which as we were spending more time in Holland might pose a problem. He was also the owner of the first Sony Walkman cassette player any of us had seen.

"Our Song" this week peaked at number seven in the Dutch charts.

Friday 13th June – Saturday 14th 1980

Our last two shows before having time off for Julie to have her baby. We were back at one of our favourite clubs, Stockton's Fiesta and as always the audiences were great. The decline in the cabaret club scene continued, where once we would perform for seven nights at the Fiesta it was now down to two.

Wednesday 18th June 1980

With just over six weeks to go before the birth of Julie's baby we had a photo session for the cover of our new album. Julie was strategically placed at the back with my large hair covering her bump.

Friday 20th June 1980

We were off to the Empire Pool Wembley to see Fleetwood Mac. Unfortunately our seats were right at the back so I needed binoculars to leer at Stevie Nicks, who made about eight costume changes throughout a great show.

Sunday 3rd August 1980

Luke with proud parents and Grandad

(Picture thanks to Julie Forsyth)

I had spent the last few weeks either fishing or working on converting the out building of our cottage into a recording studio. This evening Dominic phoned to say that at 8.20pm Julie had given birth to a boy weighing 6lb 13oz. Mother and baby, (and father) were all doing well and they had decided to call him Luke.

Wednesday 3rd September 1980

Our musical director Ray Monk phoned today and dropped a bombshell. Our band had decided to leave us and go out on their own, but would stay until we had managed to find replacements. It was a shock as Ray and drummer Dave Morris had been with us for over five years, but nothing lasts forever and in the back of our own minds we were considering the possibility of working more in Holland.

Thursday 4th September 1980

Split Enz landed at Heathrow airport, the first time they had been back in this country since January 1979. They were here to promote their single "I Got You", which had just been released, and to perform a few live shows. Mum and Dad met Nigel at the airport and drove him to Tewin. It was great to see him again but I only had a few hours as Guys n' Doll were off to Holland for a TV appearance, our first performance since the birth of Julie and Dominic's son a month ago. Luke came with us and Lynne, being a trained nurse, was on hand to look after him.

Friday 5th September 1980

We visited a Dutch trade fair and Chris Youle negotiated for us to make an appearance on the Sony stand in exchange for a brand new Sony Walkman each. Later Guys n' Dolls performed the new single "Love Lost in a Day" on a TV show, appearing with Leo Sayer.

Sunday 7th September 1980

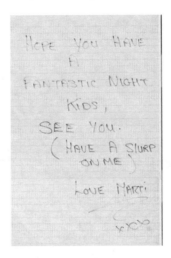

We were off to the Wellington Pier in Great Yarmouth for our first live show in three months, it was the longest period without performing since we began and a few nerves were evident. In our dressing room was a bottle of champagne and a note from Marti Caine saying *"Hope you have a fantastic night kids. See you, (have a slurp on me) Love Marti"*. It was a nice gesture and she actually popped in to see us during the evening as she was staying in Yarmouth for a summer season.

One of the support acts was comedian Lenny Henry and when he heard that our band were leaving, introduced us to a drummer friend of his who said he might be able to help. We had a chat, and the drummer (Martin) said he would see what he could do and get in touch during the week.

Thursday 11th September 1980

Split Enz on Top of the Pops. Neil and Nigel

"I don't know why sometimes I get frightened".

Before travelling to a gig in Bristol I managed to catch my brother's first appearance on Top of the Pops. Split Enz had entered the charts at 27 with "I Got You" and were making the first of two appearances on the show. The record would peak at number 12.

Martin, the drummer that Lenny Henry had introduced us to, phoned to say that he had managed to put a band together, and we arranged to rehearse with them next week

Saturday 13th September 1980

Our last gig with our old band was at the Crystal Room in Hereford, we said our goodbyes and it was a bit sad, the end of an era. Our musical director Ray Monk would eventually end up in television and be musical director for programmes like "Stars in their Eyes" and "Reborn in the USA". He has worked consistently with Des O'Connor for a number of years, but I don't hold that against him.

Wednesday 17th September 1980

Tonight we played our first gig with the new band at Park Hall Charnock Richard in Staffordshire. It wasn't bad for a first night although a bit tentative in places, but we could tell it was going to be OK.

Saturday 27th September 1980

Split Enz were playing a major gig at Hammersmith Odeon and I really wanted to go but Guys n' Dolls were performing in Birmingham. Nigel had arranged for Mum and Dad to see the show and when they took their seats, found there was a spare seat beside them. Suddenly they can see a tall, bald headed, quite intimidating looking guy striding up the aisle and Dad said, "I hope that bugger's not going to sit here", and of course he does. They strike up a conversation and discover that it is Peter Garrett the lead singer with Australian band Midnight Oil who was a huge fan of the Enz and had flown from Italy especially to see the show. His favourite song was "Shark Attack" from the True Colours album which the band opened with. I think he became Dad's new best friend.

Midnight Oil were Nigel's favourite Australian band and known for making political statements in their songs. They had a world wide hit with "Beds are Burning" which reached number 6 in the UK charts in 1989 and highlighted the plight of the Aboriginal Australians. Today Peter Garrett is a politician and member of the Australian government as minister for arts and environment, a possible future prime minister.

Monday 29th September - Saturday 4th October 1980

We were back to Holland for more promotion, appearing on a major TV show along side Telly Savalas (Kojak), who was having a major hit reciting the lyrics to the David Gates song "If".

While in Holland we performed two shows in discos singing to backing tracks for the first time. We only had to perform for thirty minutes and whereas performing with backing tracks in 1980 was unheard of in the UK, in Holland it was commonplace. This planted the seed of an idea; perhaps it was something we should think about seriously for the future.

Friday 10th October – Saturday 25th October 1980

This was a depressing two weeks when Guys n' Dolls probably came to the conclusion that their career in the UK was coming to an end. The first week was in Scotland, a promoter had put together a series of gigs in small clubs with a couple of military gigs thrown in and generally they were awful. Lynne was with us looking after Luke while we were performing and some of the places we had been booked to stay in were less than adequate.

From Scotland we drove down to Yorkshire for a series of club dates, we now had a new driver called Malcolm who drove his own Mercedes stretched limousine and had previously chauffeured Led Zeppelin's Jimmy Page. This sounds quite grand but in fact the car was very old. We'd just driven over the border and were in the middle of nowhere when the car developed a puncture, Malcolm went to change the wheel but when he tried to jack the car up, the jack went up but the car didn't. It was so rusty underneath that the jack had gone straight through the bodywork so we had to find a phone box and call the AA who eventually got us going again.

Another series of crappy club dates awaited us including Dial House social club in Sheffield, a venue I had not enjoyed when playing there with Octopus all those years ago. This really depressed me and I thought, "I don't want to be doing this anymore".

Monday 10th November – Thursday 13th November 1980

We were back on the stage of the London Palladium for four nights supporting the Danish entertainer Victor Borge. He specialised in comedy routines based at the piano and I had always found his act extremely funny, although off stage he was quite dour and hardly spoke.

I managed to catch up with Nigel on the Thursday as Split Enz had returned to the UK having spent the last five weeks touring the USA. They now had some European dates and were due to return to Australia in December.

Thursday 4th December 1980

The Griggs Brothers. Beauty and the beast. Which is which.

I drove back to Mum and Dad's from Warwickshire, where Guys n' Dolls were appearing, for a family get together before Nigel's departure for Australia. We had a few photos taken for the press in our contrasting styles. Nigel dressed in his bizarre Split Enz costume and me in my bizarre Guys n' Dolls outfit.

Friday 5th December 1980

Martine's marriage had come to an end some time ago and she was now in a relationship with our Dutch record producer Gerrard Stellard. Today she told us that she had decided to leave Guys n' Dolls in a couple of months and intended settling down, with Gerry, in Holland. It wasn't totally unexpected and now the three remaining members had to seriously sit down and discuss the next move. The doors in the UK seemed to be closing but in Holland there seemed to be new opportunities opening up.

Tuesday 9th December 1980

I had just emerged from my studio and met Lynne coming out of the house, she said, "Have you heard the news, John Lennon has been shot", I said "how is he?" and Lynne replied "I'm afraid he's dead". I just stood there trying to take it in not really believing what I had heard. The Beatles were such an important part of my life and although I'd never met the man it felt as if I had lost someone very close to me. I spent the rest of the day glued to the television watching every single detail of the events in New York over and over again. In the evening the hurriedly put together tributes began to be broadcast with anybody who had the slightest connection to John being wheeled out to give their comments. Some of the people interviewed were quite inappropriate but there was such a frenzy to obtain quotes I suppose it was down to who could be contacted at short notice. Paul McCartney had a microphone pushed under his nose while emerging from a recording studio and asked what he thought, he said "It's a drag" which sounded a little dismissive and he would be criticised for it, but it was obvious to anyone with common sense that the quote hadn't come out as intended, he was clearly distraught. The sadness of it all was that John had been back in the studio, after a long lay off being a house husband, and recently had his first top ten hit in five years with the ironically titled "(just like) Starting Over"

Like millions of other fans I was devastated, in my mind I always felt there was a possible chance of a Beatles reunion at sometime. If all four Beatles had survived and eventually put aside their differences, with the advent of the large charity shows like Live Aid and, more likely many years later Live 8, I think it may have happened, but now it never would.

Wednesday 10th December – Thursday 11th December 1980

On Wednesday evening Lynne and I drove to Leeds as Guys n' Dolls were due to appear in a TV show at nearby Yeadon the following day. We arrived in Leeds around 9.00pm and found a restaurant, the City seemed almost deserted. This was the era of the Yorkshire Ripper. Between 1975 and 1980 Peter Sutcliffe murdered thirteen women and attacked and injured several others, most of these attacks taking place in and around Leeds making it a frightened city. Three weeks ago he murdered his thirteenth and what would be his final victim. The restaurant owner told us that hardly anyone went out at night and his business and many others in the area had dropped dramatically. We finished our meal and left, I felt uneasy even walking to the car and was relieved when we reached our hotel.

Guys n' Dolls recorded their last ever UK television appearance at Yeadon town hall for a children's Christmas Day show called "A Merry Morning". We appeared with children's entertainers the Chuckle Brothers which, years later, my daughter would have been impressed by.

The Yorkshire Ripper would be finally arrested in Sheffield in just over three weeks time.

Sunday 14th December 1980

Yoko Ono had asked for a ten minute silence to remember John Lennon. In Central Park, New York, near the Dakota building where John had been murdered and in Liverpool there were huge gatherings of fans and at 7.00pm everything went silent. I sat alone in my studio observing the silence reflecting on the huge influence the Beatles had been on me, my mind went back to that day seventeen years ago when I saw them live on stage for the very first time.

Wednesday 17th - Thursday 18th December 1980

Guys n' Doll flew to Milan and from there, driven to the picturesque Lake Lugano in Switzerland for a TV show. We were appearing with Italian singer, Caterina Valente along with American dancer/choreographer Don Lurio. During rehearsals Don Lurio suddenly clutched his chest and screamed out in pain. He was rushed to hospital having suffered a heart attack. Rehearsals had to be hastily rearranged and the show went on without him. Fortunately he eventually recovered and was able to continue his career.

Friday 19th December 1980

We returned to Milan airport to find absolute chaos due to an industrial dispute. We stood in a queue waiting to check in when Lynne suddenly gasped and exclaimed "It's Nastase". Standing opposite us in the next queue was Rumanian tennis star Ilie Nastase who Lynne had a huge crush on when she was younger. She kept her cool and didn't do anything she might regret later; eventually after a considerable delay we flew back to London. We drove straight to Birmingham for a show, the last before Christmas and although we didn't know it at the time it would be our last ever show in the UK.

Wednesday 31st December 1980

It had been a year of change for Guys n' Dolls we were now signed directly with EMI Holland and had seen the cabaret circuit in the UK almost completely dry up. Martine had decided to leave the group and after careful thought we had decided to ask Julie's younger sister Laura to join us. We also decided to forget about the UK and focus entirely on Holland where our records were still selling well.

1981

Thursday 1st January 1981

Following the death of John Lennon, the first top ten of the year was dominated by three of his songs. At number one was "Imagine", at two, "Happy Christmas War is Over" and at five "(feels like) Starting Over". At number six were St. Winifred's School Choir with a song for all serious music lovers, "There's No One Quite Like Grandma".

Wednesday 7th January – Tuesday 20th January 1981

Guys n' Dolls
crazy Dutch
driver.
Long Hans

Guys n' Dolls were now effectively a Dutch group and we flew to Holland for a TV show followed by a string of live dates mostly in discos. I had spent the Christmas period recording a few extra backing tracks in my studio, our performances were around forty minutes each and sometimes we would perform two shows a day. We had a crazy Dutchman called Hans van de Velde looking after us and as he was six and a half feet tall he would be forever known as Long Hans. Despite his height his party trick was his ability to place his legs behind his head. Our last show was in the Ahoy stadium in Rotterdam and we performed in the middle of cycle race meeting, the first of what would be many strange Dutch venues.

On Tuesday 13th January, Lynne who was back in England, had phoned with the great news that she was expecting our first child in September.

Friday 23rd January – Wednesday 4th February 1981

Far left The Black Prince. I'm just about to cast off.

Lynne and I dressed for Dutch Farmers Night.

I was only home for a couple of days, last night Lynne and I met up with Dominic and Julie and then caught the night ferry back to Holland. We drove to Rotterdam, met up with Martine and Gerry and boarded the Black Prince cruise ship for a two week cruise to the Canary Islands; we were booked to perform two shows during the trip.

We had to travel through the Bay of Biscay and it's not the calmest sea at the best of times and this was January. Julie and Lynne were both sick and in Lynne's case it was difficult to tell if it was sea sickness or morning sickness, because of her pregnancy she couldn't take any medication. We performed our first show with great difficulty trying to execute our routines without falling over in quite a heavy swell. Life aboard ship was quite boring and we even resorted to playing bingo to pass the time. We visited Madeira, Lanzarote, Teneriffe and then spent two days in Grand Canaria where Lynne and Julie threatened to mutiny and jump ship. It was then a four day sail back to Rotterdam and in the Bay of Biscay we encountered a force ten gale, Lynne stayed in bed the whole time and was quite ill. Our second show was the day before we docked and this was also Martine's last live show as a member of Guys n' Dolls although she hadn't completely finished just yet. We docked at Rotterdam and immediately went to the TV studios in Hilversum to appear on the Andre van Duin show. Andre was a huge comedy star a bit like a Dutch Benny Hill but outside of Holland and Belgium he was unknown.

After six years as a member of Guys n' Dolls we said our final goodbyes to Martine, Julie and Lynne then had to endure one more sea voyage as we managed to catch the night ferry home to England. They swore they would never again set foot on a ship, although for Lynne it didn't last as we have enjoyed several cruises in recent years.

Monday 16ᵗʰ February 1981

New line up for
Guys n' Dolls
(left to right)
Paul Griggs,
Julie Forsyth,
Laura Forsyth,
Dominic Grant.

Julie's younger sister Laura had agreed to join Guys n' Dolls and today we had our first photo session and rehearsal.

Friday 13ᵗʰ March – Monday 30ᵗʰ March 1981

We had a month of frantic rehearsals with our new line up with Julie taking over singing the lead female parts that Martine had previously sung. Our first two shows with Laura were on Friday 13ᵗʰ, but no bad luck and everything went fine. It was the beginning of a run of eighteen performances which really knocked the new line up into shape. We based ourselves at the Zeider Paak hotel in Rotterdam from where we travelled to shows with Lynne staying at the hotel to look after Julie and Dominic's son Luke. We performed a couple of shows at Rotterdam's Studio 54 where we met an English guy called Scott Fitzgerald who, partnered with Dutch singer Yvonne Keeley, had a number three UK hit in 1978 with "If I had Words". Scott was trying to carve out a new career for himself in Holland and we became friends. The last gig was at a gay club in Nijmegan, which was a new experience for us, the audience went wild and the boys loved Dominic.

Our contract with EMI had been for one album only and now another company, CNR, were keen to sign us and we had a series of meetings with the Managing Director Kees Baas.

Tuesday 14ᵗʰ April 1981

We flew back to Holland to appear on a television show celebrating the ten years anniversary of the Ahoy Stadium in Rotterdam. Also on the show were Demis Rousos, Randy Crawford and Bucks Fizz who, only ten days ago, had won the Eurovision Song Contest with "Making Your Mind Up".

Saturday 25ᵗʰ April 1981

A few months ago I heard a record made by a Dutch producer called Jaap Eggermont called "Stars on 45", which was a medley of Beatles songs performed to a dance beat, this he followed with a second medley of sixties classic with the same beat. I had the idea of doing a similar thing with instrumentals by the Shadows. Unfortunately the drum machine I owned at the time was very primitive and I couldn't get the sound I wanted. I found a section on the "Stars on 45" record that featured drums on their own and recorded a two bar section on my tape machine and looped it. I held the loop on the tape machine with a pencil so it repeated over and over again and recorded this for around five minutes on to my four track machine; I suppose this could be classed as an early form of sampling. I then recorded the guitars and bass, the medley consisted of some of the best known Shadows tracks like Apache and Wonderful Land. It sounded OK and I decided to see if I could get a record company interested in releasing it.

Wednesday 27th May 1981
Liverpool beat Real Madrid 1-0 in Paris which meant they lifted the European Cup for the third time and Dave Johnson picked up his first cup winners medal.

Wednesday 24th June 1981
Split Enz were in the middle of a European tour and today arrived in London from Germany. Nigel went straight to Mum and Dad's house and I joined them later.

A couple of months ago Split Enz had released the follow up album to "True Colours" which in Australia and the rest of the world was called Waiata, the Aboriginal term for songs and singing. In New Zealand it was called Corroboree the Maori word with the same meaning. The stand out track for me was the Neil Finn song "History Never Repeats". Shortly before the album had been released, drummer Malcolm Green, (the ex. Octopus drummer) was sacked citing the usual reason when someone leaves a band, musical differences.

Wednesday 1st July 1981
This evening I took Mum and Dad to Hammersmith Odeon to see Split Enz perform. Before the show I bumped into Tim Reeves the ex. Octopus drummer, but can't say I was pleased to see him, as in my mind I blamed him for the break up of the band. He tried to con a drink out of me without success. Split Enz put on a great show which I enjoyed immensely, the place was packed and they went down a storm.

Monday 13th July 1981
Nigel brought Mum, Dad and his Australian actress girlfriend Kylie Foster, over to Tewin for a pub lunch. He was shortly to leave the UK as Split Enz had commitments in Canada and the USA before returning to Australia. Once again we did not know when we would see him again.

Friday 17th July 1981

Guys n' Dolls were supposed to be back in Holland for a string of dates starting this Sunday but today we heard that only one booking had been arranged. We needed at least three dates to make it viable as the first gig paid for the travelling expenses. The situation with our Dutch promoters had been less than satisfactory during the past couple of months so we decided to go over for the one gig and try and sort things out.

Monday 20th July 1981

Last night we performed in Valkenburg in the south of Holland and today drove to Hilversum for a meeting with a Belgian guy who had been recommended as a good booking agent, his name was Ludo Veuten and he ran a company called Rocket Management along with a Dutch rock singer called Peter Koelewijn. The meeting went well and we decided that he would take over handling of all Guys n' Dolls bookings in Holland.

I had been trying to get a release in England for my Shadows medley and had seen several companies in the UK. A couple of times I thought a deal was on the cards but until a contract is signed nothing is certain in this business. By now everybody and their mother were releasing medley type records and one of the companies I had taken my record to had the audacity to release their own Shadows medley, when I confronted them they swore they hadn't ripped me off. Unfortunately you cannot copyright an idea, and anyway I had myself, got the idea from somewhere else. Today I spoke to EMI Holland who told me that they were interested in releasing my record in Holland and would give me a definite answer in a few days.

Tuesday 28th July 1981

EMI had agreed to release my Shadows medley and today I flew to Holland with my master tape to sort out the details. I had a meeting and discussed whether my home recording was good enough or if it should be re-recorded. In the end it was agreed to use my original version but to overdub more drums so it was straight into the studio. We spent around an hour recording the drums which helped to cover up the fact that I had stolen my drums from the original "Stars on 45" record.

Wednesday 29th July 1981

While Prince Charles and Lady Diana Spencer were tying the knot in Westminster Abbey, I was in Holland mixing my record and having photos taken for the sleeve. I managed to see a little of the wedding as most of the staff at EMI were glued to TV screens, there was so much interest in Holland.

Friday 7th August – Monday 10th August 1981

We performed our first gigs in Holland for Ludo Veuten and had further meetings with CNR records who it looked increasingly likely that Guys n' Dolls would sign with. We were introduced to Hans van Hemert a Dutch record producer who he was keen for us to work with and we went to his house to listen to material. Hans van Hemert had much success with a three girl vocal group called Luv, who had broken up earlier in the year, and he played us some of the songs he had written for them. To me, although Luv had been very successful, they sounded like clones of Abba; once again I wasn't impressed and had doubts whether Hans was going to be the right producer for us. Guys n' Dolls were going through an unsettled period with us not working too much this year and Laura beginning to have serious doubts whether she had made the right choice in joining Guys n' Dolls. Mentally I was quite detached from it all with most of my thoughts centred on the forthcoming birth of my first child.

Saturday 15th August – Monday 17th August 1981

My last trip to Holland before time off to be with Lynne while she had the baby. My record, now called "Guitar Collection" had been released about a week ago and had received a few radio plays. As soon as we arrived in Holland I went straight to NCRV radio studios to be interviewed in front of a live studio audience after which my record was played and I mimed to it with a borrowed guitar (on the radio) and felt rather silly. The record would sell OK but did not make the charts due to insufficient radio plays, there seemed to be a bit of a backlash against these types of records.

We performed three gigs and then Laura and I travelled home, Julie and Dominic remaining in Holland to record our first single with Hans van Hemert without us. It now seemed increasingly likely that Laura would not be staying in Guys n' Dolls, as she did not seem to be enjoying it.

Tuesday 1st September 1981

Lynne had been taken into hospital last night but it was a false alarm. She went into labour this morning and this afternoon gave birth to our son Wayne who weighed in at 8lb 4oz. Like most new fathers I found the experience very emotional and one of the most amazing moments of my life.

Saturday 5th September 1981

Julie and Dominic came down to see Lynne and Wayne and stayed overnight. They had been working in Holland with Hans van Hemert and played me a tape of a song called "I've Got the Fire in me" which had been earmarked as our next single. It was an up-tempo Euro pop track and I wasn't convinced it was the direction we should be taking, but I was more concerned with fatherhood and didn't make a fuss.

Thursday 10th September – Saturday 12th September 1981

After the euphoria of becoming a father I reluctantly had to return to work. We were back in Holland for a couple of live shows and a TV appearance with our new record. First we had fittings for possibly the most 'over the top' costumes we had ever worn. Made from white leather with gold tassels, I referred to them as our Egyptian outfits. They were very hot, difficult to get on and off, especially if you were sweaty, and I never felt comfortable wearing them.

Tuesday 29th September 1981

Ludo Veuten (who was now effectively our manager) had been offered a trip to Indonesia for Guys n' Dolls and a Dutch singer called Jack Jersey. It would be for three weeks and would mean flying out the day after Boxing Day. We would be performing four or five shows at the Hilton Hotel in Jakarta which would pay for our expenses, and then hopefully pick up more shows out there so that we would earn from the trip. I felt it was too vague an idea and as it would mess up my first Christmas with Wayne, and didn't want a trip that would be just a free holiday. Dominic and I had a huge row about this.

There were strong links between the Netherlands and Indonesia which was once under Dutch control and known as the Dutch East Indies. It was occupied by the Japanese during the Second World War after which the Dutch never regained control and it became independent under President Sukano.

It was a sad day for me as Bill Shankly the ex. Liverpool FC manager died aged 67.

Sunday 8th November 1981

Lynne holds
Wayne at his
christening.
Julie is holding
one year old
Luke.

It was seven years ago today that Guys n' Dolls were formed coinciding with Wayne's christening at the church where Lynne and I were married, St. Peters in Tewin.

Tuesday 17th November 1981

We sang our latest release "I've Got The Fire In Me" on the Top Pop TV show, the record would peak at 26 in the chart. This was followed by a meeting at Ludo's office where Laura said she did not want to work at all in December. This created a problem as Ludo had already booked dates for us and the disputed Indonesia trip was due to begin on 27th December. Julie and Laura had a sister to sister discussion and the outcome was that Laura would leave the group as soon as we had a replacement. It had been apparent for some time that being in a group wasn't really what she wanted to do; we now had the dilemma of finding a new member as quickly as possible.

Tuesday 24th November 1981

Dominic phoned and said Julie had been in touch with a former member of Legs and Co, Rosie Hetherington, who they thought would be an ideal replacement for Laura, and she had agreed to join us. In 1976 Legs and Co had replaced Pans People as the dancers on the UK TV show "Top of the Pops" and our paths had crossed several times, Julie went to stage school with Rosie. Although I hadn't met her, I felt it was convenient option for what could have been a difficult problem.

Wednesday 16th December – Sunday 20th December 1981

Final line up for
Guys n' Dolls
(left to right)
Julie, Paul,
Rosie and
Dominic.

Laura had performed her last date with Guys n' Dolls a couple of weeks ago and Julie and Dominic had been hard at work rehearsing with Rosie. Today we were off to Holland and I met Rosie for the first time at Heathrow Airport, we had a couple of days before her first gig so had time for some final rehearsals all together. After some serious flight delays due to a fogbound Schipol airport we arrived at Ludo's office where he had arranged a party for the press to introduce Rosie.

We spent a couple of days in the studio with Hans van Hemert recording a couple of new songs and as usual I found the process boring to the extreme especially as on first day I did nothing. I was mentally going through my worst period in Guys n' Dolls as the impending trip to Indonesia was looming and so far there had been no extra dates put in, so my worst fears were coming true and it appeared to be just a paid holiday. As Wayne was only three months old there was no way we could take him and there was no way that Lynne would travel without him, all this put quite a strain on my relationship with Dominic and Julie.

On Saturday 19th December Rosie performed with Guys n' Dolls for the first time in Antwerp, Belgium. Despite the fact she was extremely nervous everything went well and she managed to fit into Laura's Egyptian costume, which she would have to make do with for the time being.

Sunday 27th December 1981

I had been celebrating a family Christmas at Lynne parent's house in Abingdon and today Guys n' Dolls were due to fly to Indonesia. Ludo had still not managed to arrange any more gigs and in my mind it was a completely pointless trip and I decided I wasn't going. We were all supposed to meet up at Heathrow for a flight to Holland and a connecting flight to Jakarta. It had been snowing, not really hard enough to stop me travelling, but I phoned Ludo's office and left a message that I had missed the plane. I later had a call from Ludo's secretary Ingrid to say I could travel the following day, but this time I genuinely couldn't get booked onto a flight to Holland as they were all full.

Tuesday 29th November 1981

I had received a stream of calls for the past two days from Rocket management and even our producer Hans van Hemert trying to get me to Indonesia and today I reluctantly decided that I would have to go. Lynne and her Dad took me to Heathrow where I flew to Amsterdam and connected with a Singapore Airlines flight to Jakarta. It was a lonely twenty hour flight and I was angry being forced to make the trip.

Wednesday 30th December 1981

My plane landed at Jakarta in a thunder storm which wasn't very pleasant and I was met by the manager of the Hilton hotel where we were working. The hotel was probably one of the best I had ever stayed in and I had a large oriental themed room, but wasn't in the right frame of mind to really appreciate it. As I hadn't slept on the plane I said a quick hello to the rest of the group, my two day delay wasn't mentioned, and went straight to bed.

Thursday 31st December 1981

Slept until 1.00pm and then discovered the complete size of our party, apart from Guys n' Dolls and Luke, there was Dominic's brother Ian who had come to help look after Luke, Dutch singer Jack Jersey, Ludo, a guy from a Dutch magazine called Joop, a Dutch DJ who had come along for a free holiday in exchange for him hopefully playing Ludo's artist's records, and a girl singer called Lisa who's main role seemed to be keeping Jack Jersey happy. There was also a Belgian guy called Jaques and I never did find out why he was there.

In Indonesia every act has to appear in front of a censor's panel to make sure the act is of good taste and yesterday, before I arrived, the other three members had to perform the complete act in full costume for this reason. Everything was fine but because I had now arrived and obviously may have brought something dubious to the act we ridiculously had to go through the whole show again, the four censors sat making notes while being fed and watered at the expense of the Hilton hotel.

This evening was our first show at the Hilton after which the manager gave us a couple of bottles of champagne to toast in the New Year, seven hours before the UK but I didn't feel much like celebrating.

1982

Friday 1ˢᵗ January 1982

Awoke at 1.00pm with a bit of a hangover from the New Years Eve champagne, had a meal and then managed to find a film in English on TV. The organiser of the tour, if you can call it that, was a guy called Pim Vroegop who this evening took us all to a party by the beach, just killing time.

Saturday 2nd January 1982

This morning we flew from Jakarta to Yogyakarta, a separate Sultanate within Indonesia. We checked into a hotel close to Mount Merapi, one of the most active volcanoes in the country. On a clear night you could see the fiery glow lighting up the sky which was impressive. The weather in Yogyakarta was diverse, in the morning there were clear blue skies but by mid afternoon it clouded over followed by huge thunderstorms when it was advised not to use the lifts in the hotel as there would invariably be a power cut.

This evening we performed our second show for charity, a bit of a waste of time as the audience was small.

Sunday 3ʳᵈ January 1982

Another day treading water with no gig scheduled, so Pim took us to a cloth factory to see the intricate Batik designs being created on traditional Indonesian clothes. This was quite interesting but it was followed by a visit to a silver factory which wasn't. It looked as if we would be performing a few shows in Surabaya in a few days time for which we would receive payment and would, for me, justify this trip.

This evening we went to watch Jack Jersey perform a show which was a disaster as there were only nineteen in the audience including us.

Monday 4th January 1982

Where's Rosie?

We visited the house of the Sultan of Yogyakarta, along with Joop the photographer from Dutch magazine Prive, and had a session dressed in traditional Indonesian costumes, including a headdress, which with my hair was a bit of a problem.

Tuesday 5th January – Friday 8th January 1982

This morning we flew to Bali for a few days off, which was a bit of a joke as we'd only performed two shows, but this was probably the part of the trip that I enjoyed the most. We were staying at an open air hotel in individual bamboo huts with no air conditioning, just a fan, a can of insect repellent and the occasional lizard crawling across the ceiling. The vegetation in Bali was stunning and the animal life amazing. During the day fruit bats with a wing span of around three feet could be seen flying above the trees and we found snails the size of tennis balls. Every night there was a pig roast and each afternoon the evening's pig was herded past our huts on its way to our plates which was a bit disconcerting. I don't know if it was the pig getting his own back but on the first night I had a touch of Bali belly.

Apart from one trip out for a photo session in the rice fields, our time was our own. We were effectively on the equator so the temperatures were in the mid forties while back in England our families were shivering in a temperature of minus eight. It was so hot in Bali that sunbathing was only possible early morning or late afternoon. We were awaiting details of our trip to Surabaya and on Friday Pim arrived with the news that the trip was off and we would be returning to Jakarta tomorrow, I wasn't best pleased.

Saturday 9th January – Saturday 16th January 1982

We flew back to Jakarta and checked back into the Hilton hotel with nothing to do for two days, and then on the Monday we performed a show for the hotel staff followed by another charity show on the Tuesday. Pim told us there was one last chance of a paid show next Saturday. We performed two more shows at the Hilton on Thursday and Friday and then guess what? The paid show did not materialise.

We were all supposed to fly home on the Monday but Pim, knowing how pissed off I was, managed to get me on a flight to Amsterdam a day early.

Sunday 17th January – Monday 18th January 1982

With my friend?
Ludo Veuten
I think I'm
pointing with the
wrong finger

Another lonely twenty hour flight but I didn't mind too much as I was going home. It's a shame I was in the wrong frame of mind for the trip, as Indonesia seemed a fascinating place, I just felt personally ripped off especially by the freeloaders who had a holiday at our expense. I was annoyed with Ludo for arranging such a pointless trip and it was a nail in the coffin of our relationship as he and I were destined not to get on.

I arrived at Amsterdam on Monday morning and caught the next flight back to London. It was great to see the family again and Wayne's facial features had changed slightly in the three weeks that I had been away.

Thursday 4th March – Wednesday 10th March 1982

Since returning from Indonesia Guys n' Dolls had got into the routine of working most weekends in Holland, travelling as far south as Brussels in the Dutch speaking part of Belgium, none of our journeys were longer than two hours. We would fly over on the Friday, perform two or three shows and return home on the Monday.

This time, as we had commitments for a whole week, I decided to take Lynne and Wayne which meant driving to Harwich and catching the ferry. We had been making our base at the Euromotel near Schipol airport but had been looking at the possibility of renting apartments on a more permanent basis.

Vinkeveen is a village about 14km south of Amsterdam and not far from Hilversum where all the TV and Radio stations are situated as is most of the music business. We were introduced to Kees Jan and his wife Marijke who owned a restaurant and chalet/apartments on the Vinkeveense Plassen, which is a large picturesque lake, and decided to rent three single story open plan chalets, one for Julie and Dominic and one each for Rosie and me. This meant we would have a permanent base in Holland and was far better than hotels which we were all getting fed up with. These would be our Dutch homes for the duration of the group's existence, with one of our neighbours being Dutch football star Johan Cruyff.

Our latest record "Broken Dreams" had been released and was climbing the Dutch charts and would eventually peak at number twelve. We appeared on a TV show at a circus and with us was American country star Emmylou Harris singing her version of a favourite song of mine "Rose of Cimarron" which had originally been recorded by Poco in 1976.

Thursday 15th April – Monday 3rd May 1982

Two of the top Dutch acts. (left to right) Andre Hazes The Dollydots

We were now firmly established in our Dutch homes and getting used to a different way of life, never managing to conquer the language as it was hard to find anyone who didn't speak English. I asked Peter Koelewijn for something to speak in Dutch during our act, he told me to say "lekker neuken niet betalen" fortunately I found out just in time that it was quite inappropriate. I am not going to translate, but for anyone who speaks Dutch I do apologise.

We appeared for three nights at the 8000 seater Jaap Edenhalle in Amsterdam along side many of Holland's home grown artist's who we were now beginning to get to know, many of them who sang in Dutch were virtually unheard of outside of the Benelux countries. Names like Lee Towers, Patricia Paay, Anita Meyer and a six piece all girl group, with attitude, called the Dolly Dots, fifteen years before the Spice Girls. It was always difficult for Dutch acts to achieve worldwide fame but I think if the Dolly Dots had been from the UK it might have happened.

Probably the biggest star at the time was a guy from Amsterdam called Andre Hazes, who sang in Dutch in a style called "levenslied" (songs of life) and in 1982 his album "Gewoon Andre" (simply Andre) had sold 500,000 copies and received five platinum awards catapulting him into superstardom. We would work with him often during the next few years. He died of a heart attack in 2004 and such was his popularity that a statue of him was erected in Amsterdam.

We had been in the studios, whenever time allowed, recording tracks for our second Dutch album. Hans van Hemert dictatorially took over complete control of the writing and content and for the first time there was no chance of me or any other members of the group having any of our own songs included. Along side this Dominic had started work on his first solo album with Hans.

There was now a third Guys n' Dolls baby as Martine had recently given birth to a girl naming her Danielle. We went to visit her and Gerry who were now living in a village called Epe. Their house was in the middle of a wood inhabited by wild pigs.

Monday 10th May 1982
As the weather got warmer life in Vinkeveen became quite idyllic with the lake virtually on our doorstep. Our landlord Kees Jan had several boats and as Dominic and I wanted to go shopping he suggested we take his small boat with an outboard motor to the village which was situated on the opposite side of the lake about mile and a half away. On the way back we ran out of petrol midway and had to sit there for what seemed like hours until we managed to attract the attention of someone on another boat who towed us back to Vinkeveen.

Sunday 16th May 1982
After Indonesia gained independence at the end of the second world war, there was a large migration of around 300,000 Indonesians into Holland over a period of twenty years. One of the traditions of the Dutch/Indo population is to hold large markets where traditional Indonesian goods are sold and entertainment provided. This is called a Pasar Malam and today we performed at one of these for the first time in a small town towards the east of Holland called Twello. We performed to a crowd of around a thousand people who gave us a great reception.

Sunday 23rd May 1982
Status Quo were appearing in Leiden and at my request our record company arranged for us to go. The rest of the group were not particularly fans but I defy anyone not to enjoy the atmosphere at a Status Quo concert.

Tuesday 8th June 1982
Split Enz had just completed a tour of Canada and were having a few free days before they started a tour of the USA, Nigel had come to England on a quick visit to see the

family. In April Split Enz had released their latest album called "Time and Tide" and a track, which would become one of my all time favourites, "Six Months in a Leaky Boat" had been released in the UK. It had been receiving a lot of airplay but unfortunately it coincided with the Falklands conflict and when HMS Sheffield was sunk with a loss of lives it was decided that the song title may cause offence and the airplay ceased abruptly just as it was about to enter the charts.

Saturday 12ᵗʰ June 1982

Dutch TV producers seemed to come up with very odd ideas on how Guys n' Dolls should be portrayed on television. Today we were driven to a BMX bike track, kitted out with all the protective clothing, and then filmed in the middle of the track singing our latest record "Broken Dreams" while a dozen kids rode around the track on bikes at breakneck speed just managing to avoid us. After this we were given bikes so that we could be filmed for our own race. Dominic and I being childishly competitive set off as fast as we could and at the first large hump Dominic and bike parted company and he went flying through the air landing heavily on the track, fortunately apart from a couple of small cuts and scratches he was OK, meanwhile I was selfishly winning the race. Boys will be boys.

Wednesday 4ᵗʰ August 1982

As well as strange TV shows we did some strange gigs. Today there was no singing; we were paid our normal fee for being driven around Antwerp on the back of a lorry signing autographs, which was much tougher than actually performing.

Saturday 4ᵗʰ September 1982

Dominic's solo single had been released and today he made a live radio appearance from the "Firato" which was a regular trade fair for the Dutch music industry. We had been performing there each night for Technics who had offered Guys n' Dolls a deal where for two years we would be the faces of the company, being featured in TV and newspaper advertising. Part of the deal meant we would be supplied with top of the range video camera equipment which in 1982 was very expensive.

Dominic's solo record "I Won't Let Me Down" would peak at number twenty three in the charts.

Wednesday 27th October 1982

Another strange Guys n' Dolls gig. Rudy Koopmans was the light heavy weight European boxing champion, tonight he was appearing at Enschede, boxing an exhibition match and we were appearing with him. We had to perform our act in the boxing ring and as the audience was all around us it was difficult to know which way to turn.

Thursday 4th November 1982

As we were working on November 5th, we decided to celebrate Guy Fawkes night at Vinkeveen a day early. We built a bonfire, made a Guy, bought some fireworks and then tried to explain to our invited Dutch friends the reason for celebrating Guys Fawkes day. We told them that Guys Fawkes and his fellow conspirators had tried to blow up the Houses of Parliament but were caught in the act and then executed, how every year it is celebrated by burning an effigy of Guys Fawkes on a bonfire. Our Dutch friends gave us a look which said "crazy English".

Tuesday 9th - Thursday 11th November 1982

My fear of flying was again evident as we travelled to Bulgaria and took our life in our hands by flying in a Balkan airline Russian built Tupelov 134 aircraft. They didn't have a great safety record and I don't know if it was me but the plane just didn't seem too safe. As we were descending there was a crash as the drinks trolley burst through a door at the back of the plane and trundled down the aisle all on its own. Despite our fears we landed safely at Sophia.

We appeared on a Bulgarian television show along side Petula Clarke who was a pleasure to work with. Fortunately our return flight was with KLM.

Thursday 2nd December 1982

We spent nine hours filming a nineteen second commercial for Technics.

Wednesday 15th December 1982

Pop music has always been dictated to by the technology available at the time and we were now into the eighties where much music was being produced using synthesisers and drum machines. Robert Moog had introduced the Moog Synthesiser in the sixties and even the Beatles had used one, albeit sparingly, on their final album Abbey Road. The early models were the size of a wardrobe, cost a fortune, and not that reliable but by now they had decreased in size and price and were readily available to everyone. The eighties were dominated by groups like Human League, Orchestral Manoeuvres in the Dark and Depeche Mode who made records entirely with machines. A British company called Simmons, based near my home town of Hatfield, introduced an electronic drum kit, each drum being hexagonally shaped. These kits were a familiar sight on Top of the Pops at the time and can still be heard today at the beginning of each episode of Eastenders. There was also the introduction of digital echo units which I felt were over used by some record producers, making many records in the eighties over produced and in retrospect it's not a time musically that I look back on with much fondness.

Today I bought my first synthesiser, a Korg Polysix and like many other musicians put the guitar on the back burner for a while as I explored the new musical possibilities now available to me.

Thursday 30th December 1982

It had now been two years since we stopped working in the UK and concentrate solely on Holland and in general it had been OK but I was still totally frustrated by our recording situation with Hans van Hemert. He had made us record some really second rate material for our latest album which had been released a couple of months ago and wasn't selling well. A single from the album, "I Heard it on the Radio" had struggled to number 36 in the charts and it seemed the Dutch public were none too impressed with the material either. I was aware I was probably appearing very negative in the studio and tried hard to just grin and bear it, but it was hard. The recording sessions were long and tedious with very little for me to do and most of the time I was just hanging around.

A few years ago there was a quote by Charlie Watts of the Rolling Stones who when an interviewer enquired "The Rolling Stones have been around for twenty five years and during that time there must have been a lot of hanging around". Charlie replied "Yes I've been playing for five years and hanging around for the other twenty". He never said very much but when he did speak it was usually entertaining.

I needed some sort of artistic outlet of my own and I had been experimenting in my studio with a Beatles song from the Rubber Soul album called "You Won't See Me". It had always been a favourite of mine and I decided to go into a studio, record a synthesizer version of the song and try to get it released. I approached Don Larking who was in business selling studio equipment but had a complete twenty four track studio set up at his premises. He had no problem with me using it in return for a share of any profit the record would make, and I could start recording next week.

1983

Tuesday 4th January 1983

We had a few days off before our scheduled return to Holland and today I went to Luton to record "You Won't See Me" at Don Larking's studio. Don supplied me with an engineer and the latest programmable "Linn" drum machine. Although my Polysix synthesiser was one of the latest models it did not have "midi" built into it. Midi (musical instrument digital interface) is a system where keyboards sequencers and computers, could be linked to communicate with each other. It is found on even the most basic keyboards today. I decided to build up the song using different sounds from my synthesiser, playing each part manually and recording them directly onto a multi track tape machine. It was a long process but I enjoyed it and by the end of the day I had recorded most of the backing track, the vocals, and even managed to play a real snare drum for the drum fills. I made a rough mix and thought that even if I couldn't get it released the experience had done me good and I felt artistically satisfied, for the present.

Friday 14th January 1983

Back in Holland, I felt honour bound to take my version of "You Won't See Me" for Ludo to hear as he was supposed to be our manager. I have said already that my personal relationship with Ludo wasn't good and I was under no illusions over what his reaction might be. I played him the track and as expected he was completely negative and said it wasn't suitable to be a single and I would have no chance of getting it released, clearly indicating that he would not try to help me with it. This reaction brought our relationship to a new low, Ludo was a good booking agent as he had kept us in good quality work since we had been working for him but as a manager he left much to be desired. A manager is supposed to direct and guide an artist's career but artistically he hadn't much of a clue and none of us ever found out what music he personally enjoyed, if any.

I left the office feeling rather annoyed, but as Ludo clearly had no intentions of helping me obtain a release, decided to pursue things on my own as I had nothing to lose.

Thursday 27th January 1983

Today I had meeting with a record company called Dureco, I played them my track of "You Won't See Me" which they liked and agreed to release it as a single as soon as possible. I negotiated a good deal which included an advance and the whole meeting lasted thirty minutes. I phoned Ludo to tell him the good news. He didn't say too much.

Saturday 16th April 1983

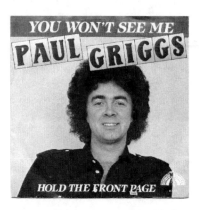

My single "You Won't See Me" had been released a week ago and had received several radio plays; today I performed the song live on one of the top shows called Los Vast.

Saturday 23rd April 1983

A marathon day, as Guys n' Dolls had been booked to perform four shows. We started in the afternoon performing at a horse show at Assen, in the North of Holland, then drove south for a show performing on a boat in Amsterdam for Technics. Next was a Pasar Malam at Dordrecht near Rotterdam and finally on to our final performance in Brussels around midnight.

There was a problem at this final show as our backing tracks were on tape, but the sound guys had brought a tape machine with the wrong sized spools. So where on earth could anyone track down the correct machine at midnight in Belgium? By this time we were all knackered and didn't really care that much but we were amazed when the organisers phoned the local dentist who miraculously owned the machine we needed. Someone went to collect it; we performed the final show, virtually on automatic pilot, then crashed out in the car and returned to Vinkeveen.

Monday 25th April 1983

My solo record had received only a couple of radio plays this past week and Ludo took great delight in telling me something I already knew, that it wasn't going to make the charts. Along with the fact that the last Guys n' Dolls single, "I Heard it on the Radio", only reached 36 and Dominic's second solo single, "Come Closer to me" had failed to chart, collectively and individually we were having a recording crisis. We would have no further hits in Holland.

The music business in Holland, which as I've already said is based in Hilversum, is quite compact with everyone knowing each other. I heard that Ludo had been bad mouthing my single and actually hindering its progress. I considered confronting him with this but as there was no real proof and knowing he would deny it, I decided to let things be.

Monday 16ᵗʰ May 1983

We were in Paris for a Technics convention and were asked to sing something a cappella so that it could be recorded on the latest digital recorder and played back to the gathered assembly which included some of the Technics directors from Japan. In the car we had often sung a three part harmony version of the traditional Irish song "Cockles and Mussels", so we decided to sing that and it seemed to work OK. We were then presented with a CD of our last album that Technics had specially pressed.

The Compact Disc was partly a Dutch development as Phillips, based in Eindhoven, had been involved with the research in conjunction with Sony. The first ever commercial release was Abba's album "The Visitor", which came onto the market only a few months ago. We now had a state of the art version of our latest album and fortunately, because of my negative feelings about it, nothing to play it on.

Saturday 18ᵗʰ June 1983

Our record company CNR had found a song that they were convinced would be a hit for Guys n' Dolls, so it was goodbye to Hans van Hemert as we were teamed up with two established producers called Pete Souer and Martin Douser. The song was called "Glory to the Beautiful People"; even the title was crap as once again I gritted my teeth and endured another painful session in the recording studio. It was an up tempo song slightly in the vein of Kid Creole and the Coconuts and once again I hated it and began giving off negative vibes.

I really wasn't trying to be difficult for the sake of it, I just wanted the group to record better material that we could be proud of and deep down I wanted to be more involved with the creative process and for us to write our own songs. I was writing quite a lot but because of my more "rock" background the songs were not obvious Guys n' Dolls material. Dominic, Julie and I had tried writing together and some time ago we wrote and recorded a song called "Answer My Question" which Hans van Hemert had rejected for our last album. It's all down to opinions but in retrospect I feel the track stands up well. I think if we had continued writing together it would have developed. Some of the Beatles early songs, i.e. "Love me Do", were not great but their writing progressed and with practise, along with the healthy competitiveness between John and Paul, the songs just got better and better.

Despite many radio plays and around half a dozen TV appearances "Glory to the Beautiful People" would fail to make any impression on the record buying public.

Tuesday 27th September 1983

We were recording at Wisselord studios in Hilversum and in the studio next door was Barry Manilow being produced by Jim Steinman. I had been mulling over the idea that when I finally left Guys n' Dolls, producing was something I might go into and Jim Steinman was a producer that I admired at the time. He had released a great solo record called "Rock and Roll Dreams Come True" and produced one of the biggest selling albums of all time Meatloaf's "Bat out of Hell". I managed to have a chat with him during a break in recording.

Wednesday 16th November 1983

Out of the blue I received a phone call from Chai the promoter from Thailand who had organized our previous tours. He had been trying to contact the group for some time as he wanted us to return to Thailand next February.

Monday 28th November 1983

The Eighties look. Julie and Rosie with Lisa Stansfield.

We had met a guy called Martin Pursey who was running Rick Wakeman's record label "Moon Records". Martin wanted to release a Guys n' Dolls single in the UK and had chosen a track that we had recorded with Hans van Hemert called "Freez" which amazingly I didn't mind too much. The record was due to be released in a week's time and today Julie and Rosie travelled to Newcastle to appear on the children's TV show Razzamatazz. The record was played and they were interviewed by a young Lisa Stansfield who was still six years away from having her first hit with "People Hold On". We had first met Lisa a few years earlier when at the age of 13 she had won a talent competition at the Talk of the North nightclub near Manchester. She had an amazing voice and it was obvious she had a bright future ahead.

Unfortunately our record was never released. We had received advanced copies but a few days after the appearance on Razzamatazz, Rick Wakeman suddenly decided to close down Moon records with immediate effect.

1984

Sunday 1ˢᵗ January 1984

Rosie catches
up with her best
friend Tracey
Ullman in
Amsterdam

Top of the British charts this week were the Flying Pickets with "Only You" followed by Slade, still having top ten hits, with "My Oh My". At number fifteen was Rosie's best friend Tracey Ullman who was on the way down after her third top ten hit with "Move over Darling". Our old label, Magnet records, had finally found a quality act to replace Guys n' Dolls, at number eighteen was "superstar" Roland Rat with "Rat Rapping".

Thursday 9ᵗʰ February 1984

As Guys n' Dolls had been working solely with backing tracks for the past few years we had to put together a live band for forthcoming visit to Thailand. The four piece Dutch band included Rosie's Dutch boyfriend Albert Boekholt and today we finalised rehearsals ahead of the impending tour.

Sunday 12ᵗʰ February – Saturday 25ᵗʰ February 1984

Our third visit to Thailand, Lynne and Wayne both came with us along with Dominic and Julie's son Luke. We performed three shows in Bangkok and then the promoter Chai once again gave us a few days holiday in Pataya which, as we all had family and partners with us, was quite Idyllic.

We returned to Bangkok for the flight home where Julie and Dominic had a problem with immigration officials. Dominic's name on his passport was Dominic Grant, Julie's was Julie Forsyth and Luke's was Luke Purdie, Dominic's real surname. They were kept for a good thirty minutes explaining the situation to officials who did not speak the best of English.

Thursday 5ᵗʰ April 1984

"Showbiz Quiz" was one of the top television shows in Holland and was a bit like UK's

"Generation Game". It was a two hour show where contestants had to participate in various games and quizzes. Today Guys n' Dolls had to sing extracts from songs and the participants had to guess which shows they came from. We sang "Starmaker" from Fame and "Staying Alive" from Saturday Night Fever. Also on the show were Rod Hull and Emu and Roger Daltrey from the Who. Roger was having a solo hit with a song called "Giving it all Away" and I was amazed that someone of his stature would agree to take part in the show. He had a contestant on stage with him and they sang the song together, taking a couple of lines each which he then repeated with another contestant followed by a vote to find the winner. Not very Rock n' Roll.

Thursday 19th April 1984

Our recording situation took another twist as we changed labels yet again. We were now with Phonogram and a new set of producers, Richard du Bois and Peter van Asten. Today we recorded our next single which was an ok but not spectacular ballad called "I feel like Crying".

Wednesday 9th May 1984

Ludo phoned to say that we were going to Korea to represent Holland in a song festival in place of the Dollydots who were unable to participate.

Friday 18th May 1984

Tim Finn from Split Enz had taken time out from the group to record a solo album called "Escapade". He and the group's manager Nathan Brenner were in Holland promoting his single "Fraction Too Much Friction". I called in at the TV studios in Hilversum to say "hello". He performed two songs on a TV show and the second song "In a Minor Key" would influence me for a song I had yet to write.

What nobody knew at the time was that Tim Finn only had a month left as a member of Split Enz.

Monday 21st May 1984

Issei Sagawa
It's in the
eyes.

Issei Sagawa
leaves the
plane at
Tokyo. I
breath a sigh
of relief.

Another song contest. We flew to Paris for an Air France flight to Seoul, in South Korea. Shortly after take off from Paris I noticed photographers taking pictures of a rather strange looking Japanese guy sitting across the aisle from me. Richard du Bois who was accompanying us on the trip said he recognised him. His name was Issei Sagawa known as the "Japanese Cannibal." He had been a student at the Sorbonne where he met and murdered a fellow student, a Dutch girl named Rene Hartvelt. He then proceeded to cut up and eat parts of her body burying the remains near the Bois de Boulogne. He was caught, tried and Psychiatrists declared him to be insane. Today accompanied by two French detectives and a posse of photographers he was being deported back to Japan. I was quite unnerved when I heard the story as there was just an aisle between him and me and he wasn't even handcuffed. He had the most evil eyes I had ever seen. We stopped over at Anchorage, Alaska, and although the detectives never left his side he was allowed to walk freely around the airport with the other passengers. I was quite relieved when we arrived at Tokyo where he left the plane to be met by a hoard of photographers.

In Japan Issei Sagawa was declared sane but guilty and due to the intervention of his influential industrialist Father was released and in effect got away with murder. Today he lives the life of a minor celebrity and seems to trade from his gruesome past.

The Rolling Stones often used a recording studio not far from the scene of the crime and their song "Too Much Blood," on their 1984 "Undercover" album was inspired by the incident.

Thursday 24th May 1984

The rehearsals for the Seoul Song Festival 84 had taken place over the past couple of days, we didn't know anyone else in the contest but we had heard of the Canadian entry, his name was Andy Kim who reached number two in the UK with "Rock me Gently" in 1974 and wrote the Archies hit "Sugar Sugar". We immediately christened him Bandy Limb, I don't remember why.

Tonight all of the contestants had to appear in a pre festival live television show. The idea for the opening was that the contestants and their entourage would walk onto a stage and then take their places sitting on the stage for the duration of the show. There were around forty people altogether and the producer made the mistake of choosing Dominic to lead everyone on. The introduction music was played and at the given signal Dominic began leading the procession. He walked up the steps, onto the stage, across the stage, and instead of turning right to take his seat, he carried straight on down the steps and off the stage the other side, followed by forty rather bemused people and a television director almost having heart failure. Have you ever laughed so much that you just can't stop, I did that night. After we had finally found our seats I totally lost it as I kept picturing the scene in my mind and bursting out laughing for the next thirty minutes. I must have looked demented and probably was.

Saturday 26th May 1984
It was the day of the festival and once again having heard all of the different entries, and differing styles from around the world wondered how the judges could pick out a winner. I needn't have worried as the voting was not entirely honest.

Our producers Peter van Asten and Richard du Bois were with us on this trip and each entrant had to supply a judge so Peter was nominated. This was where the trouble started. The judges couldn't vote for their own song so they started wheeling and dealing and making alliances to secure votes and there was a lot of bad feeling from some of the contestants. We sang our latest single "I Feel like Crying" and when all of the votes were added up Peter had proved himself to be the master manipulator as Guys n' Dolls were awarded the gold prize. I felt no emotions about winning as I thought song contests were rather pointless affairs, although I would hypocritically change my opinion in eighteen months time. There was a lot of muttering and bad vibes after the contest, even the organisers were unhappy with the way the judging had been corrupted, but it was their own fault for devising such a ridiculous system. We took our trophy, a brass model of a Korean stringed instrument, back to the hotel and drew lots as to who would keep it, Dominic won.

We received a letter after the contest thanking us for taking part and saying we would be welcome back at any time as long as we didn't bring Peter van Asten with us.

Wednesday 30th May 1984
Since the contest we had been promoting our record in and around Seoul and we were even given our own Guys n' Dolls TV special. Today it was time to embark on what would be a thirty hour journey back to Holland. For the first leg we flew in a Pan Am Jumbo Jet from Seoul to Tokyo, and encountered some of the worst turbulence I have ever experienced. The Captain came on the intercom and said "Ladies and Gentlemen due to the severe weather I am afraid we will have to close the bar". At that moment the plane suddenly dropped about a hundred feet and we heard the reassuring cry from the Captain "Jesus Christ!"

We had a four hour wait at Tokyo for our connecting flight to Paris. Liverpool were once again in the European Cup Final and when we stopped over in Anchorage I worked out that it was in the middle of the match but try as I might I could get no information as to the score.

Thursday 31ˢᵗ May 1984

Dominic holds the trophy as we try and look as if we had not been travelling for the past 30 hours.

We arrived in Paris at 7.00am and I discovered that Liverpool had won the European Cup for the fourth time beating FC Roma on penalties (Bruce Grobbelar's wobbly legs episode). Another three hour wait before our flight to Amsterdam where we were met by photographers who had heard about our "amazing" triumph? in Korea. After thirty hours on planes we were not really in a fit state to be photographed.

Sunday 16ᵗʰ June 1984

In Australia Tim Finn announced he was leaving Split Enz, a major news event in the Antipodes, even more so following the success of Tim's solo album and a much publicised relationship with actress Greta Scacchi. The rest of the band decided to carry on, with Tim's brother Neil now at the helm.

Wednesday 25ᵗʰ July 1984

Three weeks after Tim Finn had decided to leave Split Enz his brother Neil had a change of heart and decided he wanted out as well, which effectively meant the end of the band. Today they held a press conference to announce they would make one more album, undertake a final tour of Australasia and that would be the end of Split Enz.

Nigel was particularly frustrated by the decision as he felt there was a lot of music left in the band.

Wednesday 29th August – Sunday 9th September 1984

Photograph courtesy of Olaf Schrawers

As part of the deal with Technics, Guys n' Dolls performed another run of shows at the Firato music trade show in Amsterdam. This time the company had built a special stage about fifteen feet from the ground surrounded by a globe of the world. For every performance we had to climb inside and it would then open up for our show. It was quite impressive and the mechanism to open the globe did not fail and nobody fell off the stage.

Wednesday 10th October 1984

Today we took delivery of a new set of posters and hand out photographs. We had a photo session a few weeks ago, where probably around a hundred shots were taken and then much time was spent deliberating about which was the best one to use. Despite all these precautions whoever chose this picture failed to see the position of my left hand (and I can assure you it is my hand), so for ever more this was known as the "Willie" picture.

Saturday 15th September 1984

Def Leppard were recording their latest album Hysteria at Wisselord Studios in Hilversum. Drummer Rick Allen had completed his drum parts and was at a bit of a loose end. He told us that the band were going through typical Rock n' Roll extravagances spending hours experimenting with different Marshall amplifiers trying to find ones they liked. He asked if he could come with us to our gig this evening and we said no problem. He came with us to our gig in Belgium and was good company. He told us that he had recently taken delivery of a brand new American Corvette car which was his pride and joy.

Just over three months later on New Years Eve his Corvette was involved in a serious high speed crash near his home town of Sheffield and Rick tragically lost his left arm. He was determined to carry on drumming and with the help of "Simmons", the electronic drum company, a special kit was designed so that his leg could play the parts previously played by his left arm. Rick made a triumphant return to live performing at the Castle Donington Monsters of Rock in 1986 and still drums with the band to this day.

Monday 8th October 1984

Guys n' Dolls had been voted most popular "Dutch" music group by the magazine "Weekend". Considering we were British, and the way our records had been selling recently, I found this quite hard to believe. Tonight we appeared at a special award ceremony at the Marriott Hotel in Amsterdam. We performed, along with other prize winners, before receiving our award. Once again we drew lots to decide who was going to keep the award and Rosie won, which I didn't mind too much as the award was not a thing of beauty.

Wednesday 10th October 1984

Our producers Richard and Peter had come up with a song that was quite a departure for Guys n' Dolls. Describing it is difficult, suffice to say it was semi classical in parts and so far removed from anything we had done before. The song was originally called "Lonely People" but I asked if I could write some new lyrics and made the whole song about the life of Guys n' Dolls and the anomalies of the music industry changing the title to "Phoney People". We recorded it and I thought it turned out great, but I wasn't sure what the fans would make of it.

Split Enz had reached number thirteen in the Dutch charts with what would turn out to be one of my all time favourite songs. It was a Neil Finn composition from their Conflicting Emotions album called "Message to my Girl" with my brother playing a perfect understated bass line.

Tuesday 20th November 1984

A couple of weeks ago Guys n' Dolls celebrated ten years as a group, and today was my fortieth birthday. I had started to seriously consider what I would do after the group finished as I felt our days were numbered and there wasn't much I was enjoying. Song writing? Producing? These were possibilities but I felt, at the time I was ready to give up performing. I now had a family to support which would have to be my main consideration.

Thursday 6th December 1984

Split Enz had released their final album "See Ya Round" last month and their "Enz with a Bang" tour of Australasia had begun on 30th September. Tim Finn had rejoined the band for the final tour and tonight was the last show at the Logan Campbell Theatre in Auckland, New Zealand. Their final song was "Hard Act to Follow".

Paul Hester had been the drummer with Split Enz for the past year. Neil Finn would soon ask him to join his new band which would eventually be called Crowded House.

1985

Tuesday 1st January 1985

Top of the UK charts was Band Aid's "Do They Know it's Christmas" followed by Wham's "Last Christmas". Paul McCartney and the Frog Chorus were at three with his much maligned "We All Stand Together" and Madonna at four with "Like a Virgin."

Tuesday 8th January 1985

What would be Guys n' Dolls last ever single, "Phoney People," had just been released and today was our first TV appearance with the song. We appeared on Pop Shop along with Dionne Warwick, Status Quo and the Troggs. Tony Murray, who had produced the Octopus album, was still playing bass with the Troggs and it was the first time I had seen him in fifteen years. Status Quo were a great bunch and when Rick Parfitt heard that we were off to Thailand in a few weeks time he seriously asked if he could come with us. Status Quo at that time were not active, they had not broken up but had no plans for recording or touring and I think Rick was bored and needed something to do. He said he would even come along and just play guitar with the backing band. In some ways it would have been great taking him with us but Rick Parfitt was known for being a bit of a hell raiser and I'm not sure the combination of Guys n' Doll and Rick Parfitt would have really worked, so it did not happen.

In a few months time Status Quo would open "Live Aid" from Wembley singing "Rocking All over the World". This would herald a new beginning for the band.

Sunday 10th February – Tuesday 26th February 1985

We once again visited Thailand for our fourth and final trip. This time we were booked to play for two weeks at the Dusit Thani Hotel in Bangkok. Lynne and Wayne came with us and it was very enjoyable lounging by the pool during the day and popping upstairs to the Cabaret room for a show at night. We flew Alia (Jordanian Airways) and on our return we found the airline staff to be easily impressed. In return for them having a photograph taken with us, we were upgraded to first class and apart from two other passengers, plus a rather twitchy armed guard, had the whole of the upstairs section of a Jumbo Jet to ourselves.

We went from luxury to misery as we had to stay overnight in Amman in Jordan and landed in a snow storm at the beginning of an awful 24 hours. The Jordanian immigration officials were very suspicious of us and confiscated our passports. We were all dressed in summer clothes and it was freezing and had to endure a nightmare forty minute bus ride to a really dreadful hotel where the toilets were not functioning properly. The following morning there was six inches of snow on the ground and we thought we would never get away, but by midday it was all gone and with much relief we were driven back to the airport, had our passports returned, and left for Amsterdam.

Despite our record "Phoney People" having maximum plays on radio and around half a dozen TV appearances, it failed to make the charts.

Friday 5th April 1985

I had started travelling to Holland from Luton Airport. A new company called London European Airways had begun a twice daily service to Amsterdam using just one plane, a rather ancient four propeller Vickers Viscount. The fares were cheap and anyone using this airline could park their car directly outside the terminal and as it was only thirty minutes from my home it was all very convenient.

The first time I flew with London European we had been in the air only ten minutes when I noticed that one of the propellers had stopped. We had to return to Luton for repairs. Today we were only about fifteen minutes from Amsterdam when I heard the words that anyone who was nervous of flying, never wanted to hear. "Ladies and Gentlemen may I have your attention. There is a technical problem with the plane and we have to prepare for an emergency landing at Amsterdam. Please loosen any tight clothing; remove any high heeled shoes, glasses and false teeth and when you hear a whistle assume the brace position" (head down to your knees). There were around twenty people on the plane and at that moment twenty faces turned white. I had just drunk a large brandy and the stewardess had already poured me another which at the time I didn't really want. I picked up the glass and knocked it straight back, regretting it a second later realising that it's not particularly advisable to be pissed while trying to escape from a burning aircraft. By this time my imagination was running riot and I was pretty scared. Everyone had become quiet, there were two young girls dressed as punks sitting behind me and the combination of their heavy makeup and the terror on their faces was a sight to behold. I tried to work out what the problem was, it was not yet time to put down the undercarriage so it wasn't that, the two engines on my side were working OK and I couldn't hear any strange noises so what was the problem?

The undercarriage came down with a reassuring clonk and as we approached the runway at Schipol I could see the lights of the emergency services flashing in the distance. We neared the ground and a fire engine could be seen driving along side the plane. The stewardess blew the whistle and we all got our heads down. There was no problem with the landing and I expected us to have to use the emergency escape chutes, but no, we taxied in as normal accompanied by two fire engines, and came to a halt at the usual place. Nobody said anything and as I looked behind the two punk girls still had their heads in their knees; I put them out of their misery and told them it was OK to get up. We left the plane in the normal way but nobody offered any explanation as to what was wrong. I asked one of the stewardesses who said they could smell burning at the back of the plane and the pilot had a smoke indicator on in the cockpit. I was annoyed that they had put us through all of that terror for what to me seemed like a minor incident, but I suppose it was a procedure they had to carry out.

Despite this I continued flying with London European.

Saturday 1st June 1985

It was a hot sunny day in Vinkeveen and the four of us sat and had a serious discussion about the group's future. I had finally had enough and wanted to call it a day. Although our records weren't selling the work had not diminished but I was feeling like a commuter, getting on a plane each week, flying to Holland for gigs then returning home to the family, for the cycle to be repeated the following week. We probably could have continued like this for several years but I think we all needed a new challenge and Guys n' Dolls had gone as far as they could. The others agreed and we amicably decided that Guys n' Dolls would finish in December after eleven years, giving us all six months to decide what our next moves would be.

Saturday 13th July 1985

Like millions of other people around the world I spent today in front of the TV watching Live Aid from Wembley Stadium. There were some great moments but the best acts for me were Quo, Queen and Bowie. I managed to catch a glimpse of my old mate Tony Rivers providing backing vocals for Elton John and George Michael. Paul McCartney came on near the end to sing "Let it Be" unfortunately the performance was almost ruined by his microphone not working for the first part of the song. The finale was "Do They Know It's Christmas" sung by everyone who had appeared on the show and it was a bit of a shambles as these things tend to be.

Saturday 13th July 1985

A few months ago I entered a competition to write and record a thirty second commercial for TDK tapes. I suppose in my mind it was another avenue I could explore when Guys n' Dolls ended in December. I was placed third and received my prize of a Shure microphone from David Bowie's record producer Tony Visconti, at a lunch held at the

Capital Radio headquarters in London.

Saturday 10th August 1985

Our last ever appearance on the radio programme Los Vast was quite special. It was held at the Feynoord football stadium in Rotterdam and for the first time went out live on television. We performed "Rocking all over the World" with a live band in front of 40,000 people. Quite a buzz.

Wednesday 25th September 1985

Proud parents
with rather
smug siblings

Nigel had been staying with Mum and Dad, his first visit since the demise of Split Enz. Today I took him to Heathrow to catch the plane back to Australia and by a strange coincidence we bumped into Eddie Rayner, the keyboard player from Split Enz, checking in for the same flight. He had been in England working with Paul McCartney on his "Press to Play" album and Linda McCartney had just dropped him off. They didn't sit together; an ex-Beatle was paying for Eddie's ticket so he travelled first class.

Wednesday 20th November 1985

My forty first birthday. A few months ago I had written a song called "Sorry" which I felt would suit Dominic and we had been in the studio to record it with him singing lead. Since the demise of Rick Wakeman's "Moon Records," Martin Pursey had been running a label called "Bonaire." When he heard "Sorry" he asked if he could enter it for the "Song for Europe" competition. I had always looked down on song contests, especially "Eurovision" as in many quarters it was considered a bit of a joke and in general the standard of songs was poor. I suppose "Sorry" could be classed as a rock ballad and not an obvious Eurovision song but I didn't think it would do any harm to enter so I agreed.

Monday 2nd December 1985

Since Guys n' Dolls had decided to finish at the end of the year, I had been trying to decide what to do next. At the time performing live held little appeal to me as I had been gigging regularly in one form or another for well over twenty years, and thought I was ready to give it up. I had been involved with a couple of record production projects and done some work with a London based jingle company. I had also been talking to Don Larking, with whom I had recorded my last solo single, about the possibility of running his music publishing company. Today we had a meeting and it was agreed that I would start work next month. While I was there Lynne phoned to say that my song "Sorry" was in the last twenty four for a Song for Europe, from which they would chose the final eight. Suddenly the Eurovision Song Contest didn't seem quite so bad.

Wednesday 4th December - Monday 9th December 1985

Our last overseas trip was to Singapore and we performed our full set live on television, in a park, in front of sixty thousand people. Before we flew home I managed to take afternoon tea at the famous "Raffles" hotel.

Tuesday 10th December 1985

Martin Pursey phoned with the news that "Sorry" had reached the final eight for a "Song for Europe". Isn't the Eurovision Song Contest wonderful?

Thursday 19th December 1985

And now the end is near.

(Photographs courtesy of Olaf Schrawers)

Guys n' Dolls last official show was at the La Bateau in Rotterdam. It was a strange evening and although it was packed with lots of quite emotional fans, a bit of an anti climax. After the show we said our goodbyes to the fans many of whom we knew well as they were regular faces at our performances. We had a couple of drinks and returned to Vinkeveen.

Friday 20th December 1985

The Final Curtain

Wiping off the makeup or shedding a tear.

(Photographs courtesy of Olaf Schrawers)

Ludo, obviously keen to extract his last bit of commission from us, had booked one more show in Lommel, Belgium at a club called the Dancing Shaft. We spent the day packing all the belongings accumulated during our time in Holland and then set off for the very last show. The gig was OK but once again a bit of an anti climax. Our last ever song was "Sailing", which was quite appropriate as I was catching the ferry in the morning. I had few emotions at the time, I was glad the group was finishing and was looking forward to new beginnings. The club owner cracked open a bottle of champagne and that was it, after eleven years Guys n' Dolls were no more.

Looking back, although I may appear to have whinged a lot, Guys n' Dolls had been a great experience, there were lots of highs a few lows and I make no bones about struggling with the recording side of things. I often wonder what I would be doing if back in 1974, Ammo Productions' secretary Jenny hadn't rescheduled my audition when I phoned to cancel it. Through Guys n' Dolls I met my wife Lynne and my two closest friends Dominic and Julie. Over the years people have said "why don't you get back together" while others probably say "please don't". I have always said it would never happen, but you should never say "never".

Saturday 21st December 1985

This morning I said an emotional goodbye to Dominic, Julie and Rosie and with a car crammed full of belongings, a chest of drawers strapped to the roof, drove to the ferry and home. Another chapter in my life had ended.

Guys n' Dolls Statistics
8th November 1974 – 20th December 1985

Number of songs released   87
Number of UK live shows   1049
Number of UK TV appearances   70
Number of overseas live shows   584
Number of overseas TV appearances   97

1986

Wednesday 1st January 1986

Machine based bands were still having a strong influence on the charts as the Pet Shop Boys were number one with "West End Girls". At two were the Bronski Beat with "Hit That Perfect Beat" and Sweden's Aha at three with "The Sun Always Shines on TV".

Monday 6th January 1986

Luton is known for being a town associated with the manufacture of hats and even the football team, Luton Town FC, are known as the hatters. Today I started work for Don Larking whose premises were in a converted hat factory. It was a four story building and Don had given me an office on the third floor. His music publishing company was called Superwop Music a name which I felt was inappropriate so we decided to change it to Everyday Music and I had approached Dominic to design the logo. I asked him if he could draw a cartoon of an old man wearing a walkman and his design was perfect.

A music publisher acts as agent for songs trying to persuade artists to record titles signed to the company and looking after the distribution of royalties. There are two main societies that collect song writing royalties. First is the MCPS (mechanical copyright protection society) which collects all of the mechanical royalties. These are an agreed percentage of the wholesale price that goes to the publisher and, in turn, the writer when a song or piece of music is physically copied and sold. Today apart from CDs and on line downloads this extends to ring tones and even children's toys that play music. Second is the PRS (performing rights society) who collect royalties from radio TV and live performances. Every time a piece of music is played in public it has to be paid for. Restaurants, pubs and hairdressing salons all have to buy a PRS license if they wish to play recorded music.

Thursday 13th February 1986

The Song for Europe was scheduled for the beginning of April but first the song would be previewed on Terry Wogan's show in a few weeks time. Dominic had decided not to sing "Sorry" in the contest, as he and Julie were to remain in Holland as duo working under the name of Grant and Forsyth. Even though I had written the song I didn't feel it suited me so we would have to look elsewhere. Martin Pursey found a guy called Chad Brown who had been lead singer in a rock band called Lionheart and today he came along to the studio to try out the song. He was very different to Dominic but sang the song well and as the rules of the Eurovision song contest state that you can have up to six performers taking part we decided to form a band around him. Martine's ex husband Michael Richardson would play drums, with our former Guys n' Dolls band member Gary Hutchings on keyboards, myself on guitar and a bass player whose name escapes me.

Thursday 6th March 1986

Marty Wilde, who is also a Tewin resident, had a state of the art recording studio in nearby Knebworth. A week ago we recorded "Sorry" there and today we were back for the mixing.

Monday 24th March 1986

Terry Wogan's show went out live every week day, from the Shepherds Bush Empire in London. Today two of the Song for Europe entries were previewed including "Sorry". We had recorded a backing track and Chad had to sing live. It went ok except Chad decided to perform some vocal gymnastics at one point and his voice cracked. I was quite concerned as Chad had tried a few of these several times during rehearsals and seemed to be trying to show off what his voice could achieve rather than interpret the song. I have always disliked singers, mostly female divas who always seem to warble around a note before they actually hit it.

As a huge Monty Python fan I was pleased that one of the guests on the show was "Python" member and now film director Terry Gilliam.

Wednesday 26th March 1986

I flew to Holland for the first time since the end of Guys n' Dolls. I had produced a track for a Dutch artist called Rudie Crossman and was taking the finished product over to EMI Holland, who had agreed to release it. While I was there I managed to secure a sub publishing deal with EMI. which meant they would administer Everyday Music's business in the Benelux countries. They paid us an advance which was the first income I had actually earned for company.

Wednesday 2nd April 1986

It was Song for Europe day and as I headed off to the BBC television centre at Shepherds Bush I was far more nervous than I had been for years. We spent the day in rehearsals and then readied ourselves for the live broadcast at eight o'clock. I received a boxed carnation from Dominic and Julie with a good luck message and deep down, although Chad was doing a good job, I wished that Dominic was singing the song. The audience, including Lynne and Mum and Dad, took their places in the studio and the show began. "Sorry" was the fourth song and the performance seemed to go well, although Chad still managed a couple of vocal gymnastics which I wasn't keen on. Listening to all of the songs I have to admit I hadn't the slightest clue as to which one would win. We were told to all wait together in an area outside the studio while the judging took place but I managed to sneak back in and sit with my family.

Eleven regional panels of judges voted and each jury could award the songs a maximum of fifteen points. The voting began and after four regions had voted we in fourth position, Things then went downhill and after nine regions "Sorry" was in eighth and last position and I was mortified. It stayed there until the very last region gave it enough points to finish in seventh position with a total of 76 votes, not quite as bad as being last but I was surprised how bitterly disappointed I felt. The winners were a band called Ryder with a song called "Runner in the Night" which had lead all the way through and finished with a total of 145 votes. Their lead singer called himself Maynard Williams and was in fact the son of actor Bill Maynard. There was an after show party at the Video Café and although I went along with the family I really didn't feel like partying so we didn't stay long.

In the actual Eurovision Song Contest about a month later, "Ryder" were placed seventh out of twenty with the winners being Belgium.

Thursday 3rd April 1986

Martin Pursey phoned and tried to cheer me up by saying that he was starting a big campaign with "Sorry" and would try and make it a hit. I knew it would be a waste of time as I have already said, unsuccessful Eurovision entries never become hits, and even the winning song by Ryder failed to make the charts.

Saturday 22nd November 1986

Running the publishing company had been a learning curve for me. When I started in January I knew little about the business side of things but by now I was getting to grips with things. Don had set me up with a sixteen track demo studio which enabled me to make excellent demo versions of songs. For the past few months I had also been producing jingles for the local Chiltern radio station which was a good source of income for the company.

I hadn't sung in front of an audience since Guys n' Dolls finished last December and at the time thought I'd never want to perform again. The trouble was that being a performer is like a drug and once it takes a hold it's very difficult to get out of your system. The village school, which by now my son was attending, were putting on a music night and asked if I would perform a few numbers. I got together a PA system, recorded some backing tracks and performed. I really enjoyed it and realised that performing was still in my blood.

1987

Thursday 1st January 1987

Number one in the charts at the start of the year was the re-released "Reet Petite" by Jackie Wilson followed by Alison Moyet with "Is This Love". At three was the Gap Band with Big Fun.

Monday 16th February 1987

A film had just been released called "Peggy Sue Got Married" which featured the Buddy Holly song of the same name. I had recorded a version of the song and decided to try and obtain a release. I took it to a small record company called Spartan based in Wembley who liked the idea and agreed to release it. They decided I should change my name as they thought that Griggs was not suitable, (they had a point) so I took my second name and went as Paul David. It was clear that Spartan were a small label and I was concerned that they would not have sufficient funds to promote the record adequately as they had asked me to approach the publishers of the song to help with promotion.

Thursday 9th April 1987

My version of "Peggy Sue Got Married" was due for release tomorrow and I had a meeting with Spartan to discuss promotion. It was obvious after the meeting that the company was not in the best of financial positions and that money for promotion was not available. The most important thing at that time was to have your record played on Radio 1, which wasn't easy. There were a handful of record pluggers who had the ability of achieving this but their services didn't come cheaply. Spartan supplied me with a hundred copies of the record for me to handle the promotion myself. Over the next few weeks I promoted it as best I could but without support there was not too much I could do. I secured a few plays on local radio stations but soon realised that it was a lost cause.

Thursday 30th April 1987

As a publisher I would be sent details of various song contests that took place around the world. After my experiences in a Song for Europe I had decided never to take part in a contest again. Today I changed my mind. I received details of the Buddy Holly Song contest and the criterion was to write a song in a style that Buddy Holly might sing. As the letter came from MPL, Paul McCartney's company, I thought it was an opportunity I couldn't miss. I had a song called "No More Tears" which sounded more Beatles than Buddy but it was all I had at the time and the closest I was going to get, so I sent it off.

Paul McCartney's company MPL, were part owners of Buddy Holly's copyrights.

Friday 19th June 1987

I received a letter informing me that my song had been selected for the final of the Buddy Holly Song Contest and would I be available to attend the awards lunch to be held on 9th September in London. I checked my diary which was a waste of time. There was a chance I was going to meet a Beatle and even if I had been going to the moon I would have cancelled. I phoned MPL and said I'd be there.

Friday 26th June 1987

I had first met Bev Walker back in 1980 when I was still working in the UK with Guys n' Dolls. He managed sports personalities and we had kept in touch and met socially several times. Bev had been trying to persuade me to come and work for him as he wanted to set up a music production and publishing company. I had finally decided to take him up on his offer and today was my last day with Everyday Music. Don Larking was very good about it and as a leaving present gave me a Vox AC30 amplifier, which had once, belonged to Francis Rossi of Status Quo.

Today I received an invitation for two from Paul and Linda McCartney to the Buddy Holly Song contest.

Monday 29th June 1987

My first day working for Bev Walker. I travelled down to his office in Haywards Heath for a meeting. The plan was that he intended to buy a recording studio that would be the base for the business. We had found a couple of studios that we intended to take a look at, but for a few days there was nothing to do so I stayed at home kicking my heels. I didn't realise at the time just how much heel kicking I would be doing over the next few months.

Wednesday 9th September 1987

Paul McCartney signs my award.
(Picture by Lynne Griggs)

I give Paul McCartney some advice on song writing, while Duane Eddy looks on.
(Picture by Lynne Griggs)

The day of the Buddy Holly Song Contest awards and Lynne and I set off far too early as we were the first ones to arrive at the Dolphin Brasserie in Belgravia. We were told we could sit anywhere except at the large table with a reserved sign. Realising this table was probably for the host and hostess we sat on the table next to it. The guests began filtering in and we were joined on our table by Mike Maxfield who was an original member of Billy J. Kramer's Dakotas, and guitarist Mick Green who I had last seen playing with Johnny Kidd and the Pirates in my youth club back in 1963. Another guest was Peter Waterman who had come a long way since his days working at Magnet records and was now Mr. big time record producer with hits pouring out of him.

Suddenly eyes were turned to the door as Paul and Linda McCartney walked in with their daughter Stella. They were accompanied by Twiggy, her husband actor Leigh Lawson and Ruby Wax and took their places at the large reserved table. It was a nice lunch, veggie of course, the music was supplied by Mike Berry's band who performed mainly Buddy Holly songs and two of Buddy Holly's original Crickets, Jerry Allison and Joe B. Mauldin, were in attendance. Next was the actual award ceremony which was conducted by Jonathan Ross. I didn't win first prize, and I honestly didn't mind as it was great just being there, but I did received a framed runners up certificate. I wanted Paul to sign my award and a short while later he went around the room talking to old friends. He passed by our table and here was my chance, he took my award, turned it over and said "No More Tears, good song". Now whether he meant this or whether he was just being polite I will never know, but he said it and that's good enough for me. It is difficult to know what to say to one of your own all time heroes, saying that you're a huge fan and you've bought all the records is a bit obvious. I managed to bring my brother's band Split Enz into the conversation and we chatted about them. While this was going on Lynne managed to take a couple of photos which included fifties legendry guitarist Duane Eddy. I thanked Paul for a nice meal and as he was walking away managed to blurt out "and thanks for the inspiration", but I expect he'd heard it all before.

Paul decided he wanted to get up and sing with the band, so along with Alvin Stardust and DJ Tony Prince he took to the stage and gave us a rendition of the Jerry Lee Lewis classic "There's Whole Lotta Shaking Going On". Shortly after this things started winding down and everyone began drifting off. As we travelled home with me clutching my signed award I had to say that meeting Paul McCartney had been one of the great moments of my life. He probably felt the same about meeting me.

Wednesday 18th November 1987

I had been working for Bev Walker for almost five frustrating months, frustrating because in that time very little had happened. We had seen several studios and expressed interest in buying them but then everything would go quiet and I wouldn't be able to contact Bev for days at a time.

Tonight I as due to meet Bev Walker in London to see a great little band that I had found called "Scared of Heights". I originally was going to travel by train but at the last moment decided to take the car. I was driving along Euston Road approaching Kings Cross station when the traffic slowed to a crawl and I could see fire engines ahead, and smoke. This was the night of the Kings Cross underground fire, at the time the road had not yet been closed but white smoke could be seen coming up from the subway entrances each side of the road. As I passed the smoke suddenly turned black and billowed out and this must have been the moment that a fire ball engulfed the escalator and ticket office. When later I found out the full extent of the disaster, 31 people perished, it really shook me up. If I had taken the train it would have been to Kings Cross and I may well have been catching an underground connection at that time. Life is full of what ifs.

1988

Friday 1ˢᵗ January 1988

Belinda Carlisle started off the year at the top of the UK charts with "Heaven is a Place on Earth" followed by the Pet Shop Boys with a cover of the Elvis Presley song "Always on my Mind". At three was Krush with "House Arrest".

Thursday 4ᵗʰ February 1988

I was still doing a lot of heel kicking working for Bev Walker. Since I had joined him last June I had achieved very little within the company and the problem seemed to be financial. We were still no nearer buying a recording studio and I had found a couple of very promising bands but with nothing concrete to offer them these projects just fell by the wayside. For the past few months I had returned to gigging locally, performing solo gigs playing guitars and singing to backing tracks and I could not believe how much I was enjoying it. I was my own boss with no one else to answer to.

Julie Forsyth had decided to enter a "Song for Europe" with a composition of hers called "Go". Our friend Scott Fitzgerald was singing it and today she learned that it had reached the final twenty.

Tuesday 23ʳᵈ February 1988

Bev Walker desperately needed finance for his company and today David Frost came to the office as a potential investor. Everyone who worked for Bev, including myself, had a meeting with Frost outlining their plans for the company. The outcome would be that he did not see enough potential to persuade him to invest.

Julie heard that she had reached the final of a Song for Europe and I was so pleased for her hoping that she would fare better than I did.

Monday 14ᵗʰ March 1988

I had a phone call from Bev Walker giving me the news I had feared for some time. The bank had withdrawn his credit facility and he was in deep financial trouble and would have to let me and several other members of staff go. It was not unexpected and in some ways a great relief, I had been working for Bev for nine months and because of his financial dilemma I had done very little and it been a situation I had found frustrating and unsatisfactory.

The question was what was I going to do next? I was gigging quite a lot and at some of the venues where people would ask me if I knew of other acts who could play for them and this was when I began to think seriously about becoming an entertainment agent.

Friday 25th March 1988

Julie and Scott receive their awards from Terry Wogan.

It was two years since I had reached the final of a song for Europe and tonight it was Julie's turn. For the first year the result would be determined by the public with phone in votes. Scott had been drawn eight the last song to be performed, he did well and now was the wait for the phone voting to finish. The votes were announced in order and "Go" won with 93,271 votes, a clear winner almost twenty thousand votes ahead of the second song. This meant it would be representing Great Britain in the Eurovision song contest in just over a month's time.

Monday 11th April – Friday 15th April 1988

I was asked if I would like to accompany Scott Fitzgerald on a few days radio promotion for "Go" and as I needed something to do I said "yes". We flew to Aberdeen collected a hire car and began a gruelling but enjoyable few days visiting local radio stations up and down the country. On the first day we covered Aberdeen, Dundee and Glasgow before driving to Preston for the night. Over the next few days we covered most of country ending up in Wales and finally Bristol. In Cardiff we bumped into Rolf Harris and my memory is of Scott and Rolf singing "Flower of Scotland" in full voice, in the BBC Wales reception area.

Saturday 30th April 1988

This year the Eurovision Song Contest was held in Dublin and I watched the programme keeping my fingers crossed for Julie. There were twenty one entries and Scott had drawn the penultimate position. He sang well with Julie and Dominic providing the backing vocals. Each country provided a panel of judges who could award twelve, ten, eight and then down to one for their ten favourite songs. As the last few countries voted it was clear the contest was between Scott Fitzgerald singing "Go" and a then unknown singer called Celine Dion singing "Ne Partez Pas Sans Moi" and representing Switzerland. With just one set of votes to come Scott Fitzgerald had 136 points and Celine Dion 131. Yugoslavia were the last jury and gave Celine Dion six points giving her a one point lead, surely not enough, surely Great Britain would win. Amazingly as the final points were announced

Yugoslavia had decided to give Scott nil points and so Celine Dion won by a single point. What a disappointment. A few years later Bruce Forsyth appeared on "Room 101" where guest celebrities choose things they hate and banish them forever into the imaginary Room 101. Bruce tried to get Yugoslavia put in for giving Julie nil points. Holland also gave the British entry nil points and considering that Julie and Scott were well known in the country and worked there for a number of years it seemed a little odd. Maybe it was sour grapes as they were representing Britain.

Wednesday 27th July 1988

I had a call from Bev Walker who, although I wasn't working for him, asked me if I would come to a meeting at "spoon bender" Uri Geller's house. He wanted me to meet a world famous American concert pianist called Byron Janis who he was trying to become involved with. I had never heard of Byron Janis and knew nothing about the world of classical music but I said I would go along to give him some support. I drove to Uri Geller's home in Sonning on the River Thames and Bev introduced me to Uri and his wife and to Byron Janis who was married to film star Gary Cooper's daughter Maria. We sat around and talked for a couple of hours, and with Uri Geller present the conversation was a bit cosmic at times. I had a strong desire to ask him to bend a spoon but common sense prevailed. I tried to make all the right noises but at the end nothing was really achieved and I really couldn't see why I was there.

I stopped writing a daily diary towards the end of 1988 but continued to keep an appointments diary.

1989

Thursday 3rd August 1989

Julie and Dominic were married today at Egham in Surrey on their son Luke's ninth birthday. It was a bit of a Guys n' Dolls reunion as past members Martine, Rosie and of course Julie's sister Laura were all present along with Guys n' Doll musical director Ray Monk and drummer Dave Morris. As one would expect the bride's father made a brilliantly hilarious speech.

1990

Tuesday 29th May 1990

A joyous day, my daughter Vicki was born, and as with my son Wayne nine years earlier the birth was an amazing experience. She was a month premature and had to stay in special care at the QE2 Hospital in Welwyn Garden City for nearly two weeks.

Monday 23rd July 1990

Most of my gigs were normally quite close to home. I enjoyed playing but travelling held little joy for me. I made an exception when Alan Field our agent from the Guys n' Dolls days offered me six weeks work performing cabaret on the Olau line sailing between Sheerness in Kent to Vlissingen in Holland. I would join the ship on Monday perform two shows a day until Thursday. My son Wayne came with me and had the time of his life. Some of the Dutch Guys n' Dolls fans joined the ship for the round trip and it was good to see many familiar faces. This would continue every summer for the next three years.

1992

Monday 2nd November 1992

Away from music my love of steam trains continued unabated and for an early birthday present Lynne arranged for me to have a two hour driving experience on the world famous locomotive the Flying Scotsman. This was at the Birmingham Railway Museum and there were three of us on the footplate with an experienced driver taking it in turns to drive up and down a stretch of line. When the driver was sure I knew what I was doing I was allowed complete control and I could not believe the power that was unleashed when the steam regulator was opened. For me it was another one of life's great experiences and I arrived home complete with sweat shirt bearing the words "I have driven the Flying Scotsman" and a stupid grin on my face.

Wednesday 2nd December 1992

I was friends with a guy called Henry Harrison a former member of the New Vaudeville Band who had several hits in the sixties. He said he was going to see Chris Barber with Lonnie Donegan making a guest appearance and would I like to come along. I hadn't seen Lonnie perform for years and this was his first show since he suffered a heart attack earlier in the year. He was appearing at the Forum theatre in Hatfield where I had played with Guys n' Dolls years earlier.

We sat talking to Lonnie in the dressing room and he was on top form reminiscing about the old days and itching to get out and perform. He only sang around half a dozen songs including, "Grand Coulee Dam" and "Bring a Little Water Sylvie" but at 61 years of age he had lost none of that old excitement and energy, it was a great performance. In recent years I had rediscovered Lonnie and had begun buying all of his available material on CD realising again just how good it all sounded.

I met a guy called Mel Roberts who had been involved with Lonnie since the sixties and was one his closest friends. Lonnie, who now lived in Spain, would always stay with Mel and his wife Linda at their home near Peterborough when he was in the country. Mel started off as a fan like me and we both knew far too much about Lonnie for our own good so were able to have many in depth discussions about him.

1995

Monday 27th April 1995

"Rockin' all over the World" Dominic's there somewhere

Dominic and Julie were now performing in Holland as Grant and Forsyth. A few years ago they had recorded a country album which was incredibly successful and since then had achieved continued success in the same genre. They were in the middle of a theatre tour of Holland and I flew over to stay with them for a couple of days to see one of their shows. Julie's Dad and his wife Winnie also came over and when he saw me, made a typical Brucie comment, "I knew you were coming but it was too late to cancel". We went to the show at a place called Etten-Leur with Julie and Dominic giving a great two hour performance and dragged me on stage (I didn't need much dragging) at the end for "Rockin' All Over the World".

Wednesday 6th September 1995

Mel Roberts informed me that Lonnie Donegan was about to record another album and was looking for material. I decided to try and write him a song and came up with "I Don't Wanna Lose You" which rhythmically derived some of its inspiration from a favourite song of mine "Copperhead Road" by Steve Earle. I let Mel have a tape of the song to hear, he thought it would be ideal for Lonnie and sent it off to him in Spain.

Thursday 14th September 1995

I was working in my studio when the phone rang and as I was busy decided to let the answer phone kick in. I heard a voice saying "Hello this is Lonnie Donegan in Spain, I would like you to fax" ---- I grabbed the phone. Lonnie told me he liked my song and said it had a kind of "Cajun" feel to it. He asked me if I could fax the lyrics over to him and I said that I would send them immediately.

Thirty minutes later the phone rang again and it was Lonnie. He said he was interested in recording the song but wanted me to change a few of the lyrics. He then went through the song line by line pointing out those that he felt were a bit ambiguous and which he felt needed altering to make it more of a story. I said I would get working on it and fax back the new lyrics.

Sunday 17th September 1995

For the last three days I had been labouring over the corrected lyrics for "I Don't Wanna Lose You". When I write a song it usually takes about thirty minutes to write the lyrics, Lonnie had only wanted a few lines changed and I was desperate for him to record my song and wanted to get them right. I faxed the amended lyrics to Lonnie and hoped for the best.

Wednesday 15th November 1995

It had been almost two months since I faxed the amended lyrics of my song to Lonnie Donegan and I had not heard a word from him. I was dying to know if they were OK so I decided to ring him. I phoned and tentatively asked if he had received the lyrics and if they were OK. He said "Lyrics? – oh yes they were fine and I've already recorded the song". To say I was pleased is an understatement, one of my all time heroes had recorded a song I had written. It doesn't get much better than that.

Monday 4th December 1995

Released today was the first new Beatles single in twenty five years. It was called "Free as a Bird" and was a result of Yoko Ono giving the remaining three Beatles a very rough tape of John's and they, with the help of Jeff Lynne, turned it into a brand new Beatles record. It received its first radio play on my fifty first birthday a couple of weeks ago and in general had not been that well received. I think the problem was that because of the quality of the original tape, John's voice is a little indistinct. Personally I thought it was fantastic, it was the first Beatles song where John, Paul and George all take a lead vocal and George's guitar solo was spot on. It is definitely in my top ten of Beatles' songs and the video that accompanied it, with images representing many Beatles songs, was stunning.

1996

Tuesday 5th November 1996

I had phoned Lonnie Donegan to see what progress was being made with the release of his album. It had been over a year since he recorded my song and there seemed to be one delay after another with the record label, Carlton. He said that there had been major changes within the company and it was no longer their policy to release full price albums, they would in future concentrate on budget re-releases. Lonnie was back to square one and looking for a new outlet for his album. He asked if I had any contacts within the business and I said I would give it some thought.

The problem was that it had been many years since I had contact with anyone in the UK music business and as there are always personnel changes within the industry with no one staying in the same position for very long I had no idea where to start. I remembered that the Beatles had been originally inspired by Lonnie Donegan, especially George Harrison who had his own label Dark Horse. I thought I had nothing to lose so I wrote to George Harrison to see if he was interested in releasing Lonnie's album.

Thursday 7th November 1996

Two days after I had written to George Harrison I was amazed when a letter dropped onto my door mat with "Harrison" stamped on the back. I quickly opened it and read.

Dear Mr. Griggs,

Re. Lonnie Donegan.

*I must unfortunately decline your offer of Lonnie's anniversary album as
My 'label' is only a vehicle for my own recordings. There are no other
artists on the label and, in fact, no employees to run it. Give my regards to Lonnie and I
hope you are successful in your endeavour to help him out with
this project.*

Sincerely,

George Harrison.

I was quite staggered that I had received a reply at all, let alone so quickly and I was even more staggered that I had actually received a letter from a Beatle. By the end of the day the letter was unashamedly in a frame and on my wall. Today it is a treasured possession.

1997

Monday 6th October 1997

I had been invited to appear on the TV show "Never Mind The Buzzcocks" to stand in the line up as an ageing pop singer to see if the panel could identify me. At first I wasn't too keen as people who appear in the line up tend to be ridiculed mercilessly and having been in a group like Guys n' Dolls I would probably be an easy target. They said they would send a car to collect me and take me home and when they told me the fee, I immediately said "Yes". Martine Howard, my ex. colleague from Guys n' Dolls was also to appear.

We had to arrive at the BBC Television Centre at exactly six o'clock so we could be hidden away in dressing rooms out of sight of the panellists. The BBC looked after us well and we were fed and watered. Apart from Martine and I there were four others in the line up two who were supposed to look like me and two like Martine. Before we went on Martine had the idea of us all holding carnations which had been a bit of a Guys n' Dolls trademark. I thought this was a crap idea so as we were walking out for our spot I conveniently managed to lose mine. As we stood in the line up a far too helpful floor manager came running out with my carnation saying "I think you dropped this". Mark Lamar had a theme going when he named the members of the line up and for the boys it was Lenny. There was a Lenny Bruce, a Lenny the Lion and when he reached me he ironically named me after the comedian who had pissed us off at the first ever live Guys n' Dolls show all those years ago, Lenny Bennett. Trying to identify us were Phil Jupitas, Brian Molko from the band Placebo and Bruce Dickenson from Iron Maiden. Phil Jupitas correctly identified us by saying, "It's three and six which is about what they're worth these days". Afterwards we spent some time in the green room where Bruce Dickenson was a bit sniffy and obviously felt it was far beneath him to associate with the likes of members of Guys n' Dolls, but Brian Molko was a nice guy. When we left I managed to get away with my number three badge.

After the show I had phone calls from people saying that they thought the panel was rather rude to us but people who take part in the show are aware that they are going to be made fun of and to be honest I think we got off rather lightly.

Monday 27th October 1997

In a weak moment I wrote a song called "All I Want for Christmas is a Spice Girl", much to the embarrassment of my family. Amazingly I managed to secure a deal for my version to be included on a Christmas line dance album, as there was a country feel to it. I played it to Julie and Dominic and after they had fallen about laughing Julie said she would try and get a Dutch act called "Gompie" to record it. Gompie was in fact Peter Koelwijn who was a partner in our old management company in Holland. He had recently had a hit with "Living Next Door To Alice" (Alice who the f--- is Alice) and in a lack of good taste, subsequently agreed to record my song.

Sunday 9th November 1997

(Photo Courtesy
of Olaf
Schrawers)

Today Julie and Dominic were holding their Grant and Forsyth fan club day at Maarssen near Utrecht and had invited me across to make a guest appearance. It was a most enjoyable day with lots of the old Guys n' Dolls fans in attendance and at one point the three of us sang a few songs together for old time's sake.

1999

Monday 4th January 1999

Almost three years after Lonnie Donegan had recorded my song, his album, now called "Mule Skinner Blues", was finally released yesterday on the BMG label and today I received a copy from them. I have never believed anything is certain in this business until it is one hundred percent confirmed. I looked down the track listings and there it was, my little song, "I Don't Wanna Lose You". I was knocked out especially when Mel Roberts told me that over the years George Harrison, Brian May and Chas n' Dave had all written songs for Lonnie and none of them were ever released.

2000

Thursday 30th April 2000

I arrived at a pub called the Fox in Harpenden for an evening gig. It was my first time there and I went in to see where I should set up. There was an elderly gentleman sitting at the bar who I recognized immediately and I blurted out "John Cunningham". He seemed a little startled by my outburst but I explained why I recognised him. John Cunningham was the chief test pilot at the De Havilland Aircraft Company where my father worked for most of his life and I had often seen his photograph in the company magazine which Dad would bring home when I was a small boy. He was famous for being the first pilot ever to fly a jet airliner when the Comet, built by De Havillands, made its maiden flight on the evening of 27th July 1949 witnessed by me at four years of age from my back garden at Hatfield. John Cunningham passed away on 21st July 2002 aged eighty four.

2001

Tuesday 16th October 2001

I went along with Tony Rivers to see Lonnie Donegan at the Stables in Wavenden near Milton Keynes, a small theatre owned by Johnny Dankworth and Cleo lane. It was a great show, Lonnie seemed like a fine wine, maturing with age and his band were excellent. His set list consisted mainly of his traditional Skiffle numbers with no room for "Dustman" or "Chewing Gum". I have never had a photo taken with Lonnie so I took a camera along to rectify this. Unfortunately there was a problem with the camera and so this was not possible, I thought "next time". I was talking to Lonnie's bass player Peter Oakman after the show when Lonnie prodded me in the back and said "Get writing, I'm going to record another album". He suggested that we might try and write something together saying "you've got my number and I'm often in England". I thought there would be nothing I'd like more than to sit down with Lonnie and try and come up with a song. Sadly it would never happen as that was the last time I ever saw him.

Thursday 29th November 2001

Today my son Wayne came into the office and gave me the sad news that I had been dreading for some time. George Harrison had died of cancer in Los Angeles. George had been diagnosed with cancer in 1997 and had undergone surgery to remove a cancerous lump in his throat. It seemed that the cancer had been caught in time but earlier this year there began to be reports that George was having more treatment in Switzerland and America. A few weeks ago Paul McCartney and Ringo Starr had made a special visit to see George in Los Angeles and it didn't take much reading between the lines to know that the end was near.

George Harrison was my favourite Beatle and a huge inspiration to me. I had learned every note of every guitar solo he played with the Beatles and I've already mentioned that it was George who composed my favourite Beatles song, "While My Guitar Gently Weeps". George Harrison was the first to be disillusioned with being a Beatle and soon tired of the frenzy that surrounded the group. He must have found it hard writing songs in the shadow of Lennon and McCartney but his writing just got better and better and two of the best songs on the final Beatles' album, "Abbey Road", were written by him. They were, "Something" and "Here Comes the Sun".

George was the first Beatle to have a solo number one hit in the UK when "My Sweet Lord" swept to the top of the charts in January 1971. John Lennon didn't reach the number one spot until 1980 when, in the frenzy of buying his records immediately after his death, he had three number ones in the space of two months. Although Paul McCartney reached number one with Mull of Kintyre as a member of Wings in 1977, he had to wait until 1984 for his first solo chart topper with "Pipes of Peace".

2002

Monday 4th November 2002

Possibly the last photo of Lonnie Donegan taken at The Nottingham Royal Concert Hall on 30th October 2002 four days before he died. (left to right) Vince Eager (Guesting with Lonnie) Peter Oakman (Bass) and Lonnie.

(Picture Courtesy of Vince Eager)

November seemed to be a bad month for people I admired. One year on from George Harrison's death a friend phoned with the sad news that Lonnie Donegan had died from a heart attack in the early hours of yesterday morning. I was completely shocked and immediately switched on the TV, and the news was confirmed. I phoned Mel Roberts who told me the whole story. Lonnie and his wife Sharon had been staying with Mel and his wife Linda in between dates of a British tour he was currently undertaking. Lonnie had just been invited by Eric Clapton to appear at the Concert for George Harrison due to take place on November 29th at the Royal Albert Hall and they had spent Saturday evening discussing what he should sing. In the early hours of Sunday morning Lonnie went upstairs to the bathroom and suddenly called for Sharon. When they reached him he had collapsed and never regained consciousness. Two of my greatest influences gone in a year.

Thursday 14th November 2002

Lonnie Donegan, MBE
(1931-2002)

Order of Service

Peterborough Crematorium
Thursday 14th November 2002

Celebrants: Pauline Southam
and Ernest Eyncha

I was privileged to attend Lonnie's funeral at Peterborough crematorium just ten days later. His coffin was carried into the chapel accompanied by a small jazz band in traditional New Orleans style. There were many musicians in attendance who like me had started out their musical lives bashing out Lonnie Donegan songs, people like Joe Brown, Chas n' Dave, Albert Lee and members of Lonnie's band some of whom had been with him for many years. Joe Brown gave an address and spoke of the influence Lonnie had been on him and all of us, Lonnie's wife Sharon spoke followed by his two youngest sons Peter and David who paid glowing tributes to their dad. David just managing to get through before the emotion overwhelmed him. At one point Lonnie's version of "Over in the Gloryland" was played and we were all asked to stand and sing along which lightened things up a little.

After the service we all went outside to see the many floral tributes from, among others: The Rolling Stones who's card read *"With fondest memories and thanks for the inspiration"*, Van Morrison, *"A great loss of a fine friend and an inspiring musician"*, Elton John, *"A man who will never be forgotten love Elton & David"*, Brian May, *"Long live the King"*.

Almost every member of the bands from the sixties British pop music explosion started out in Skiffle Groups singing Lonnie Donegan songs. The earliest known recording of John Lennon is of his Skiffle Group the Quarrymen singing "Putting on the Style". Lonnie took his influence from folk and blues artists like Huddie Ledbetter and Woody Guthrie and created a style of music that earned him over 30 top twenty hits during the fifties and early sixties, including three number ones. He had the first band to use the line up of lead guitar, rhythm guitar, bass and drums which became and still is the recognised basic line up for rock and pop bands. Groups like the Beatles, the Stones, the Shadows,

Dire Straits, and Oasis all used that same line up of instruments started by Lonnie Donegan all those years ago.

Rest in peace Lonnie we will all miss you

2003

Thursday 8th May 2003

A memorial service for Lonnie Donegan was held at the actor's church, St. Paul's in Covent Garden. It was a celebration of Lonnie's life and began with his son Peter and Sam Brown singing "Amazing Grace". There were readings and addresses by Lonnie's wife Sharon, Mel Roberts, Peter Oakman and Lonnie's heart specialist Dr. Graham Jackson who apologized to us all for not being able to keep Lonnie with us for a while longer. There was music from Chas n' Dave, Lonnie's sons and finally Brian May who sang his favourite Lonnie song "I'm just a Rolling Stone". As we left the church Lonnie's version of "The Party's Over" was played, which wasn't one of my particular favourites but seemed appropriate.

Tuesday 22nd May 2003

I was fortunate enough to see Paul McCartney's show "Back in the World 2003" at Earls Court, and I have to say it was the best concert I have ever been to. I know I am biased being a huge fan of the Beatles but, having seen them live ten times and almost every concert Paul McCartney has performed since then, this was close to perfection.

The man was on stage for over two and a half hours non stop performing 36 songs of which twenty two were Beatles classics, and his voice was awesome. The concert began with a hippy, trippy piece by around twenty performers which I can only describe as a bit odd, but suddenly there appeared on a giant on stage screen the silhouette of Paul McCartney with his trade mark Hofner Beatle bass guitar. The screen was raised and Paul with his four musicians went straight into "Hello Goodbye" one of the songs he had never performed before. From then on it was like a giant party with the whole audience joining in as soon as they recognised the introduction to a particular song. The earliest song was

"I Saw Her Standing There" from the first Beatles album "Please Please Me", to "Lonely Road" from his last album "Driving Rain". Apart from Paul "Wix" Wickens, who had played with Paul McCartney on his last two tours, it was a brand new band with Rusty Anderson (Guitar), Brian Ray (Guitar/Bass) and Abe Laboriel Jr. (Drums) and they were superb. Abe Laboriel Jr. was a show all on his own.

Some people question why he still bothers to tour, because he is over sixty years of age and incredibly wealthy, but you can see why, it's because that's what he does and he loves it, and when he talks to the audience between songs, it's like he's having a chat over a cup of tea. In the early years after the Beatles he had a problem with singing Beatles' songs but he gradually sang more and more with each tour and now he is totally comfortable with being an ex. Beatle. If I could pick out a highlight, which is difficult as there was so many, I think it would be "She's Leaving Home", another song he had never performed live.

After two and a half hours, two false tabs and around half a dozen encores we were into "Sgt. Peppers Lonely Hearts Club Band" followed by "The End" and that was it. I had sung every word, and was exhausted so God knows how he felt having performed the show for four nights out of the last five. It was, to quote a cliché, "the soundtrack to my life".

2004

Saturday 25th September

Three days ago Lynne and I celebrated our silver wedding anniversary and today we held a party for family and friends. Dominic and Julie came along as did Rosie and the four of us, which was the final line up for Guys n' Dolls, got up and performed a couple of numbers.

2005

Friday 6th May 2005

Bruce's wife Winnie checks to make sure Dominic has sculpted the chin to the correct size

(Photograph courtesy of Loes Derks)

Dominic had always been involved with art but had never taken it too seriously. In the Guys n' Doll days I remember him producing some excellent sculptures and then leaving them lying around until they disintegrated. Some time ago he took some of his work to a very successful artist called Roy Petley. Roy took him under his wing and began selling Dominic's Bronzes at his galleries in Mayfair and Monte Carlo and this had given Dominic a new direction.

Julie came up with the idea of Dominic making a bronze bust of her Dad that could be placed in one of the bars at the London Palladium which was Bruce's second home. Dominic had spent months getting the image just right and had started again from scratch a couple of times, but now it was ready to be unveiled. There was a ceremony to unveil the bronze in the Cinderella Bar at the Palladium in front of friends and family. Bruce was on top form when he gave his speech saying that Dominic now had a new career, followed by, "and by God he needed one".

Thursday 14th July 2005

My brother Nigel had been living the quiet life in Australia and now resided in a small town called Emerald about forty minutes from Melbourne. He seems to be more interested in gardening than music these days but was enticed away from his vegetables to take part in the induction of Split Enz into the Aria Hall of fame which took place at Melbourne's Regent Theatre.

They performed live for the first time in twelve years with two songs, Tim Finn's "History Never Repeats" and Neil Finn's "Poor Boy". There was some speculation that they may reform for a short tour next year.

2006
Wednesday 7th June – Friday 16th June 2006

| **Wayne backstage with his Uncle Nigel** | **On stage with the Enz 2006. A rare smile from my brother.** |

The "True Colours" line up of Split Enz, Tim Finn, Neil Finn, Noel Crombie, Nigel Griggs, Eddie Rayner and Malcolm Green, reformed for seven major concerts in Australia. My son Wayne was on a back packing holiday at the time and managed to see his Uncle Nigel on stage in Sydney the day before he returned home to the UK

2007
Friday 23rd February 2007

The Griggs family with far right Bill Aylward who is Vicki's Consultant at Moorfields Eye Hospital. Standing in front of the plaque that The Queen has just unveiled

There has been a fair amount of "name dropping" throughout this book, some of it to the very highest standard, but I've left the best till the end.

My daughter Vicki has been a patient at Moorfields Eye Hospital since the age of four and was very privileged to be invited to the opening of the new Richard Desmond Childrens Eye Centre by Her Majesty The Queen.

Her Majesty spent forty minutes touring the new hospital and stopped to talk to Vicki, and my wife and I in the out patients department on the fourth floor. It was an amazing experience for all three of us and quite a surreal moment when the Queen walked up to us and shook our hands. Unfortunately there was nobody there to take a photograph, the cameras were all down on the second floor swarming around Jordan and Peter Andre, but for Vicki it was an experience that will remain with her the rest of her life.

We were able to look around the new hospital and it is quite an amazing place and much needed, as the old children's ward was very cramped and outdated. Vicki met up with many of the staff that she has got to know during her time at Moorfields. A special person to the three of us is Vicki's consultant Bill Aylward who has looked after Vicki so well over the years.

2008
Friday 21st March – Saturday 22nd March 2008

GUYS n' DOLLS 2008
(left to right)
Thereze Bazar
David Van Day
Martine Howard
Paul Griggs
Julie Forsyth
Dominic Grant

For around two years there had been talk about a possible reunion of the six original members of Guys n' Dolls for some concerts in Holland. I had some reservations and didn't think it was likely to happen due to the geography of various members' homes and the past differences we had, but how wrong could I be.

There had been an invitation for the original Guys n' Dolls to appear on a major TV show called "Mooi! Weer de Leeuw", starring Dutch comedian Paul de Leeuw. This would be preceded by a day of interviews and promotion for projected concerts. The six original members Dominic Grant, Julie Forsyth, Paul Griggs, Martine Howard, David Van Day and Thereza Bazar had all agreed to take part.

I arrived at the hotel in a small Dutch village called Breukelen and everyone was already there apart from David who, we had been told, was on his way. Thereza had flown over from her home in Sydney Australia and I hadn't seen her or David since we all met at the High Court during our case with Ammo Productions twenty seven years earlier. There were no problems as we all sat down and began discussing families and what we'd all been up to since we had last met. David arrived and we spent the rest of the day being interviewed by press and TV and having several photo sessions. We managed to cram in a quick rehearsal for the TV show where we would have to sing two songs live with the studio band.

On the day of the TV show there was only time for one rehearsal with the band before the broadcast. The band were fantastic and we performed our biggest Dutch hit "You're My World" followed by the opening song from our act in the seventies "Love Train". Apart from Dominic missing the first couple of words, as it was difficult to hear the intro, it went really well. We had a farewell drink, said our goodbyes and headed off home in various directions.

Saturday 31st May 2008

The Author and family
31/5/2008
Vicki's
eighteenth
birthday party.

IN CONCLUSION

At sixty three years of age I consider myself lucky to be still gigging every week and thoroughly enjoying it. The idea for the Guys n' Dolls reunion concert is gathering momentum and it looks as though we may be performing sometime during 2008. As long as it does not take over my life again I have no problem with this and maybe it will give a boost to my pension fund.

Music has been a major part of my life which has taken some twists and turns during its course. I don't think I have many musical ambitions left except perhaps one. I'd like to sit down with Paul McCartney, a couple of guitars and sing the harmony part to "All my Loving" with him, I could then die happy. So Paul, if you're reading this------

Acknowledgments

First I would like to thank my wife Lynne and children Wayne and Vicki for tolerating me living in the past while writing this book.

Thanks to my brother Nigel for his invaluable help and advice and stopping me constantly referring to him as "my brother Nigel".

I would also like to thank Dominic and Julie for their patience with me continually phoning with "do you remember ---" questions, and for their friendship.

A big thank you to the following people who have helped me make this book as accurate as possible.

Daren Aldwinckle, Danny Bacon, Dave Cash, Malcolm Collins, John Cook, John Cowan, Tony Dangerfield, Dolf & Loes Derks, Alan Field, Bruce Forsyth, Alan Goldsmith, Peter Green, Geoff Harrison, Keith Hayward, John Kincade, Peter Koelewijn, Ray Monk, Peter Oakman, Dennis Pugsley, Dave Radcliffe, David Johnson, Mel Roberts, Olaf Schrauwers, Freddie Starr, Tony Upson.

Thanks to Lonnie, John, Paul, George and Ringo for their inspiration.

For further information on Lonnie Donegan and his influence on British popular music, you may enjoy reading, "Vince Eager's Rock n' Roll Files."

Every effort has been made to trace the ownership of photographs used in this book.

www.paulgriggs.com